The Films of
Budd Boetticher

ALSO BY ROBERT NOTT
AND FROM MCFARLAND

The Films of Randolph Scott
(2004; paperback 2008)

*Last of the Cowboy Heroes:
The Westerns of Randolph Scott, Joel McCrea,
and Audie Murphy* (2000; paperback 2005)

The Films of Budd Boetticher

Robert Nott

McFarland & Company, Inc., Publishers
Jefferson, North Carolina

Unless otherwise noted, all illustrations are from the Johnny D. Boggs Collection.

ISBN (print) 978-1-4766-6707-2 ∞
ISBN (ebook) 978-1-4766-3521-7

Library of Congress cataloguing data are available

British Library cataloguing data are available

© 2018 Robert Nott. All rights reserved

No part of this book may be reproduced or transmitted in any form or by any means, electronic or mechanical, including photocopying or recording, or by any information storage and retrieval system, without permission in writing from the publisher.

Front cover: Poster art from the 1956 film *Seven Men from Now* (Warner Bros./Photofest)

Printed in the United States of America

*McFarland & Company, Inc., Publishers
Box 611, Jefferson, North Carolina 28640
www.mcfarlandpub.com*

Table of Contents

Acknowledgments vii
Introduction 1
Biography 5

THE FILMS 23

Television 167
Bibliography 185
Index 189

Acknowledgments

As is the case with most books—particularly nonfiction works—a lot of people end up lending a hand or two, well aware that they will be lucky if they get a "thank you" out of the deal. So, in no particular order, my thanks to:

The late film historian and author John Cocchi, who encouraged me to write the book, gave me some stills and located a copy of the hard-to-find 1943 Columbia film *Good Luck, Mr. Yates*, in which Budd Boetticher plays a bit part as a boxer.

Tom Weaver, one of the best film historians around, provided moral support, contact information for interview sources, and miscellaneous articles from Budd's career.

Boyd Magers' *Western Clippings* website is a must for anyone writing about Western films. He probably has interviewed more people involved in the making of American Westerns than any other historian or author living today. He also self-published three volumes of Western film reviews, a collection I recommend to any Western film fan.

The late film historian, author and literary agent Jon Tuska was of immense help, pointing me in the right direction when it came to finding interview sources and material on Boetticher, and in providing a series of stream-of-consciousness letters in which he recalled his impressions—not always favorable—of Boetticher. Jon's widow, Vicki Piekarski, sent me a VHS copy of the 1985 film *My Kingdom for...*, which is technically Boetticher's final cinematic project, though it was never released theatrically.

Sue Gossett, author of *The Films and Career of Audie Murphy*, put me in touch with Michael Dante and Ron Masak and sent me a few letters that Boetticher sent to her regarding *A Time for Dying*. She also provided me with some photos for this book.

I received the expected high-quality assistance from Ned Comstock and his staff at the University of Southern California's Doheny Library, which houses both the Universal studio archives and the Warner Bros. studio archives. Those archives are a treasure trove of fascinating behind-the-scenes tidbits.

The staff at the Margaret Herrick Library at the Academy of Motion Pictures Arts and Sciences helped me navigate a collection of articles, reviews and clippings about Boetticher's career. The James Karen collection at that library includes a number of screenplays that Budd wrote and never produced, as well as a shooting script for *A Time for Dying*. That collection also includes a hodgepodge of correspondence, studio archive materials and articles on Budd's career.

While I was visiting Los Angeles to research the book, film editor and film historian Peter Kaminski put me up. He also viewed a video copy of a rare 1955 television pilot that Boetticher directed, *Alias Mike Hercules*, and provided a write-up for this book.

New York City's Lincoln Center for the Performing Arts has a formidable clippings file on Boetticher (as well as Burt Kennedy and Randolph Scott).

Ronald L. Davis, former college professor, author and former curator of the Film Oral History Project at Southern Methodist University in Dallas, Texas, remains an unsung film historian. He interviewed dozens of film artists, including Budd and Burt Kennedy, during his lengthy career and still found time to write a number of good books, including one on John Wayne and another on John Ford. You can find his vast collection of question-and-answer interviews with these artists at the Southern Methodist University Library.

Zoran Sinobad and his staff at the Library of Congress in Washington, D.C., were of immense help when it came to viewing one of Boetticher's most elusive movies, *Youth on Trial*.

I was fortunate enough to interview Budd Boetticher for about four hours one autumn afternoon way back in 1997, using an old-fashioned cassette-playing tape recorder. He and I would sometimes talk by phone over the ensuing years until his death. I also interviewed Burt Kennedy about the films he made with Budd and Randolph Scott. I also interviewed Rand Brooks, Harry Joe Brown, Jr., Bill Catching, Cora Sue Collins, Johnny Crawford, Rhonda Fleming, Nancy Gates, Roy Huggins, L.Q. Jones, Ron Masak, Virginia Mayo, Steve Mitchell, Terry Murphy, Noreen Nash, Gregg Palmer, Michael Dante, Walter Reed, William Reynolds, Ann Robinson, Craig Stevens, Jack William and H.M. Wynant.

Sean Axmaker interviewed Boetticher for the essay "Ride Lonesome: The Films of Budd Boetticher," much of which was later distilled into a *Filmfax* article. Many of the Boetticher quotes I used in this book come from that interaction, and I have done my best to credit Axmaker throughout.

Santa Fe novelist and former assistant film editor Tom Clagett, author of a book on the films of director William Friedkin, was kind enough to give the manuscript a close read and offer a lot of smart suggestions that made it better.

Western novelist and film historian Johnny Boggs helped collect stills and lobby cards, provided me with a copy of the rare 1956 Berkley Publishing Company paperback *of 7 Men from Now* and—as a historian and author of books about films featuring Billy the Kid and Jesse James—weighed in with some historical perspective on Boetticher's 1951 Western *The Cimarron Kid*.

James Donovan, author of *The Blood of Heroes: The 13-Day Struggle for the Alamo* (Little, Brown & Co., 2012), and novelist and Seminole expert Lucia St. Clair Robson also provided some historical context for my sections on Boetticher's 1953 releases *The Man from the Alamo* and *Seminole*.

Emmy-winning Santa Fe–based screenwriter and producer Kirk Ellis walked me through a screening of John Sturges' edited version of Budd's *Arruza* and pointed out the differences between it and Budd's original film, which is nearly impossible to access today. He did the same for a screening of Budd's rarely seen *My Kingdom for...*

If I have missed anyone else who contributed to *The Films of Budd Boetticher*, forgive me. It's been a long trail to ride, and I may have nodded off once or twice along the way.

Introduction

When I first saw Henry Silva gun down Arthur Hunnicutt, I was about 12 years old in a bowling alley–bar in Fishkill, New York. That was a defining moment in my appreciation for both Randolph Scott and Budd Boetticher. I had wandered into the bar at the old bowling alley because my dad, Bruce Nott, Sr., was bowling in a Sunday afternoon league there that day. It was a cold, rainy autumn day and the local New York sporting events were rained out. This is probably why the gruff middle-aged bartender had *The Tall T* playing on the old television set mounted on the wall behind the bar.

There were a handful of men sitting at the bar and at some nearby tables—local drunks, I think, and not tournament bowlers. Most of them were watching the film in respectful silence. I had gone into the bar to order a ginger ale, and I sat at a table near the bar to watch the film, commercials and all, for the next hour. I'd missed the first 20 minutes or so, but it didn't matter: I was hooked.

I did not know that Budd Boetticher had directed the film, as I missed the opening credits, but I kept my eye out for Randolph Scott titles in the weekly issues of *TV Guide* that we used to buy, and sure enough, some eight or nine months later—on a sunny summer Saturday afternoon, when I should have been out playing baseball or biking through the nearby trails—I caught *Comanche Station* on a local television station. I liked Randy Scott's style: laconic, sensitive, mysterious. I caught the credits and made note of the names of director Boetticher and screenwriter Burt Kennedy.

The Boetticher-Scott (and-sometimes-Kennedy) Westerns of the mid– to late 1950s spoke to me in a way that then-current Westerns did not. They were short, violent and to-the-point. They had a story to tell, and they told it as directly as possible. The hero was flawed but determined and the bad guys were equally flawed but determined, and they all knew how to kill. The introduction of these sometimes-comic villains introduced a new type of bad guy, one whose amoral approach to living life to the fullest by killing was at odds with the so-called Code of the West.

Budd Boetticher was all the rage in those days. He had returned just a few years before from a lengthy self-exile in Mexico, and all the noted film historians and critics were rediscovering the Scott Westerns and writing salutary essays and articles about Boetticher. The Scott Westerns still seemed relevant in an ever-changing American landscape of free love, political scandals and civil protests and demonstrations against an increasingly unpopular war. You didn't know what was going to happen out on the streets, and you didn't know what was going to happen in a Budd Boetticher-Randolph Scott movie. On screen, Scott would overcome anarchy in the end, but in the sometimes riotous America of the late 1960s and early 1970s, the outcome was not so clear.

I met Budd once, in the autumn of 1997, spending four hours with him taping an interview about his work with Scott and Kennedy, and his relationships with Audie Murphy, with whom he made two not-particularly good films. He was living in Ramona, California, and his wife, Mary, ran out to a local deli and brought me a roast beef sandwich to eat while we talked. Budd was Budd: animated, funny, proud, egotistical and open to telling pretty much the same old stories he had already polished to perfection. I was mostly interested in Scott and Murphy—and to a lesser degree Joel McCrea, with whom Budd worked briefly on the 1943 comedy *The More the Merrier*—because I was conducting research for my book *The Last of the Cowboy Heroes: The Post-War Westerns of Randolph Scott, Joel McCrea and Audie Murphy*. Budd wrote that book's introduction, and over the ensuing years he would call me just to talk about this thing or that, as though we were friends. We weren't, but it was nice to think that maybe we could have been.

In late 2000, Budd was slated to come to Santa Fe, New Mexico, where I worked as a journalist for *The Santa Fe New Mexican*, to receive a Maverick Award from the Santa Fe Film Festival. The festival ran a restored print of *Seven Men from Now* (1956) and *Bullfighter and the Lady* (1951) and Budd participated in a phone interview for a newspaper story I wrote on his career. Shortly before the festival, Budd fell ill and called me and asked me to accept the award on his behalf. I threw together a collection of clips from his Scott Westerns for projection on the big screen in the hotel ballroom where the awards ceremony was held, and I rattled off a story about how Budd had once jumped into a lake to rescue a stuntman who Budd thought was drowning. (He wasn't.) It got a laugh, as did some of the filmclips, and when I called Budd a few days later to tell him how it had played out, he seemed pleased. That was the last time we ever spoke. He died about a year later of what we would likely call natural causes. I'm sort of amazed that the hard life he lived didn't do him in sooner.

It took me some time to decide that I wanted to write about his films: all of them, not just the ones that critics and historians keep coming back to, like the Scott Westerns and the bullfighting triage and a few of the noir titles. His filmmaking career can be divided into five phases: First, there are the five one-hour programmers made for Columbia. In the late 1940s came a series of even cheaper Eagle-Lion and Monogram movies that gave the impression that he had un-learned everything he picked up at Columbia. The third phase is his Universal period (1951–1953) during which he made nine relatively entertaining features covering everything from World War II to rodeo life to a search for an undersea kingdom.

The fourth phase is the marvelous series of Randolph Scott Westerns, mostly penned by Burt Kennedy and mostly produced by Scott's business partner Harry Joe Brown. The seven pictures were shot cheap and fast. *Seven Men from Now, The Tall T, Ride Lonesome* and *Comanche Station* are now seen by just about every serious film critic and Western movie historian as four of the finest Western dramas ever made. Another, 1958's *Buchanan Rides Alone*, is like the *Casablanca* of B Westerns, both in the way it was put together on the set day-by-day and the intricate double-crossing and finagling in which the on-screen characters engage. The other two, 1957's *Decision at Sundown* and 1959's *Westbound*, are watchable disappointments though Boetticher sometimes referred to them as "crap."

I gotta be honest here: There's a lot of "crap" in his film canon. He was first and foremost a studio-system director, turning out films of varying quality because of his unpredictable approach to life, his disdain for studio politics and the fact that he jumped from studio to studio over the years, never quite anchoring his storytelling ship in any one port. There is a reason he is best known for the Randolph Scott films: They're the best things he ever made, though a few of the others, notably *Bullfighter and the Lady,* are pretty damn good.

This is a film-by-film look at that career, replete with anecdotes, film archive material, critical responses and synopsis. I can't put Budd up on a pedestal of great filmmakers. I can say that even his worst films—*Killer Shark* comes to mind—are worth watching at least once. This is not a biography of Budd, though I have included a lengthy biographical section. Budd was a professional, an assembly-line craftsman and a creative artist all in one. He was also just as much of a showman as P.T. Barnum or Cecil B. DeMille. Despite his public scorn of producers—"They can lick you or they can fire you, and once you know that, you're not afraid of anybody"—he had enough political savvy to find a way to work with or around them without antagonizing them. Unlike Sam Peckinpah, Budd did not put off that many important people on his rise to the top. He and contemporary Anthony Mann came of age in the middle of the Golden Age of Hollywood, and they learned to adapt to the studio system and take advantage of it when possible.

Boetticher's Randolph Scott Westerns provide a direct link between the Anthony Mann-James Stewart Westerns of the early 1950s (I find it interesting that their collaboration ended in 1955, the same year Budd was directing his first Scott film, *Seven Men from Now*), and the 1960s Western films of Sam Peckinpah. Budd was not good friends with either Mann or Peckinpah, though he knew them. Peckinpah once said he didn't like Boetticher's Westerns but did not say why. But Budd was basking in a lengthy afterglow of his achievements in the early to mid-1970s, when Peckinpah's career began floundering. One day the two men got together to talk over a beer. According to Budd, the talk went this way:

> SAM: "Jesus Christ, you don't have to do anything more, do you?"
> BUDD: "What do you mean?"
> SAM: "Shit, look at all you've done."
> BUDD: "Yeah, but you've made three or four pictures and everybody knows about them and I don't know anyone who's seen my pictures."
> SAM: "Don't worry, they've seen them."

They sure have.

Biography

When journalist Patrick Francis of the *LA Weekly* phoned Budd Boetticher late in 2001 to set up an interview for an article called "Wise Guys," Budd told him, "I think it's a great idea to start your article by saying this isn't going to be completely truthful."

Therein lies a challenge for any writer attempting to compile an accurate biography of the late cult film director and bullfighter, whose mantra seemed to be, "Let's make it up as we go along." Budd had a way with playing with the truth that sure made it sound truthful, even if it wasn't. He expounded, exaggerated and probably outright fibbed about various details of his life and career, and it's difficult today to confirm or deny many of those reports. Studio archive material and interviews with people who worked with Budd certainly help in confirming some of his film-related stories. But they cast doubt on others.

When it comes to his personal life, one almost has no choice but to take Budd at his word that what he said happened *did* happen, even if it didn't.

A birth certificate tells us he was born July 29, 1916, in Chicago, Illinois. Oscar and Georgia Boetticher adopted him. Oscar was at that time a fiftyish businessman who ran a successful hardware retail operation. Georgia, some 20 years younger, basically did nothing, according to Budd. Asked by one interviewer whether his mother was a homemaker, Budd incredulously replied, "A homemaker? She was never a homemaker. She was the countess of whatever you want to call it. She was something very special to me."

Yet in his autobiography *When in Disgrace* (1989), Budd writes that he never trusted his mother after the age of six when, in an effort to deceive him into going to the dentist to have his tonsils removed, she told him she was taking him to the circus. His reply, upon arriving at the dentist's office, was, "Where are the elephants?"—the title of his second, still unpublished autobiography.

Though Budd was born in Chicago, the Boettichers raised him in nearby Evansville. If his mother did indeed sometimes dress him up in Little Lord Fauntleroy attire as Budd has testified, it is no wonder he got beat up a lot. He learned quickly how to run fast, and he learned even more quickly how to hit back. Running and hitting became two traits that would come in useful when it came to bullfighting and making movies. "It wasn't a great youth," he said years later. "I was spoiled rotten." It didn't help that his father and mother did not have a strong relationship, perhaps in part because of the large age difference between them. Years later, when Budd learned he was adopted, he said he felt relieved: "And that's pretty terrible."

He played football in high school and learned to box at a local gym. Photos of Budd as a child on horseback bear out his claim that he was partially reared on horses. His father, a member of a local hunt club, would hook Budd onto the back of his horse when chasing foxes. "I was raised on horseback as a hunter and a jumper," Budd told interviewer Ronald L. Davis in 1988. "Cowboys to me were a far cry from everything I did. There were no cowboys in evidence in Indiana.... I never saw a western saddle until I came to California."

He spent his weekends at the local bijou, like so many other kids, watching the matinee idols of the day (including the cowboy heroes) engage in weekly dust-ups. But Budd never claimed to have gravitated specifically towards Westerns during his youth. Seeing movies, he said, was "what we did on Saturday afternoons when we were in grade school and on Sunday afternoons when we were in high school."

In the mid–1930s he spent two years at Culver Military Academy in Indiana, where he first met Hal Roach, Jr., son of film producer Hal Roach, best known for his comedies featuring the "Our Gang" kids and Laurel and Hardy, among other screen comics. (That friendship paid off a few years later when Roach, Sr., offered Budd his first real job in the motion picture business.) From Culver, Budd moved on to Ohio State—"to play football," he later said—and there he rubbed shoulders with future Olympic champion Jesse Owens. "I would have gone there [Ohio State] to run but I didn't figure I was going to catch up with him," Budd joked.

A football injury at college was a turning point. To recover, he agreed to join his pal Tom Joy on a road trip to Mexico. Tom's wealthy family ran the Packard Motors enterprise in Grosse Pointe, Michigan. That vacation was planned as the first part of a lengthy South American sojourn that would include a visit to Vera Cruz. The year was 1939, and Budd would never make it past Mexico. There he fell in love with a woman he identified as Ruth D'Laurage. He later estimated her age to be between 30 and 40, and for a randy college student, she was no doubt an excellent mentor and teacher for him when it came to the ways of the world—and love. She told him she was the madam of Mexico City and ran seven houses of prostitution there. She was also an *aficionada* of bullfighting and invited Budd and Tom to attend their first *corrida*. There, famed matador Lorenzo Garza had decided to fight six bulls in a row. Preparing to watch his first bullfight, Boetticher recalled that he felt "as if I were back in Rome to witness the Christians being thrown to the lions. Or worse—being a devout animal lover—I wondered if I could stomach a noble beast being tormented. But no matter, I felt a strange excitement in the pit of my guts."

That afternoon, Boetticher fell in love with the sport (or "the art," as he called it) and with Garza's confidence and talent. He also enjoyed Garza's taunting of the crowd, which had no respect for him after he reportedly lost his nerve in some previous bullring encounters. Garza's flashy and unexpected comeback that day inspired a mini-riot in the stands, which Budd and his beloved narrowly escaped thanks to a couple of pistol-wielding bodyguards that the madam kept on hand. Thinking back on the experience, Budd wrote, "Never had any single event made such an impression. Perhaps it was because the art of the bullring was so dangerous. Or perhaps it was because it was so damned medieval. As a callow youth I'd always played at 'knights.' Maybe I saw in 'Lorenzo the Magnificent' the resurrection of King Arthur, or Lancelot, or El Cid."

The next day, according to his memoir, he told Tom that he wanted to be a bullfighter. "Overcoming danger is what it's all about," he explained. Ruth helped by introducing him to General Maximino Avila Camacho, the brother of future Mexican President Manuel Avila Camacho and yet another bullfighting aficionado. "He was intrigued with the idea of an American athlete actually wanting to become a *torero*," Budd wrote. "At the time I never considered that he also might have been intrigued with the thought of an American athlete getting himself killed."

He didn't get himself killed but he was gored at least once. "I should have died but I didn't," Budd told Patrick Francis for the "Wise Guys" piece. "I refused to, for years."

Camacho introduced Budd to Lorenzo, one of several mentors who taught Budd the ropes, and the capes, and the swords all at once. During this time, Budd first met matador Carlos Arruza, a "cute-looking, skinny kid with a big gold tooth right smack dab up front," and a new prospect for bullfighting stardom. Budd and Arruza cultivated a personal friendship and professional camaraderie; some 20 years later, Budd began work on a film about Arruza.

Personal troubles followed: Tom Joy was killed in an airplane accident and Ruth ended the romance with Budd. Learning the trade of *El Toreo* provided a welcome distraction. When Garza got gored in the groin during a bout, Budd was given the chance to step in and fight female bulls. The third time he faced off against a three-year-old bull, he got gored in his rear end. He realized, in retrospect, that he had tried to imitate Garza by performing a kneeling pass with his *muleta* (cape). The bull's right horn caught him under his knee, throwing him into the sand where the bull hit him again from behind. "It didn't hurt!" Budd wrote. "It did feel hot down there. But it didn't hurt. Then I remembered a lot of pink capes swirling to my rescue, and things went black." Later, he said, he compared the feeling to "being run over by a herd of stampeding elephants—twice."

But he loved the high of fighting bulls and would return to the ring and Mexico for years to get in the arena again. Photos bear out the fact that Budd did this at least into the early 1950s. In a November 1955 issue of *The Hollywood Reporter*, Budd penned a piece called "Time Out for Bullfighting" in which he said he had recently returned to Tijuana to "fight the brave bulls at the city's big annual charity event." In that article, he said that making films can become an "ulcer-provoking business. As for me, I don't have ulcers. Nor do I visit a psychiatrist. I fight the bulls instead."

The goring bought him respect from his peers. "Now I had finally joined the group," Budd wrote. His scar was not visible when he was clothed, but he would willingly drop his pants to show curious friends and acquaintances his bodily badge of honor.

News of Budd's goring reached Georgia Boetticher's ears, and she and her husband decided they were not going to let Budd get killed. Budd's dad wanted him to come into the hardware business, but Budd declined. His mother convinced him to go to Hollywood where she secured his first job, he said, as a technical advisor on the 20th Century–Fox production *Blood and Sand*, a bullfighting movie starring Tyrone Power and Rita Hayworth. And that's how Budd got into motion pictures.

Well, not exactly. Budd himself often confused the timeline with which he returned to the States and went to work in Hollywood. By his account, his mother called Hal Roach, an old family friend, and asked him to call Darryl Zanuck, head of Fox, to suggest Budd work as a technical advisor on the film. Budd tells this story in *When in Disgrace*. Budd recalls that *Blood and Sand* led to a job at the Roach studio, which in turn led to a job at Columbia.

Not so. Fox produced *Blood and Sand* from January to April 1941. But the Hal Roach archives housed at USC document Budd's work on a number of Roach productions starting in the summer of 1940, a full half-year before the Fox picture started shooting. Budd and some Boetticher historians said he started at the Roach lot on the 1939 production *Of Mice and Men*, starring Burgess Meredith and Lon Chaney, Jr. Budd's name is not listed on the daily call sheets for that film, though he may have been one of the nameless "horse wranglers" who worked on the film. He disputed that claim years later, suggesting such work was beneath him and insisting he was an assistant to the assistant director. Maybe. But maybe not. Since that picture was shot in the summer of 1939, and there is no record of Budd working for Roach until June 1940, one must question whether he worked on *Of Mice and Men* at all.

USC's Hal Roach documents reflect a flurry of work for Budd in a variety of capacities, from second assistant director to second-unit assistant to performing sound and photography tests of actors to no job title at all, from the summer of 1940 through the summer of 1942. The list of 17 pictures he worked on ranges from *Captain Caution* (1940) to *Road Show* (1940) to *Fiesta* (1941) to the absolutely weird and surreal *The Devil with Hitler* (1942), in which Hitler, Mussolini and Tito are reduced to performing Three Stooges–type comedy, including engaging in a pillow fight with an energetic orangutan! The majority of the Roach films were called "streamliners" and ran 45 to 50 minutes. They were meant to fill the bottom half of a double bill. Budd also put in time on two Roach-produced War Department movies shot and released months before the December 7, 1941, Japanese attack on Pearl Harbor.

Prior to Budd's time at the Roach lot, Roach had briefly tried to break into the A rank of studios with major motion pictures like *Of Mice and Men*, *One Million B.C.* and a trio of *Topper* comedies. But as an independent producer releasing his product through United Artists—which did not own any theater chains—Roach found himself in financial trouble by the early 1940s. Much of his output during the years when Budd worked there may best be described as "blandly pleasant." Laurel and Hardy, arguably Roach's biggest draw in the 1930s, left the Roach lot by 1940, and as author Richard Lewis Ward noted in his book *A History of the Hal Roach Studios* (Southern Illinois University Press, 2005), Roach's "non–Laurel and Hardy features proved to be inconsistent box office performers." Of the "streamliners," Ward wrote that they "seem oddly rushed. Scenes end virtually in mid-sequence." They were budgeted around the $100,000 mark and produced in two to three weeks.

The experience proved invaluable to Budd. He watched as mostly second-rate directors like Gordon Douglas, Kurt Neumann, Glenn Tryon and George Archainbaud put actors like Victor Mature, William Bendix, Noah Beery, Jr., Joe Sawyer and William Tracy through their paces. Roach, for the most part, hired actors on the verge of stardom—Mature and Bendix come to mind—or actors who would never quite gain stardom, like Carole Landis and John Hubbard. The rest of his ensembles were made up of character actors like Zasu Pitts and James Gleason. These were the sorts of performers who populated most of Budd's features at Columbia, Universal and other studios in the future.

Budd said he started at Roach, located in Culver City, as a messenger boy at $46 a week. Soon he was promoted to a reader, and then to an assistant or second assistant director. He described that last job as being one in which he was expected to snitch on the director by telling the producer what the director was doing wrong, but he insists he never did that. "I was not a very good assistant director on any of my pictures because I was always on the director's side," he told Ronald L. Davis in the late 1980s. In his autobiography, Budd says he learned a lot from the studio's four "Honest-to-God assistant directors," Barney Carr, Harve Foster, Holly Morse and Eddie Montagne. "These were the men who shaped my career but I'm sure I drove them all crazy."

During his tenure at Roach, Budd first met Chicago-born actor John Hubbard, who was being groomed for a stardom that he would never attain in the screwball comedies *Road Show* and *Turnabout*. A May 1941 *Sun-Baltimore* story by Ted Gill, "Synthetic Bull Fighting," paints a picture of Budd and Hubbard creating a miniature arena and dummy bull in the backyard of one of their homes for fun. The bull was mounted on a wheeled platform and apparently Budd was practicing all the time. The article said the two men often bused across the border to Tijuana on weekends to watch bullfights in Mexico; Budd told Gil he had killed 18 bulls to date.

After working for Roach for several months, Budd went over to 20th Century–Fox to help on *Blood and Sand*. Directed by Rouben Mamoulian and based on the 1908 book by Vicente Blasco Ibanez, the picture was a colorful epic about a young and arrogant bullfighter (Tyrone Power) who lets success go to his head and pays for it with his life in the ring. "Everything in the book was downbeat, everybody was dying," Budd said of the book. In his autobiography, Budd devotes about 12 pages to his experiences on the film, which, in his recollection, started in September 1941 when he showed up at Fox to prove he could fight bulls and nab a job as the picture's technical director. Zanuck told Budd he had five minutes to show him, Mamoulian and screenwriter Jo Swerling everything he knew about fighting bulls, to which Budd said, "Mr. Zanuck, that's like a bunch of atheists telling a Catholic he has five minutes to tell them all about Catholicism."

Within 15 minutes, by Budd's own account, he and Zanuck were taking turns playing bull with a chair and making passes. Zanuck hired Budd at $150 a week to teach Power "how to look and move like a bullfighter," as Budd put it. Budd told journalist Lyn Sherwood of *Bullfight World* that Mamoulian "was out of his element making a bullfight picture. He didn't know anything about it. And he didn't make a very good picture. Some call it a classic, but it wasn't. Technically it was so wrong." Budd said that he continually offered Mamoulian technical advice but was ignored until, about two-thirds of the way through the picture, he stopped making suggestions.

But Budd grew to admire Mamoulian's style of directing actors and realized he had his own vision for the film. Likewise, Budd liked Power—"the most beautiful man you ever saw in your life"—as well as Rita Hayworth and co-star Linda Darnell. Editor Barbara McLain taught Budd the editing ropes after she asked him to sit in on some of her editing sessions to ensure that the sequences involving the bulls were cut the right way. "She taught me more about film editing in those two weeks than I could ever have learned in a four-year college course," Budd recalled. (McLain is not credited with working on the film as an editor—Robert Bischoff is.) Budd later said the picture afforded him the first opportunity to insert a personal touch into the story when he demonstrated to assistant dance director Geneva Sawyer how to stage *a torero's paso doble* dance in which the man plays the matador while the woman dances the part of the bull. Hayworth and Anthony Quinn danced it in *Blood and Sand*, and it is a memorably erotic piece of choreography.

The experience was vital in shaping Budd's career. Budd fell in love with moviemaking on the set and later said it was the project that kept him anchored in Hollywood and made him want to be a director. And he felt sadness on the last day of the shoot, "like being graduated from a school you sincerely love. You say goodbye to people you may never see again … you get a strange empty feeling in your stomach and it hurts."

Budd returned to Roach, where he worked on a number of films into the summer of 1942. His last known job there was on the service comedy *Yanks Ahoy* (1943), in which Budd put in 16 days in July and August 1942. By that time, Roach had entered the U.S. Army as a major and signed a deal to lease his studio to the Army to make military-themed shorts and documentaries. The Roach Studio effectively shut down production by September 1942 with an eye toward revitalizing its efforts once the war started. But that didn't exactly pan out as Roach expected, as Budd would find out when he returned to the lot in 1946 following a stint in the Navy.

Budd went to work for Columbia. Why? "Because they wanted me," he simply told one interviewer, as if that was that. One wonders if his credentials at Roach gained him entry, or whether Roach himself made another phone call to help Budd out. Or perhaps Budd's penchant for making friends outside the studio, encountering the likes of George Stevens and Frank Capra at various athletic clubs in town, helped secure him a toehold at Columbia. In his autobiography, Budd said that director George Stevens requested him as the second assistant director on the comedy *The More the Merrier* with Joel McCrea, Jean Arthur and Charles Coburn. *The More the Merrier* began shooting in September and wrapped by year's end.

Budd also said that he worked one day on Charles Vidor's Western *The Desperadoes* (1943), produced by Harry Joe Brown and starring Randolph Scott and Glenn Ford. By Budd's account, he was on hand for the saloon brawl sequence, which spotlights Ford and Guinn "Big Boy" Williams but not star Scott. Vidor asked Budd if he could throw a chair over the bar and hit the big mirror on the wall behind it—a staple of Western saloon brawls, it seems. Budd said yes. Then he threw the chair, hit Ford and got fired. Since *The Desperadoes* was shot from June to August 1942, as Roach was preparing to close up shop, it is possible that Budd wrangled a one-day job at Columbia, which was probably his introduction to the Gower Gulch studio. It also makes sense that if he was only on the set one day, he likely did not meet producer Brown or star Scott, both of whom would play major roles in revitalizing his career and cementing it into cult film history when they hired him to direct a series of Westerns at Columbia in the 1950s.

Fired or not, the gutsy director-in-the-making still had the moxie to get back on the Columbia lot and eventually back onto a Charles Vidor set, but only after working for George Stevens. By the autumn of 1942, Budd was working steadily on the Columbia lot, a studio that best served him during his roughly 15-year career as a director in Hollywood.

Created and controlled by Harry Cohn (1891–1958), Columbia sprang up in the center of what was then known as Poverty Row because of the number of low-budget studios located in that area. Clive Hirschhorn in *The Columbia Story* (Hamlyn, 1999) writes that Cohn

> knew he would have to begin modestly, and no place was more modest in the Hollywood of the 1920s than the small area just off Sunset Boulevard—near Gower Street and Beachwood Drive—known as Poverty Row. Without as yet a studio of his own, the only way for Harry Cohn to become a producer was in the tried-and tested Poverty Row tradition of borrowing money from a sympathetic banking house. Next, he would have to find a story that could be shot mainly out of doors [and] find an actor who was either on his way up or on his way down (and so did not cost too much).

Budd must have learned a lot from Cohn, because this approach speaks to his film career as well.

For a few years, Cohn rented studio space. Then, in 1925, he purchased two stages and an office at 6070 Sunset Boulevard which eventually expanded into Columbia Studios. In the late 1920s, Cohn hired director Frank Capra, thus displaying a talent for drawing top-flight talent to the studio, albeit on short-term contracts. As Hollywood ushered in the sound era, Cohn and Columbia relied on B+ stars like Jack Holt, Ralph Graves (does anyone remember him?) and Buck Jones to draw crowds. Cohn was shrewd enough to build up some female stars of his own, notably Barbara Stanwyck, Jean Arthur and Rosalind Russell. Later still, Cohn turned the likes of Rita Hayworth and Kim Novak into stars. Still, "'Making the most with the least' might have been the studio's motto," Hirschhorn wrote. "With its rapacious need for escapist entertainment, [the 1940s] was the decade in which Harry Cohn became the powerful equal of Messrs. Warner, Mayer, Zanuck and Zukor."

In the days when movie house exhibitors were anxious to book two new titles a week for a solid double-feature offering (not to mention short subjects, cartoons and newsreels), Columbia prospered. In 1944, Columbia produced 45 films and released another six produced by outside entities. In 1945, it produced 42 titles and released another 11 shot by others. It was the era of the "film series" featuring recurring fictional characters like Blondie, Boston Blackie and the Crime Doctor. In the 1940s, the studio also produced low-budget Ann Miller musicals, Judy Canova comedies and medium-budget Westerns starring the likes of Scott, Glenn Ford and Larry Parks. Its stable of not-quite-A-level stars also included Cornel Wilde and Nina Foch. Columbia remains well known for its popular, long-running series of Three Stooges shorts.

Bernard F. Dick, writing in *Columbia Pictures: Portrait of a Studio* (University Press of Kentucky, 1992), said that Columbia "produced some of the world's most honored films. It also, of course, made its share of schlock." Guess which type Budd made for the studio in the mid–1940s?

There was a method to Cohn's financial madness. "Cohn understood that quality and big budgets were not identical; quality could be achieved for as little as $750,000 or as much as $2 million," Dick wrote. At that time, the studio's few "big" pictures a year cost somewhere in the $1 million to $2 million range: *The Talk of the Town* cost $1 million, *A Song to Remember* $1.5 million. The rest—the 10- or 12- or maybe 18-day wonders—could be easily produced for a half-million or less.

Unlike most of the major studios, Columbia had no theater chain to distribute its wares, but this would work to the studio's advantage in the early 1950s when the government forced the bigger studios to divest themselves of those chains, citing conflict-of-interest concerns. Nor did Cohn, in the 1930s and 1940s, employ a lengthy list of "A" level stars and directors. Cohn could attract quality film artists on one- and two-picture deals: George Stevens, Howard Hawks, Cary Grant and later producer Sol Spiegel all worked there briefly. And Cohn had a knack for spotting talent and nurturing it. Budd got his first real break at Columbia, as did directors John Sturges and Phil Karlson. "[Cohn] found that the people like Capra and Stevens were not getting any younger and he wanted to develop new talent," said director William Castle, who also got his start at Columbia. Cohn, Castle said, "was my father, my brother, my boss. I feared him, I loved him … he was a fantastic man, the movie mogul of those days, he ran people's lives." Phil Karlson echoed those words, saying there was no one tougher in Hollywood than Cohn and that the studio boss said to him one day, 'You're going to be the biggest director in this business and I'm going to make sure you are.'" Budd said that Cohn was "always 100 percent [honest] with me … he called me his resident *torero*."

For the most part, Budd enjoyed the experience of working on *The More the Merrier*, a comedy about the wartime housing shortage and how it works to the romantic advantage of McCrea and Arthur. Though McCrea had made a few Westerns before this picture, he was not yet typed in that genre as peer Randolph Scott was. Budd found McCrea to be a gentleman who was interested in Boetticher's background. "I always arrived at his dressing room a little early so that we could visit," Budd recalled. "I am extremely sorry that I never had the opportunity to direct one of his films." Some years later, Budd expressed surprise to learn that producer John Wayne had sent the script for *Seven Men from Now* to McCrea before settling on Randolph Scott for the lead.

Budd recalled that George Stevens hated Cohn and would annoy the mogul by bouncing a tennis ball against a big backboard whenever Cohn visited the set, "at about $100 a bang."

One day Cohn came on the set when Stevens was away and said to Budd, "Tell that fuckin' director of yours I want to see him."

Budd said, "I'm sorry, sir, Mr. Stevens is busy."

To which Cohn said, "Listen, you son of a bitch…"

Budd cut in and told Cohn that if he called him that again, he would knock him on his ass. When Cohn asked Budd if he knew who he was speaking to, Budd said yes, but added, "Compared to those black bulls coming out of those black holes, you look like the Virgin Mary."

Cohn ordered Budd to come to his office at six o'clock, following the end of the day's shooting. Budd showed up, certain that he was about to get fired. There, Budd apologized, telling Cohn that had he (Cohn) not insulted Budd that way in front of the entire crew, he would not have threatened him. Cohn liked Budd's gutsy attitude and said, "I guess I'm the son of a bitch who is going to have to make something out of you."

Columbia kept Budd employed as an all-around handyman, just as Roach did, putting him to work as a second assistant director here and a bit player there. Yes, that's Budd performing an unbilled silent role as a surly boxer in the 1943 B drama *Good Luck, Mr. Yates* (Tom Neal knocks him down in a boxing match). He worked as an assistant on Vidor's *Cover Girl*, starring Rita Hayworth and Gene Kelly, for much of the latter half of 1943. Some historians say that Budd worked as an uncredited assistant director on Columbia's *Submarine Raider* (1942) but this is unlikely, as it was shot from late February to mid–March 1942 when he was still working pretty steadily at the Roach studio.

By Budd's account, Cohn called him early in 1944 to tell him he wanted him to direct. He assigned Budd to watch director William Berke on a 12-day B called *The Girl in the Case*, typical World War II nonsense about a locksmith involved in a complicated plot to ferret out some Nazi spies. Berke mostly made C movies involving the likes of the Falcon, Jungle Jim and Don "Red" Barry. Boetticher spoke well of Berke: "[He] didn't mind my nosing around on the set. And he went out of his way to help me learn the art of making a full-length film in two short weeks. Believe me, it's not easy!"

Cohn then put Budd to work assisting Lew Landers on *U-Boat Prisoner*, shot in two weeks in April 1944. In his autobiography, Budd said he directed the first two days on that film. Later, he amended that story to say he actually directed the last two days. In yet another interview, Budd said Cohn fired Landers and let Budd direct the whole film, uncredited. But given the fact that Landers remained at the studio into the mid-1950s, knocking out cheap Jungle Jim films, among other titles, I find the latter claim questionable.

By May 1944, Cohn was ready to give Budd his chance to direct on his own with the Boston Blackie series entry *One Mysterious Night*. Budd later claimed he was not afraid of the responsibility: "All they can do is fire you or shoot you." His first film is arguably the best of his 1940s offerings, moving at such a snappy clip that you don't much care if it makes sense. Right away Budd was in his element, directing has-been stars (Chester Morris) and up-and-coming nobodies (Janis Carter). He bluffed his way through all five of the Columbia films he made in 1944:

> In those days when anyone offered a suggestion to me, I didn't dare take it because I figured they'd be right. And once you do that, everybody starts to direct the picture. And when I would make a suggestion, and they would look at me like, "You've got to be kidding," I would pat them on the shoulder and look into their eyes and say, "You really don't know what I'm doing, do you?" and walk away. And they would say, "My God, maybe this guy is another Orson Welles," and they'd leave me alone. And I walked away *knowing* I didn't know what I was doing.

Budd loved Columbia and the freedom that Cohn gave him. "It was a small studio, they were making wonderful pictures," Budd told Ronald L. Davis. "They had Capra, they had Stevens, they had Bill Seiter, and they had a lot of good B directors. They had a B unit, the Briskin unit, where they gave us the opportunity to direct 10- and 12-day pictures and learn our business. Those pictures cost $100,000." But, he added with honest insight, "The B pictures that I made were D, E and F pictures."

Between May and December 1944, Budd—billed as Oscar Boetticher, Jr.—knocked out five of these pictures, all designed for the bottom halves of double bills. He said he taught himself to get better after watching his first movie and saying, "Good God, don't ever do that again." The pictures, he later explained, were easy to dismiss. "They cost so much, they made so much and that was that." Film historian and author William K. Everson put it this way: "One of the hallmarks of Boetticher's Bs at Columbia, especially *Escape in the Fog* and *The Missing Juror*, is that they were good enough to make one wish they had been given the budgets so that they could be even better."

Boetticher learned how to stay within his budget and his shooting schedule. He called his time at Columbia "a montage of actors, producers, actresses, cameramen, movies and mistakes. Everything involved with my first five films at Columbia was a learning experience."

Before Columbia could renew its option to keep Budd on contract, he applied for, and received, a commission from the U.S. Navy. He soon found himself in uniform in Washington, D.C., working at the Photographic Science Laboratory with the likes of Gene Kelly, Richard Carlson and Charles Marquis Warren. During this time, Budd made short war films for the science lab and met Emily Cook, whose family had established a well-known beer and champagne business.

Actress Martha Raye introduced Budd to Emily, who Raye nicknamed "Cookie." In his memoir, Budd says he was attracted to a small scar on Emily's face (a birthmark had been removed) and that he didn't realize she was raised in Evansville and used to play with his brother. He dedicated a few pages of his autobiography to his courtship of her and the joy they shared in those early days as they fell in love. She disappears from his narrative for a long time before he returns to the end of the marriage—because of his love affair with actress Karen Steele, around 1957. When Emily divorced Budd in 1957, she claimed that Budd and she had two wedding ceremonies, one in Tijuana in August 1946 and a second in California in July 1949. The couple had two daughters, Georgia and Helene.

During this wartime period, Budd also found out the truth about his real parents, a pair of New Yorkers: His mom died giving birth to Budd and then his father, in despair, walked to his death in front of a fast-moving trolley car. Budd continued to harbor a mysterious resentment toward Georgia Boetticher, calling her an "unhappy enigma" who kept chasing his girlfriends away. Still, he claims at this point that he decided to honor both Georgia and his father by making them proud of his career—one reason he returned to Hollywood following his Naval service.

Among Budd's film-related jobs with the U.S. Navy, he directed the Office of War Information's *The Fleet That Came to Stay*, which covered the Operation Iceberg invasion of Okinawa on Easter Sunday, 1945. "It was the Fourth of July in reverse on Jap airfields, carriers and military targets," the film's narrator tells us. "One hundred thousand Yanks were rattling the locks on Japan's front door." The combat footage, including some startling Japanese Kamikaze aerial shots, was provided by the Navy, Army and Marines. Budd shot fictional opening shots involving the inner thoughts of some of the Marines about to engage in the operation before the picture segued into real-life footage with a voiceover narrator providing details. Budd realized years later that his war film work did not match what had been done by John Ford, Frank Capra or George Stevens, but said, "I just did the best I could with what they gave me, which wasn't much."

World War II ended in September 1945, and by early 1946 Budd was a civilian again. He said that Columbia was happy to let him out of his contract because his five movies there were not exactly winners. Hal Roach, Sr., and Jr., asked Budd to come to work at Roach again, signing him and three other directors to seven-year contracts to make 50-minute films. "The studio set us up in beautiful bungalow offices," he recalled, "And we sat and sat and sat waiting for our individual films to be scheduled."

Roach resumed production of the streamliners in the spring of 1946 but only made four more films. Budd did not work on any of them. He just sat around for a year, finding time to write a screenplay called *Tomorrow's Almost Over* with the hope that Roach would produce it. The story involves a man framed for murder who breaks jail to either clear his name or—according to an outline housed in the Hal Roach Archives at the University of Southern California—"kill some irrelevant person and be adjudged insane." Just as our hero is about to kill a woman who has agreed to help him in his quest, the real murderer confesses, saving the day for our two protagonists. Reader Everett Hayes read the script for Roach and encouragingly reported on May 31, 1946: "The story is above the level of the usual murder story ... replete with suspense." He initially suggested the studio hire Val Lewton or Alfred Hitchcock to direct it, with perhaps Dane Clark and Betty Field starring. But then Hayes reversed course, saying there was not enough in the actual script to justify adding it to the studio's production schedule. A second reader, unnamed, liked the story more than Hayes, calling it "one of the most cinematic screenplays I've ever read ... excellent." The project went nowhere, which was more Roach's fault than Boetticher's, given the state of the studio in the postwar years. But it is interesting to see how Budd attempted to take control of his career by branching out into screenwriting—a field he would return to more frequently in the 1960s and 1970s, with little success.

Roach's days as a film producer were over by 1948, despite efforts to set up distribution and financing deals with both United Artists and MGM. Instead, he and his son wisely branched out into television, keeping the studio alive for another decade. The studio would cease production in 1959 and eventually the Roaches sold it. It was torn down in 1963.

One of the reasons that Boetticher's pre–*Bullfighter and the Lady* career is so erratic is because of the jump from studio to studio and the two years he lost to military service and idle time at Roach. It didn't help that he was about to make a pit stop at Eagle-Lion before ending up at low-rent Monogram. At the end of 1947, Oscar Boetticher, Jr., was hardly an in-demand director when his agent, who he identified as Herb Tobias, called him to say he had set up a deal for Budd to direct two films for producer Bryan Foy for the fledging Eagle-Lion Studios.

Here's how Budd said that scenario played out:

> "I got you a two-picture deal," Tobias told Boetticher. "I told Brynie (Foy) that you were the gentile Sammy Fuller."
>
> "Jesus Christ, Tob," Budd replied. "I'd rather be the Jewish John Ford!"

That's another amusing Boetticher anecdote, but if it is true, he must have got the timing wrong. Budd began working on his first Eagle-Lion film, *Assigned to Danger*, in December 1947, a year and two months before Lippert Pictures released Fuller's first movie, *I Shot Jesse James*, early in 1949, so it's unlikely that Tobias, Boetticher or Hollywood had any awareness of who Sam Fuller was in 1947.

In fact, the two pictures Budd shot for Eagle-Lion were under the guidance of producer Eugene Ling, who wrote and produced a slew of low-low-budget films featuring down-and-out actors through the 1950s. (In 1961, he wrote and produced the semi-cult horror stinker *Hand of Death*.) Budd called the two Eagle-Lion films "fun, nothing more. They were produced by a delightful young fella, Eugene Ling. He and his pretty wife, Betty, became close friends of ours and he was one of the few producers with whom I ever cared to spend time." *Assigned to Danger* pretty much stinks, and the second film, *Behind Locked Doors*, while adequate, did not further Budd's career. Anthony Mann flourished at Eagle-Lion and made a name for himself while Phil Karlson made a couple of decent pictures there and then took a step up to Columbia and United Artists to initiate a series of still-respected melodramas and noirs. But Budd came and went at Eagle-Lion without making a splash, and then took a big career step downward: He moved over to Monogram.

Located at the corner of Hollywood Boulevard and Hoover Street, Monogram was close to the bottom in the Hollywood food chain of studios. "Monogram was a little studio that nobody paid much attention to," director William Castle said. "They'd try to make deals with stars cheaply, stars who were out of work at the time or were starting.... [T]hey'd take newcomers that were under contract to other studios and borrow them."

Karlson, who worked at Monogram in the late 1940s, said of the studio, "They had very little money. They knew what they were doing because there was a certain class of picture they were going to make and they weren't going to make anything any different. They had the Charlie Chans, the Bowery Boys, the East Side Kids and they had the Shadows and

A smiling Budd Boetticher in uniform, circa 1945. Serving in the military for two years threw Budd's still-evolving film career off track.

they had Kay Francis over there for a couple of pictures." He recalled being under contract to direct at Monogram for $250 a week, and it's unlikely Budd got more than that for the three pictures he directed for producer Lindsley Parsons.

Budd's career could have died at Monogram had he not turned it around by finally telling a story he wanted to tell: that of a cocky American who wants to become a bullfighter and pays for his arrogance. In retrospect, the stopover at Monogram was vital to Budd's success, because it was while shooting the abysmal *Killer Shark* (1950) there that he met Andrew McLaglen, whose father Victor had worked with both John Ford and John Wayne. Andrew said that about this time, Budd was talking about an idea he had for a movie about an American sportsman who goes to Mexico and becomes fascinated by bullfighting. McLaglen said that he told Budd he would pass the story on to John Wayne, who had just started producing some movies, if in return Budd hired McLaglen as assistant director for one of the Monogram pictures.

And that is how Budd's story outline for *Bullfighter and the Lady* got into John Wayne's hands. Wayne asked his writer pal James Edward Grant to write a screenplay based on the story, and then Wayne and Budd went to Herbert Yates, head of Republic Studios, to pitch the story with Budd as director. (For more background, see this book's section on *Bullfighter and the Lady*.) By the spring of 1950, Budd Boetticher was directing his life story—with lots of Hollywood trimmings added—down in Mexico, far from the prying eyes of studio executives and with the Hollywood weight of producer John Wayne behind him. Though John Ford cut over 35 minutes out of the film so Yates and Wayne could comfortably sell it as a B-picture, the critics and the public responded to its authentic insight into the mysterious and dangerous world of the *toreros*. Budd netted his only Oscar nomination for Best Story for this film, which in turn drew the interest of Universal Studios.

More importantly, *Bullfighter and the Lady* was the first picture on which Boetticher took directorial credit as Budd, rather than Oscar Boetticher, Jr. That was because, he said, "It was the first good picture I made."

"I don't think any other director in film history has switched so suddenly, so dramatically or so successfully from 'B' to 'A' production in one leap," William K. Everson wrote. *Bullfighter and the Lady* made Boetticher's career.

And then he signed with Universal and found himself back on the assembly line. Like Columbia, Universal had been around since silent movie days. Like Columbia, it did not boast a strong list of contract players and stars on the scale of an MGM, Fox, Warner Bros. and Paramount. And like Columbia, Universal did not have its own chain of theaters and understood the importance of making medium-budget escapist films.

When Budd joined the Universal fold in May 1951, it was home to Abbott and Costello, Francis the Talking Mule, Ma and Pa Kettle, up-and-coming stars Tony Curtis and Rock Hudson, sultry Yvonne De Carlo and studio contract directors including Joseph Pevney, George Sherman, Charles Lamont, Frederick de Cordova and Douglas Sirk. Production heads Leo Spitz and William Goetz ran things with the help of studio manager Edward Muhl, wisely focusing on turning out relatively inexpensive and colorful stories that entertained audiences looking to get two features for the price of one. The studio, located in the San Fernando Valley, produced 33 or 34 films per year in 1951, '52 and '53.

During Budd's time there, Decca Records acquired an interest in the studio, and in the summer of 1952 Muhl became the studio head. Clive Hirschhorn's *The Universal Story* (Octopus Books, 1983) calls the ensuing years the studio's "golden period" due to the creative input of producers Aaron Rosenberg and Ross Hunter—who had acted in one of Budd's Columbia programmers, *A Guy, a Gal and a Pal* (1945). Budd stayed at Universal for two years (May 1951 to May 1953) and made nine movies, six of them Westerns. He said Universal wanted to type him as a Western director because he looked like one. He kept within budget and schedule except on the problematic *The Man from the Alamo* (1953). Despite his scorn for

Boston Blackie star Chester Morris (right) visits with Budd Boetticher on the set of Budd's only out-and-out comedy, *A Guy, a Gal and a Pal* (Photofest).

some of the upper brass, he did his job well. His shooting schedules for these pictures was usually 30 days and the budgets ranged from roughly a half-million dollars to just under a million. He worked with studio stalwarts Audie Murphy, Rock Hudson and Jeff Chandler and on-loan talent Glenn Ford, Van Heflin and Robert Ryan.

One of the nine Universal pictures, *Bronco Buster*, allowed Budd to express his creative voice and anticipates his later work with screenwriter Burt Kennedy and actor Randolph Scott. *The Man from the Alamo* plays up the notion of "a man alone" trying to get a job done, another thematic point seen in the later Scott films. But for the most part, Budd took what was assigned to him, never turning down any projects, and it is difficult to find a theme running through these nine works.

Film journalist Sean Axmaker, who knew Budd well and interviewed him for a lengthy piece on his career called "Ride Lonesome," accurately wrote that Budd was looking for his voice during his years at Universal and began to find it with *The Man from the Alamo*. Budd described Universal to Axmaker as being "like a country club where I was having a good time but I was never going to graduate into becoming a good director."

Budd, in his autobiography, said of his time at Universal,

> When you work for an operation that eventually manufactures a studio tour that deglamorizes the entire industry, you have to learn something. For instance: "biting the hand that feeds you!" The producers at Universal, with one shining exception—Aaron Rosenberg—beat their brains out trying to teach me that motion pictures were not

an art form but a business venture. Still, I never believed them. For one hundred and four weeks of the first two years, with only Sundays off, I directed nine major Universal films. Katy Jurado complained that I was "making pictures like tortillas," and she was correct.

True, but several of these pictures are solid, if not better, and the worst of them are respectable time-fillers. (Well, except *City Beneath the Sea*, a real clunker.) The actors appearing in them appear to be pushing themselves a little harder under Budd's guidance. Had he stayed with the studio, would Boetticher have graduated to bigger pictures with higher budgets and grander stars, perhaps directing James Stewart or Cary Grant? It's impossible to say, but probably unlikely. Most of the studio's contract directors of the 1950s—Joseph Pevney, Nathan Juran, Jesse Hibbs, Jack Arnold and Charles Lamont, for example—stayed within the realm of the fast-and-furious B-level genre movies that they proved to be successful at.

Budd was antsy to move on, to tackle another personal project, and so he left Universal to make *The Americano* with Glenn Ford in Brazil. He later said that one reason he had to get away from Universal was because he fell hopelessly in love with actress Julie Adams, who was married and who appeared in three of his movies. On a personal level, Budd experienced two personal losses when, in December 1953, his father Oscar died at his Santa Monica home at the age of 86. A year and a half later, in May 1953, his mother Georgia, in her mid–60s, died suddenly of coronary thrombosis.

The Americano was a disaster for Budd as production delays, bad weather and even worse luck held it up. It became the only film that he started that he did not complete, and that lack of closure haunted him the rest of his life. (William Castle completed the picture and receives credit.) Boetticher returned to Hollywood uncertain of where he stood or what he would do. He passed time shooting some episodes of the television series *Public Defender* before jumping from one independent film production to another in 1954 and 1955. The first two—*The Magnificent Matador*, a failed attempt to capture the past glory of *Bullfighter and the Lady*, and *The Killer Is Loose*, a taut B noir—did nothing to restore his reputation.

But the third, Burt Kennedy's *Seven Men from Now*, did. John Wayne, despite his differences with Boetticher, wisely saw his potential and approached him about directing the picture for Wayne's Batjac Productions in the summer of 1955. Budd said he both loved and hated Wayne, but credited Wayne with saving his career twice. "He played John Wayne better than anybody in the world," Budd told Herb Fagen for the book *Duke: We're Glad We Knew You* (Citadel Press, 1998). "The man had style. He was Duke and he was fascinating and he was tough. But I don't think I could have directed him. I couldn't have lasted halfway through a picture with him. Either I would have quit or Duke would have fired me. But he did produce two of my best pictures, *Bullfighter and the Lady* and *Seven Men from Now*."

Seven Men from Now—and many of the follow-ups Budd made for Scott and his partner Harry Joe Brown—made Boetticher's reputation as a cult director. Everything he had learned along the way at lesser studios suddenly proved invaluable, particularly as, for the most part, he worked on these pictures with minimal studio interference. "We were left alone because we weren't really anybody," he said of the films he made with Scott. By 1955, Budd had learned to shoot fast and loose and improvise, all talents that came in very handy as he and Kennedy worked together to revamp the scripts and come up with new material on location. Budd shot in sequence as often as possible, which worked well on the Lone Pine pictures where characters got killed off along the way and thus actors could be let go as their characters expired. He also kept his coverage footage to a minimum to ensure that a John Ford didn't come along to cut a half-hour of beloved footage out of these projects. "He had a John Ford complex," said actor-stuntman Jack Williams, who worked with Budd on several projects. "He tried to cut with the camera so he'd end up with a short picture."

Boetticher had already learned to adapt to—or ignore—interfering producers. And, as several actors who worked with Budd have attested, he had a psychologist's mind when it came to understanding the people around him. He had survived bulls running at him, so making end runs around Randolph Scott, Harry Joe Brown and the like was not so very difficult.

"I fell in love with Randolph Scott and Harry Joe Brown," Budd said in a late 1960s interview. Scott, who had turned to making Westerns full time in the late 1940s, teamed up with producer Brown in 1947 to form a company called Producers-Actors, which made inexpensive ($500,000 to $750,000) color Westerns starring Scott. The duo made a deal with Columbia to split both the costs and profits of these pictures. (Singing cowboy Gene Autry made a similar deal with Columbia around the same time.) For seven or eight years, these pictures brought in three to four million dollars, resulting in a tidy profit for Harry Cohn, Brown and Scott. But by the mid–1950s, the creative duo were looking to not only freshen Scott's screen image, but change it. And in Boetticher and Kennedy, they saw the perfect partners with whom to do just that.

Scott liked Budd, and visa versa. Scott was Southern royalty on horseback, a modern-day Lancelot and a man Budd would have likely pushed into the bullfighting ring had he been 20 or 30 years younger. Scott, Budd said years later, had something very few people in the industry had: class.

The resulting films charged the normally stone-faced Scott's well-known Western character with a sense of purpose that bordered on the deadly. Film historian and author Jim Kitses wrote, "The Boetticher hero as created by Scott can be said to possess (or be moving toward) a great serenity, the knowledge that we are fundamentally alone, that nothing lasts, and what matters in the face of all this is living the way a man should [live]."

Seven Men from Now's surprising financial

(From left) Budd Boetticher, Audie Murphy and Beverly Tyler watch as one of Budd's bullfighter compatriots (possibly Carlos Arruza, though it is tough to tell) shows off on the Universal backlot during the shooting of *The Cimarron Kid* (1952).

and critical success led business partners Scott and Brown to hire Budd to direct five films for their company. Those pictures, as well as a one-off that Budd directed for Scott at Warner Bros. called *Westbound*, have informally become known as the Ranown Cycle after the production company Scott and Brown put together to make the last two in the series, *Ride Lonesome* and *Comanche Station*. Burt Kennedy supplied the script for four of the seven and worked uncredited (and only briefly) on two others. It was a happy team made up of people having fun and taking chances far away from the confines of a studio on location in places like Lone Pine and Old Tucson. The tight shooting schedules didn't scare Budd: "I think when you really know what you're doing, you put a lot more into 12 days—artistically, physically and mentally—than you do into 90 days, just because it's impossible," he told Eric Sherman for *The Director's Event* a decade or so after the last of the Scott films was produced. "You're really not making a 12-day picture because you're giving it 24 hours a day."

Boetticher was in his element, and mostly in control. "I prepare my pictures the day before I shoot. And I think there's that spontaneous feeling when you see them," he said. There is an element of potential surprise in many of the Boetticher-Scott films: You don't really know what is going to happen next, and often what happens is jarringly violent.

Budd didn't like the over-analysis of his Westerns but he always liked the attention he got for making them and wisely played that up in later years when he became a celebrity on the film festival circuit. He praised Burt Kennedy's scripts and Kennedy's ability to adapt to Budd's wishes when it came to adding or eliminating or changing something. "The reason that people understood the Westerns I made with Randy Scott is that they were simple, and in their simplicity I had a couple of goals to reach," he said. "I knew where those goals were and what I was striving for.... Nothing in those Scott pictures would make the audience say, 'What did he mean? What was he trying to say?'"

This period remains the peak of Boetticher's career and the Scott pictures remain the best-regarded. The series probably could not have gone on much beyond 1960, the year the last of the films, *Comanche Station*, was released. The studio system was dying fast, Scott was over 60 and ready to retire, Kennedy wanted to direct and Budd wanted to make a film about Carlos Arruza.

One senses that Boetticher was a man who was easily bored, and that may be another reason his overall cinematic career doesn't hold up as well as Anthony Mann or some of his other contemporaries. He worked at one studio for a while, left to take a break, worked at a studio which was not even as good as the first, bounced over to a third studio for a picture, landed at studio #4 for a while, went to make a picture in Brazil that didn't work out, returned to make a few independents, shot some Randolph Scott Westerns, made some TV shows, and then spent too many years focusing on an impossible-to-make reality-film production about the life and career of Mexican matador Carlos Arruza. He married actress Debra Paget and divorced her just as quickly.

And somewhere along the way, many people think, he kind of lost his mind.

About 290 pages of Budd's roughly 390-page autobiography covers his years in Mexico, his own bullfighting experiences and the Homeric saga behind the making of *Arruza*. By his own account, he began filming background bullfighting footage in the spring of 1958. He put together a first draft of a script roughly a year later. Again by his own account, he shot the last sequences for the movie in February 1967. It took another four years to get a mostly finished print together to premiere in Tijuana, Mexico, and another year before the film received limited distribution in May 1972. It's not unfair to say that *Arruza* comprised a 14-year odyssey for Budd, one that took him out of the American spotlight and cost him his bankroll, marriage and career. He claimed it gave him confidence to realize he was a good director.

"In the long run, I now have a much better concept of what I want to do," he said in *The*

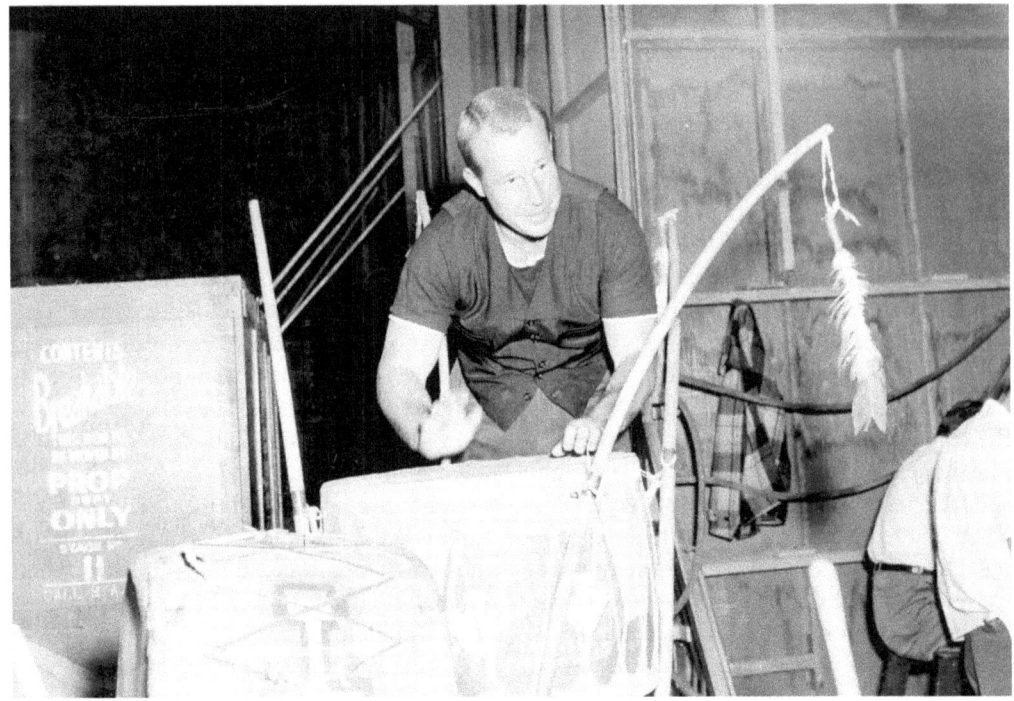

Budd Boetticher clowns around on the Universal lot, circa 1952 (Photofest).

Director's Event. "I sure as hell understand people a lot better. I was terribly hungry and terribly cold, but I'm delighted things turned out like they did, because I remember those times now." In that same interview book, he said, "I don't think you can improve on *Arruza* as a documentary.... [I]f you've made 31 features, and then you make a documentary, you sure as hell should have learned something. If I have, it's all in *Arruza*."

"Now I think there's a chance I might be a good director," he said in one interview around 1970. In another interview around that time, for *Film World*, he said, "I would like to be considered before I die one of the best [directors]."

The problem is, in terms of resuming his Hollywood career, he had lost his footing. Audie Murphy, looking to stage a comeback for himself and work his way into the business as a producer, asked Budd to direct *A Time for Dying*, a script Budd had written some time around 1966 or 1967, for Murphy's new production company. But the low-budget film featuring no-name actors did not get released before Murphy's death in May 1971, and after that everyone involved with the production seemed to have lost interest in trying to do anything with it.

Meanwhile, Budd wrote the screenplay for *Two Mules for Sister Sara* with a Mexican film production in mind, but then switched gears and offered it to Universal with his name attached as director. It was all looking good as a strong comeback film for Budd, possibly starring Robert Mitchum as the gunfighter and Elizabeth Taylor as the prostitute posing as a nun. (Audie Murphy's son Terry, as well as Budd, also said that Audie Murphy was in the running for the lead male part.). But a series of somewhat difficult-to-follow circumstances led to the studio hiring cult director Don Siegel, who had recently scored a couple of hits with the crime drama *Coogan's Bluff* and *Madigan* (both 1968) to direct. "I'd been gone for seven years and Universal felt that I had lost whatever I had—which is highly probable," Boetticher said around the time of the film's release. He hated the finished product. Universal did, at least, pay Budd off to avoid a lawsuit, and that money allowed Budd to live comfortably for some time. He also got a story credit on the film.

Budd's favorite story about *Two Mules* revolved around a phone call he received from John Ford shortly before Ford died in late August 1973. Ford had apparently caught the first television screening of *Two Mules* and called Boetticher the next day to ask, "Did you make that piece of crap I saw on the tube last night?"

"No, Jack," Budd replied. "I had nothing to do with that except the title."

"I didn't think so," Ford replied before hanging up.

Arruza was released in select cinemas in the spring of 1972. Critics mostly praised it, with some overrating it because they were so happy to see Budd Boetticher back. But it did not get him any more work. Budd talked about making a comeback with any number of film projects: *A Horse for Mr. Barnum*, a screenplay he wrote about a trio of cowboys who travel to Spain to buy some Andalusian horses for Barnum's circus; *When There's Sumpthin' to Do*, a World War I–era Western set in Mexico that Budd wrote, in which five Americans get caught up in a plot to steal a steamboat full of silver, and the little-known *Feather Nest*, a 1930s drama about a Midwestern-born athlete who goes to a military academy, heads off to Mexico for some adventures and ends up working for the obscure Eberly Studios in Hollywood. Budd apparently wrote that script before he penned his autobiography as it is a thinly veiled fictionalized version of his own life. Despite repeated media reports that Budd was about to film one or more of these pictures into the early 1990s, nothing came of any of these proposed projects.

Nor did Budd carve out a niche as a character actor in the manner of a John Huston or Orson Welles. In the spring of 1985, *Variety* announced that he would play a small role in *Two Jakes*, a sequel to *Chinatown*, but it did not happen. He did play a small role as a judge in Robert Towne's nourish *Tequila Sunrise* (1988) but he so detested the experience that he vowed never to return to Hollywood ever again.

Budd retired to Ramona, California, with his third and last wife, Mary Chelde, who he met during the production of *A Time for Dying*. There he raised horses, gave countless interviews about his career—mostly focusing on the Randolph Scott Westerns and his trio of bullfighting films—and became a film festival circuit celebrity. Now and then his name popped up in the trade magazines in connection with some project, such as a 1981 *Variety* piece about his plan to direct *Califa*, starring James Coburn and Yvette Mimieux, about the breeding and training of Portuguese Lusitro bullfighting horses. That project never materialized.

"I'm not interested in making *Halloween IV*," Budd told *Hollywood Reporter* journalist Kirk Ellis in 1984. "I can afford to sit back and wait until there's room for my kind of picture again."

The problem is, his type of movie would never come back, and he would wait until he died some 17 years later. In the interim, he wrote his autobiography *When In Disgrace*, published by Neville in 1989, and then wrote a second autobiography, *Where Are the Elephants?*, which has not been published to date. He talked at one point of making a film out of *When in Disgrace* but said, "Who the hell could play me?" He oversaw the 1986 restoration of *Bullfighter and the Lady*, with the help of David Shepard, Director of Special Projects at the Directors Guild of America, and Robert Gitt, then head of the University of California at Los Angeles' Film and Television Archives, as well as the movie's star Robert Stack.

In December 2000, Budd agreed to work with filmmaker Bruce Ricker on the documentary *Budd Boetticher: A Man Can Do That*. Ricker said at the time that Clint Eastwood helped get the picture made. Eastwood always had respect for Boetticher's work. In a 2005 interview with the *Los Angeles Times*, Eastwood said of Budd, "I don't think he fit in. A lot of these [B directors] get used to being in that size of film and producers don't see you doing anything larger…. Boetticher never got to do any big ones."

In a 2005 interview with the *Santa Fe New*

Mexican Pasatiempo magazine, Ricker said of Budd, "I don't think he could ever look outside of himself. He could never figure out a way to stop and say, 'Maybe I'll have to compromise.'"

Budd died on November 29, 2001, at his Ramona home at the age of 85. David Binder, in his *New York Times* obituary, wrote that Budd directed 38 films which "display an eye for vivid landscapes and were noted for a sharp contrast between heroes who were men of few words—the strong, silent type—and voluble villains." He quoted Budd, from a 2000 interview, saying, "I hate macho, even though that's what I was all my life."

Budd's widow Mary Chelde later relocated to Nevada, where she lives as of this writing.

Asked late in life what his filmmaking style was, Budd Boetticher said, "Honest. Tough. Perhaps unpredictable because that's the point of telling your story.... I think I have always been a storyteller."

But, he added, "I didn't get to tell a lot of the stories I wanted to tell."

The Films

One Mysterious Night (Columbia, 61 minutes, released in September 1944) Director: Oscar Boetticher, Jr. Producer: Ted Richmond. Screenplay: Paul Yawitz. Cinematographer: L.W. O'Connell. With Chester Morris (Boston Blackie), Janis Carter (Dorothy Anderson), William Wright (Paul Martens), Richard Lane (Inspector Faraday), George E. Stone (The Runt), Robert Williams (Matt Healy), Robert E. Scott (George Daley) and Dorothy Maloney (Eileen Daley).

Synopsis: When cunning thieves steal the highly prized "Blue Star of the Nile" out from under the watchful eyes of both the police and museum officials, Boston Blackie is suspected of the crime. To clear himself, he hunts down the culprits.

> *My first picture had a wonderful review and I realized I had a great career because I couldn't go anywhere but up. The review said, "This film wasn't released. It escaped."*—Budd Boetticher, 1969

Budd Boetticher had a tendency to put down his mid–1940s Columbia pictures, once calling them "terrible pictures" made on the quick. "We had all these people who later became stars, or didn't, like George Macready and Nina Foch, and you never had anybody any good. I don't mean that they weren't good but they weren't then, and neither were we," Boetticher said in 1979.

He's being hard on his first full-fledged directorial credit, *One Mysterious Night*, originally titled *Boston Blackie's Appointment with Death*. It *should* have been titled *One Mysterious Phone Call*, because that is what gets the whole plot going. It's a briskly paced one-hour programmer that does exactly what it sets out to do: keep the patrons engaged while they wait for the main feature. Pulp writer Donald Boyle had created Boston Blackie in a series of short stories that later became a full-fledged novel in 1920. Columbia optioned the rights and, starting in 1941, created 14 inexpensive "series" programmers starring Chester Morris as good-bad guy Boston Blackie, a hood who always evades the law by joining it to solve crimes. "More so than any other contemporary sleuthing series, 'Boston Blackie' relied on humorous moments to carry the routine crime-solving pictures," wrote James Robert Parish in *The Great Movie Series* (A.S. Barnes, 1971). "Morris gave the characterization a snappiness and pep, albeit on a low intellectual level, so sadly missing from the 'Crime Doctor' and 'The Lone Wolf' films [also produced by Columbia]."

Parish is right, and Boetticher can be credited with adding some of that "snappiness and pep" to *One Mysterious Night*, which often plays like a comedy and shows just how inventive Boetticher could be even at this early stage in his career. In one shot, he has the camera do a double-take after it casually passes by the upside down figures of Boston Blackie and his sidekick The Runt (George E. Stone) tied to the bottom of a Murphy Bed standing in a wall. Boetticher urged the two actors to do the stunts themselves after giving them a firsthand example of what he wanted. In a June 1944 U.P. piece by Frederick C. Othman, "Ex Office Boy Loses Pants But He Directs a Movie," Boetticher said, "I tried to show my actors how to do it [hang upside down] and I split my pants all the way off." Othman added,

Chester Morris as Boston Blackie (left) helps a squeamish "Runt" (George E. Stone) learn how to fire a gun in this publicity still for Budd's first film, the fast-paced *One Mysterious Night*.

"In case you're wondering about his first name, it's Oscar, though he doesn't go around advertising it."

There is more than a little fun to be had in watching *One Mysterious Night*. It's amusing to see how the clever masterminds behind the broad-daylight theft of the Blue Star pull off their brazen robbery by simply getting two bratty kids to struggle over a pinwheel, which in turn leads the miscreants' shrewish mothers to engage in verbal warfare. "Police Baffled! Public Aroused!" one newspaper headline declares. Soon there is consensus that while 20,000 police officers cannot solve the crime, Boston Blackie can. His long-time nemesis, Captain Faraday (well played by Richard Lane), calls a press conference and tells the eager journalists that Boston Blackie pulled off the job.

This is just Faraday's ruse to draw Blackie into the case. He gives Blackie a police badge and full freedom to go after the bad guys, and soon our hero is pulling off magic tricks (something Morris was adept at in real life) and posing as a professor, a geologist and a telephone repairman to get his man.

Carter plays an unethical reporter who has no qualms about pulling the old "There's something in my eye" routine to distract another woman and switch handbags in order to get a key to the other woman's apartment.

One Mysterious Night also includes one darkly absurd bit where two police officers, assigned to watch over a seriously wounded man, bide their time by playing gin rummy over his prone body! Oh, the stuff you could get away with in 1940s Columbia B films.

This was the seventh in the 14-strong Boston Blackie series, which ended in 1949. Several notable directors, including William Castle and Edward Dmytryk, cut their teeth making Boston Blackies, and there must have been worse ways to earn a living in Hollywood in those days. In a six-degrees-of-separation scenario, the film gave Boetticher the first chance to work with producer Ted Richmond, who would oversee two Boetticher Universal films in the 1950s, and it was scored by Mischa Bakaleinikoff, who later composed scores for three Boetticher-Randolph Scott films. Bakaleinikoff worked at Columbia for nearly two decades before dying in 1960, shortly after *Comanche Station* was released.

Actress Dorothy Malone, billed as Dorothy Maloney, played a small role. Budd later referred to her as one of several stars-in-the-making who he worked with when they were still nobodies.

When interviewer Wheeler Winston Dixon asked Boetticher if he did any planning on the Columbia Bs, Boetticher replied,

> No, I didn't do anything like that. I just figured I was the director and I'd go on the set and direct the picture. Listen, you don't learn to be a director; you either are or you aren't. And you better damn well be able to deal with people. I would look at the scene, rehearse the scene with the actors, and then shoot it ... but I didn't design anything. I just went on the set, I was the boss, and I did it.

One Mysterious Night is probably the best movie Boetticher made in the 1940s. But the critics were not impressed. Maybe they were tired of the series already, based on some of the reviews. According to *The Independent* (September 16, 1944), "A routine cops and robbers yarn has been rehashed for this whoodunit to offer little other than plenty of action." In his September 21 review, the *New York Herald Tribune's* Bert McCord wrote, "I suspect it will be seen by many thousands of theatergoers who will enjoy and promptly forget it."

The *Motion Picture Herald* critic, who caught the film in a surprise preview screening at the Pantages Theater in Hollywood, said the matinee audience which had come to see an Abbott and Costello comedy as the main feature gave the secondary offering a tepid reception. That reviewer credited Budd with managing to "inject a certain amount of suspense and some comedy" into the film. The normally supportive *Hollywood Reporter* (August 21, 1944) wrote, "This is one of those pictures which provides a growing sense of irritation as it unfolds.... The script has more holes than Swiss cheese."

The *New York Times* critic said Columbia seemed intent on killing off the series with this entry, which was "as unsatisfying as a blank cartridge in a gunman's gat. The redoubtable Blackie too, has the look of a man whose patience is being sorely tried. Although this slow fiction about a stolen diamond offers two murders and an occasional bit of gunplay, it still adds up to too much sound and very little fury."

Talking to Ronald L. Davis, Budd said of Columbia B pictures, "You can't learn to be a great quarterback sitting on the bench. But they let us make $100,000 pictures and make terrible mistakes because they knew they were second features. If you had a *Cover Girl*, you'd have a *Boston Blackie* with it. And nobody stayed through it unless you got in in the middle of it, so it didn't make any difference."

The Missing Juror (Columbia, 66 minutes, released in November 1944) Director: Oscar Boetticher, Jr. Producer: Wallace MacDonald. Screenplay: Charles O'Neal. Story: Leon Abrams. Cinematographer: L.W. O'Connell. With Jim Bannon (Joe Keats), Janis Carter (Alice Hill), George Macready (Harry Wharton), Jean Stevens (Tex), Joseph Crehan (Willard Apple), Carole Mathews (Marcy), Edmund Cobb (Cahan) and Mike Mazurki (Cullie).

Synopsis: After a jury wrongly convicts Harry Wharton of murder, the psychologically tortured prisoner takes his own life. When someone starts killing off the jurors one by one, ace crime reporter Joe Keats (Bannon) gets on the case.

A so-so picture with a decent premise, *The Missing Juror* benefits from George Macready's nuanced performance as a falsely accused man driven to insanity. The film is shot with flair, suggesting it was directed by someone who knew what they were doing, and it includes a pre–*T-Men*-like sequence in which our hero is locked in a steam room and left to die. That scene, and the presence of familiar noir figure Mike Mazurki (as a poetry-spouting masseuse!) makes one wonder why Boetticher, despite some decent chances, did not rise to the ranks of Anthony Mann—who directed *T-Men* and other noir classics at Eagle-Lion and MGM.

The Missing Juror does keep the suspense going, and for a while you will be guessing who the killer is. The newspaper headlines showcased in these kind of pictures warrant a laugh: "Revenge from Beyond the Grave!" and "Jury Members Quake in Fear!"

The script is the culprit here, with one far-fetched situation after another: The police are dumb enough to immediately believe a weirdo who claims to have committed all the crimes; a dying man, saying he has little time left to explain what happened, gabs away incessantly, and our reporter hero convinces the police to let him interview a prime suspect. The script doesn't make Bannon's character look too bright in the first place.

Bannon, star of radio's once-popular series *I Love a Mystery*, is pleasantly bland in the same manner as so many B-level actors who never became stars. Bannon essayed Red Ryder in a series of Eagle-Lion Westerns around the time Budd was making a couple of noirs for that studio; his career fizzled out by the end of the decade.

Carter was never destined to become a star. Boetticher, in his autobiography, says she was his first love in Hollywood but that his attention was not returned. "She was just so darn nice and so much fun," Boetticher wrote. "And the fact that her legs made Betty Grable's legs look…. Well, Miss Grable's just weren't as pretty." (Studio cheesecake photos of Carter from that period do reveal a shapely figure and inviting smile.) Casting director Max Arnow had a thing for Carter, and while she was apparently rebuffing his advances, Arnow thought Budd was succeeding, so Arnow ended up hating Budd. Boetticher said that Carter "could have been a star—if she had wanted to. But I'm happy she was too smart to play that game." Star or not, Carter hung on at Columbia into the 1950s, surviving the *Whistler* and *Lone Wolf* series programmers and later co-starring with future Boetticher star Randolph Scott in 1951's *Santa Fe*. She left the business by the mid–1950s, and died in North Carolina in 1994.

Another future Randolph Scott co-star, Macready anchors *The Missing Juror*. A former newspaper reporter, he bore a facial scar from a car accident in the early 1920s. It gave him a distinctive look but led producers and directors to cast him as a villain more often than not. It's possible he did not mind, telling *TV Guide* in the 1960s, "Everyone has a little evil in them." Boetticher would refer to Macready as a classically trained Shakespearean actor (his great-grandfather was Shakespeare performer William Macready), but time and again his rather puffed-up emotion left him looking like "American's Greatest Ham Actor," as one blogger put it. In an interview with Winston Wheeler Dixon, Budd said Macready "was great. And that was his first really big performance…. From that picture,

Jim Bannon and Janis Carter pretend to act for this obvious publicity photo for Budd's second film, *The Missing Juror*.

George Macready (left, in jail cell doorway) does some over-emoting to the bewilderment of (center, from left) Edwin Stanley, Joseph Crehan and Jim Bannon in *The Missing Juror*. **The actors at left and right are unidentified.**

he went on to be one of the top character actors in Hollywood. He had a scar on his cheek that was real; I don't know if it was from a car accident or a dueling accident or what, but it really added to his personality on the screen, and I liked him very much."

The Missing Juror is breezy but nonsensical. With a bigger budget, bigger stars and a slightly longer running time, it could have been a contender for one of those unsung 1940s noir gems.

It's a great premise for a real noirish tale. It's only too bad that no one involved in the production of this movie knew how to produce a real noirish tale, nor even how to tell a tale that makes any more sense than this one does. There are enough holes in the story to sink a battleship, and no one in the cast ever stops to make the obvious questions—with the answers equally obvious—if there are any.—Steve Lewis, The Mystery File *blog, 2010*

Escape in the Fog (Columbia, 63 minutes, released in April 1945) Director: Oscar Boetticher, Jr. Producer: Wallace MacDonald. Screenplay: Aubrey Wisberg. Cinematographer: George Meehan. With Otto Kruger (Paul Devon), Nina Foch (Eileen Carr), William Wright (Barry Malcolm), Konstantin Shayne (Schiller), Ivan Triesault (Hausmer), Ernie Adams (George Smith) and Mary Newton (Mrs. Devon).

Synopsis: Ex-servicewoman Eileen Carr (Foch) has a dream in which she sees two men attempting to kill a third man on the Golden Gate Bridge. Shortly after waking up, she ends up on that bridge where her nightmare becomes a reality.

There may be some who consider *Escape in the Fog* a fair noir deserving of more credit than it receives, but to me, it's a potentially interesting picture that quickly slips into absurdity because of the many illogical plot points and sometimes unintentionally funny dialogue. It's tough to take a story seriously when

Escape in the Fog

Bad guys Ivan Triesault (left) and Konstantin Shayne, both with guns, have the upper hand over hero William Wright and heroine Nina Foch in *Escape in the Fog*, a disappointing noir.

it includes a sequence in which a somber Harbor Patrol captain says his crews might be able to find a floating packet in the river if they "compute the speed of the current together with the wind drift in relation to the tide running at the hour the object was lost and send one of our boats to search the area." Incidentally, they don't find the package.

But what a start: Lovely Eileen Carr (Nina Foch) wanders into the fog. A ship's foghorn is heard. A taxi pulls up. There's a struggle. Somebody pulls out a knife. Then a scream. "You never can tell what will come out of the fog," a passing police officer tells Eileen.

Then she wakes up from this nightmare and meets a man destined to take her back into it: Barry Malcolm (William Wright), an undercover American spy who, like Eileen, is recuperating from what we today might term post-traumatic stress disorder. Before he can swoop Eileen off her feet (and into bed), he's called back into service by top-billed Otto Kruger, who is supposed to be the local head of American intelligence but who stupidly lets German spies set up a radio bug in his grandfather clock. Kruger wants Wright to undertake a secret trip to Hong Kong to deliver an even more secret packet, and in no time at all we are caught up in a plot reminiscent of a World War II–era Republic serial.

It's pretty silly. German spies, who are hip to the Allies' plot, pop up in taxi cabs, telephone booths, clock repair shops and Chinese restaurants to bedevil our heroes. At one point, desperate to find the missing packet, the German spies place a personal ad in the local newspaper's Lost and Found section. "I am overlooking nothing!" the head Nazi snaps to his disbelieving subordinates—and the funny thing is, his ploy works!

Part of the problem with Boetticher's 1945 noir *Escape in the Fog* is that the hero (William Wright, center) is continually outwitted by the bad guys (Ivan Triesault, left, and Konstantin Shayne).

Characters flash phony-looking police badges and are immediately accepted as top brass. Strange people get on the phone and pretend to be someone else, and the next thing you know, some stupid motorcycle cop is transporting the coveted package to them. Foch's character, watching Wright tear up a top-secret missive, says, "Give it to me for safety," and puts all the torn pieces into her purse, where a Nazi later finds them and easily pieces them together. A manhole cover leads to a carefully planned-out underground secret passage that the authorities and sewer workers have somehow overlooked. And all our hero does to avoid expiration is to duck as two bad guys shoot at him and kill one another instead.

What is most disappointing is that this is about the only Budd Boetticher-directed film with a female protagonist. Foch's character slowly recedes into the background as the plot plays out, and she is, at best, well-meaning but dumb. Women generally played subsidiary roles in Budd's movies, and sometimes they barely showed up at all, so it's a shame that *Escape from the Fog* doesn't do more to play up the potential for a female lead to act the part of hero.

"This minor programmer is notable only because of the fact that the director later changed his name to Budd Boetticher," accurately wrote Arthur Lyons in *Death on the Cheap: The Lost B Movies of Film Noir!* (Da Capo Press, 2000).

In its May 22, 1945, review, *The Hollywood Reporter* curiously reported, "The timely film, under the knowing director of Oscar Boetticher, Jr., displays a cast whose craftsmanship is notable." That reads like Nazi code for "It's not very good, but some of the people in it went to acting school."

Variety said, "Script and good playing maintain interest against a background of San Francisco fog and war intrigue…. Wright and Miss Foch team excellently with good performances. [Konstantin] Shayne, [Ivan] Triesault and [Ernie] Adams are expert menaces." But in those days, the trade magazines were expected to say nice things about almost any picture to prove that movies were better than ever.

Of his Columbia pictures, Boetticher wrote in his autobiography,

> These little black-and-white pictures were made in 12 days for $100,000. They were called "fillers." They filled the bill consisting of a major motion picture and a second feature designed so that, for a minimal ticket price, the patrons who were worried about our probable participation in World War II could spend the entire afternoon in the theater. I suspect folks bought a lot of popcorn when my pictures came on.

Boetticher shot the movie in two six-day work weeks, finishing up a few days before Christmas 1944, and it was in theaters by the spring. Originally titled *Out of the Fog* (which makes little sense to me, given Warner Bros. had released a film with that very title in 1941), *Escape in the Fog* was originally intended for director William Castle, who was also cutting his teeth on B Columbia films at the time.

Youth on Trial (Columbia, 59 minutes, released in January 1945) Director: Oscar Boetticher, Jr. Producer: Ted Richmond. Screenplay: Michel Jacoby. Cinematographer: George Meehan. With Cora Sue Collins (Cam Chandler), Eric Sinclair (Denny Moore), David Reed (Tom Lowry), Georgia Bayes (Meg Chandler), Mary Currier (Judge Julia Chandler), Robert Williams (Officer Ken Lowry), John Calvert (Jud Lowry), William Forrest (Robert Reynolds), Florence Auer (Maude "Mac" McGregor), Boyd Davis (Mayor Townsend) and Joseph Crehan (Commissioner Ryan).

Synopsis: Small-town Judge Julia Chandler tries to convince city leaders to invest in a youth center to put a damper on rising juvenile delinquency cases, unaware that her daughter is one of the teen culprits.

An unintentionally amusing exploitation film, *Youth on Trial* tries to shed light on what was then a serious problem: juvenile delinquency during World War II. Various accounts from that time period report that "acts of mischief" and "sex delinquency" among teen girls were on the rise for reasons that authorities tied to the fact that America was engaged in a war. If Dad was away serving his country and Mom was working, there were likely no parents around to keep an eye on the kids. That's still a relevant issue, but *Youth on Trial* does not delve into these challenges, choosing instead to focus on the high-powered antics of its antagonist-as-protagonist, Denny Moore (Eric Sinclair). If nothing else, *Youth on Trial* holds a tenuous tie to Budd's 1961 gangster film *The Rise and Fall of Legs Diamond* in spotlighting the questionable, selfish motives of its lead character and playing up the consequences guys like him face when they break the law. And you might argue that its theme even relates to 1969's *A Time for Dying* in that the lead character is a callous teen with no older mentor to serve as a moral anchor.

Columbia produced the film in October 1944 under the racy working title *Our Wandering Daughters*. Screenwriter Michel Jacoby had just written a similar exploitation piece called *Are These Our Parents?*, which Monogram produced in 1944. Aside from getting credit for his original story for Warner Brothers' lavish *The Charge of the Light Brigade* (1936), Jacoby's work was mostly for the smaller studios; his next two scripts would also be for Monogram.

Youth on Trial has disappeared from view and it's unlikely anyone has caught it, even on late-night television, in decades. The only copy I could track down resides at the Library of Congress in Washington, D.C. Maybe one day it will pop up on television or DVD, but in the more likely case that it doesn't, I'm going to give the whole plot away, because it's a lot of fun to think that Budd Boetticher could be associated with something like this—it's so atypical of his work.

The setting is an anonymous-looking high school somewhere in America. The teens, mostly played by actors in their early 20s, drink such fountain shop specialties as the Bazooka Special (which cost 25 cents) at The Hang Out, where Billy Benedict (of Bowery Boys fame) works as the counter boy. When a customer orders a ham and Swiss cheese sandwich and then asks to change it to American cheese, Benedict yells out to the off-screen cook, "Naturalize the Cheese!"—about the only intentionally funny line in the entire film.

A storm gathers over our happy campers in the form of Denny Moore, who runs a loaded dice game in a dark enclave of the school. Moore is also pitching woo to innocent Cam Chandler, played by former child star Cora Sue Collins. "Let's wrap ourselves around a couple of double malts!" he enticingly says to Cam, slowly winning her over to the dark side. She'll be drinking a lot stronger stuff than that by nightfall, much to the dismay of her more straight-laced beau Tom Lowry (David Reed).

Moore's fixed game is just one small problem for Cam's mom, Judge Julia Chandler, who has to contend with dozens of cases just like that in the course of one day. The judge tells her hatchet-faced female bailiff Mac that she is going to ask the city commissioners to invest $100,000 into a youth center to keep these unruly kids off the streets. "Be careful—those commissioners have very sharp teeth," Mac tells the judge.

"Don't worry, my grandfather was a lion tamer!" the judge responds with a laugh.

But the council is not easily tamed. "The fact that Judge Chandler had 27 cases today… is no indication that this problem is on the increase," the mayor says in what might best be described as an act of serious denial. The council gives the judge the bum's rush.

Undeterred, the judge teams with the sympathetic police commissioner to arrange a police raid on Romano's Farm House, a rural roadhouse where teens converge to jitterbug and consume spiked Cokes. Little does the judge know Denny has brought her daughter up to this den of iniquity. The cops arrive and tell everyone to come along quietly, and then there's a hilarious pause of about ten seconds

Hot headed Denny Moore (Eric Sinclair, with gun) has some explaining to do to a surprised Mario (Muni Seroff, left) as Denny's dad (John Calvert) slowly expires in *Youth on Trial*.

in which nobody moves, as if the actors were waiting for Budd to say, "Okay, action—now run fast, everybody!" Then the entire lot of kids hightail it, chased by clumsy-moving cops who are easily thwarted by screens, chairs and plates being thrown in their path. Our lovebirds escape, but the other teens, facing the wrath of Judge Chandler the next morning, rat out Cam in court. The local newspaper headline says it all: "Judge Chandler Orders Own Daughter's Arrest!"

Tom and the well-behaved kids of town, who run their own youth court to judge their peers, ostracize Denny and Cam. The football team gives Denny the boot and Cam is kicked out of a theater production, which is doubly sad because, as she pleads with the director, "I wrote the play!" The director coolly tells Cam they will find another script to produce.

Denny and Cam also get the cold front when they visit The Hang Out, with soda jerk Benedict giving them the stink eye. Tom pulls Cam aside to confront her about the visit to the roadhouse. "News certainly travels fast," she angrily tells him.

"Not as fast as you're traveling," he responds.

The two outcasts decide to leave town and get married. Denny tries to stack the deck in his favor by robbing his own father Jud (John Calvert), who runs a shady restaurant. When Jud catches Denny red-handed, the volatile teen draws a pistol he found in Jud's office and, in a struggle, shoots his father. He then picks up an unsuspecting Cam and goes on the lam, hiding out at a cheap roadside motel. The duo's sojourn there is interrupted by a news flash on the radio: Police are looking for Denny Moore, who shot and killed his father. Denny denies all to a hysterical Cam, and then, when she tries to escape, he slaps her silly until she faints. Then he gets drunk.

Cam wakes up and tips off the motel owner

Angry youth Eric Sinclair fires away at the police while a concerned Cora Sue Collins looks on in this lobby card for Columbia's *Youth on Trial*, an exploitation film that is often unintentionally amusing despite its good intentions.

before returning to Cam to keep him occupied until the cops show up. That ruse doesn't work and soon bullets are flying all over the place. Judge Chandler, alerted to the crisis, speeds to the site of the shoot-out. There the local police officers tell the judge not to worry about their bullets hurting Cam. "We're shooting in the air," they explain, though that didn't seem to be the case just seconds before she pulled up.

Rather than wait for the fast-shooting Denny to run out of bullets, Cam inexplicably runs out the door and blunders in front of Denny's loud-talking handgun, getting a bullet in her shoulder for her efforts. An anguished Denny rushes out and blasts away at the officers, who gun him down.

The next shot sees our young lovebirds lying in bunk bed cots in the ambulance. Cam is on top. "Aren't you sorry?" she asks Denny.

"Lot of good it's gonna do me to be sorry now," he responds. "But I am." Then he passes out.

Cam survives and her mom forgives her. It's not clear what happens to Denny. The mayor and his cronies show up at the judge's house to say they support her efforts to build a youth center: "Drop in tomorrow! Let us know how you want to spend that hundred thousand!" The judge turns to the camera and says, "It's the parents who are delinquent." To underscore this message, a title card appears to admonish parents: "You—You!—The Mothers and Fathers. Are you meeting the challenge of youth today? Or will you have to stand trial for them tomorrow?"

All this in 59 minutes.

For all the fun I poke at it, *Youth on Trial* is somewhat ahead of its time in its depiction of the restorative justice youth court program, now a popular alternative method of keeping first-time teen offenders from a life of crime. And the film tried to tackle a subject that was bedeviling many an adult in America during the war years. The U.S. Department of Labor reported in 1943 that instances of juvenile delinquency were "intensified, aggravated and given new emphasis under the pressure of war," and some cites around the country saw these rates rise by 15 to 20 percent. Britain had the same problem during the war years.)

In the middle of all this nonsense, Budd stages a beautifully played sequence between the judge and her daughter in which they talk about the need to take responsibility for your actions, and how they once enjoyed an intimate relationship in which Cam told her mom everything, even stuff about boys. It's really a wonderful little bit in the circus of dementia that surrounds it.

Cora Sue Collins embodied a naturalness that is refreshing to watch. Eighteen in real life, the actress, who was under contract to MGM and made *Youth on Trial* as a loan-out, seems more in tune with her high school senior's wants and fears than the rest of the ensemble. She retired from films the same year that *Youth on Trial* was released, choosing instead to life the simple life of a housewife. "I can just be myself," she told one interviewer about the decision. Had a studio produced a film version of the popular comic book *Betty and Veronica* (which debuted in 1942), she could have played either role, because in this film she starts out as a nice-hearted Betty and slowly turns into a devious, dark version of Veronica.

Her co-star Eric Sinclair, then 23, plays a one-note variation on James Cagney throughout. Though he exudes energy, one can see why his starring days were short-lived. He worked as a character actor into the late 1980s. David Reed is bland as the equally bland Tom Lowry, and it's no surprise his film career was pretty much over by the end of the 1940s. The rest of the cast is made up of people who seemed to be passing through the Columbia lot for this one picture (such as Georgia Bayes) or experienced veterans like Calvert, Auer and Benedict, who are given little to do but do it well.

Cora Sue Collins told me,

> I don't remember how I got the part. I don't know if Budd wanted me, or someone at Columbia requested me. It was a loan-out, and I was loaned out a great deal. MGM was like an orchestra and Columbia was like a one-man band. Columbia was a smaller, more crude

version. I will say that MGM had a superb wardrobe department but Columbia's was every bit as good as MGM's at that time.

I loved that part. I never got to play a teenager. I was always playing Miss Goody Two Shoes, and I wasn't in that film. I thought Budd was a very intelligent man, very down-to-earth and very unassuming. I spent my entire life up to that point working with grown professionals, and some of them were nice, and some of them were not so nice. Budd was one of the good ones.

And he was very helpful. I had never taken any drama lessons of any sort. I was what they called a "natural" and usually directors wanted me to just be "natural." But when I needed some assistance, Budd was wonderful. He helped me a great deal with projecting emotions I had never been asked to play before. I enjoyed working with him.

Here's one thing I remember from that film. I am an acrophobic. I am scared of heights and afraid of falling. When I was six or seven or eight years old, I had to fall down a flight of stairs in a film. Instead of having a double do it, the director wanted me to do it. They made the stairs out of foam rubber to cushion the blow, but it didn't ease my anxiety. I had to fall down them—over and over and over again. From that point on, I was terrified of falling down, even on film. But I had to fall down when I got shot in [*Youth on Trial*]. I never felt I did it well. I looked at that scene in the rushes and felt I had not done it well. It was terrifying for me to do, and it's still terrifying for me to fall.

I would love to see that film again. I haven't seen it since it was released, and I'm not even sure I saw it then. In those days, we worked six days a week and if you think I wanted to spend my seventh day—me being a Roman Catholic who attended Mass on Sundays—doing that or watching one of my movies, you better believe I wasn't going to watch one of my movies.

Variety, in its March 16, 1945, review, liked the movie: "Manages considerable interest and suspense despite a familiar theme." The *Motion Picture Herald*, in its February 24, 1945, review, more accurately noted, "The effects of juvenile delinquency are depicted vigorously but the cases aren't explored with equal force in this melodrama which attempts to prove that children reflect the care or neglect given them by their parents." Good point. There seems to be little reason for Cam to start acting out so much, given her hard-working single mom appears to have been there to support her throughout her challenging adolescent and teen years.

Interestingly, after filming four melodramas in a row featuring gangsters, goons, gunmen, gamblers and Germans, Budd Boetticher was about to shoot his one and only comedy, *A Guy, a Gal and a Pal*.

A Guy, a Gal and a Pal (Columbia, 62 minutes, released in March 1945) Director: Oscar Boetticher, Jr. Producer: Wallace MacDonald. Screenplay: Monte Brice. Story: Gerald Drayson Adams. Cinematographer: Glen Gano. With Ross Hunter (Jimmy Jones), Lynn Merrick (Helen Carter), Ted Donaldson (Butch), George Meeker (Granville Breckenridge), Jack Norton (Norton), Will Stanton (Barclay), Russell Hicks (General), Sam McDaniel (Archie—Train Porter), Dudley Dickerson (Porter) and Alan Bridge (Mayor).

Synopsis: World War II hero Jimmy Jones takes a train to Washington, D.C., to receive the Medal of Honor for his actions in combat. He slips into screwball comedy territory once he gets involved with a woman, posing as a movie star, who is mistaken for his wife.

An often-delightful little comedy, *A Guy, a Gal and a Pal* suffers from weak scripting and the miscasting of Ross Hunter—later to make a name as a producer of high-gloss romantic comedies and dramas—as an Audie Murphy-like hero. The film looks cheap, particularly in its train station sequences, and the first third includes a lot of bits in which everybody tries to make material that isn't funny, funny. But as the roughly one-hour comedy unfolds, it may win you over with a by-the-numbers romantic comedy tale of two misfits thrown together by fate on a train. Had Budd been given a better script and Joel McCrea and Jean Arthur for his lead players, it's possible he would have turned out a minor comedy classic that may have shifted the direction of his career. But then maybe we wouldn't have gotten all those great Randolph Scott Westerns.

The movie includes a wonderful Capraesque bit of business in which our protagonists, accompanied by a pair of drunken hunters, attempt to stay dry in a pitched tent

The jig is up for (from left) Ross Hunter, Lynn Merrck and Ted Donaldson in Boetticher's only out-and-out comedy, the often delightful *A Guy, a Gal and a Pal.*

that is slowly filling with water from a torrential downpour. Budd and cinematographer Glen Gano then give the audience a wonderful reveal when we discover the characters have camped on a golf course which is being heavily watered by sprinklers. The script by Monte Brice, a veteran of B-level comedy who sometimes got to contribute to class-A Bob Hope vehicles in the 1940s, includes some clever gags and jokes ("I think we should ask questions first and shoot later," one drunken hunter says to another as they plan for a fracas with Hunter and Merrick), and some reworked physical gags from Laurel and Hardy movies. There's also some Three Stooges–like scare comedy nonsense set in an isolated cabin in a thunderstorm that never quite plays out the way it should, but that's offset by a very creative camera pan in which characters move from room to room and Gano's camera follows them from the audience point of view, revealing all the false fronts of the film set as if we were watching a stage play.

When the plot gets us off the train and out into the expanse of the new West, it's clear that Budd is having fun with a lengthy chase sequence played for action, not laughs, and some neatly performed byplay between Hunter and Merrick on the stairs of an isolated railroad station. For every step forward taken by *A Guy, a Gal and a Pal*, it takes a step backward, but at least it's not two steps backward. The script borrows a bit from *It Happened One Night*, and the cast is chock-full of familiar comic character types including perennial drunk Jack Norton (playing a character named Norton), Dudley Dickerson as a befuddled porter and the underrated Mary McLeod as a gabby news reporter more interested in what is happening in real life than in netting a front-page story. Also good is African-American Sam McDaniel as a train porter who immediately creates a real human bond with Hunter's serviceman. The character is not played for stereotypical laughs as many African-American characters were at that time. Look fast for bit player Joseph Palma, later to gain cult fame as the "fake Shemp" of mid–1950s Columbia short subjects (he filled in for the late Shemp Howard in a few films).

But in the lead roles, both Ross Hunter and Lynn Merrick are too inexperienced as actors to know what to do with some of the ripe material they handle. And the story wraps up a little too neatly, without any real climax or sense of comic tension.

Of interest in that it is Budd Boetticher's only out-and-out comedy (and his first "journey" film, predating the Randolph Scott Westerns of the 1950s), *A Guy, a Gal and a Pal* may lead you to ask why Columbia decided to try him out on material so at odds with everything else he had done for the studio. But that was life in the studio system in those days. Most actors, directors, writers and technicians were just human components of an assembly line designed to give them experience and make audiences happy. *A Guy, a Gal and a Pal* must have made audiences at least a little happy.

As with *Youth on Trial*, Budd rarely mentioned the film in later years, probably because no one had seen it. (Grover Crisp, Executive Vice President for Asset Management, Film Restoration and Digital Mastering at Sony-Columbia Pictures, was kind enough to arrange for a DVD to be sent to me, given the film has pretty much disappeared from view.) "[Ross Hunter has] always been a friend of mine," Budd told film historian and author Ronald L. Davis. "He and Doris Day and Rock Hudson made some wonderful pictures. But Ross was not cut out to be a physical leading man, he was more artistic than that."

Hunter's career as an actor, which started in 1943, was pretty much over by 1946, when he appeared in the Monogram musical-comedy *Sweetheart of Sigma Chi*. He turned his career around by producing low-budget Westerns, sword-and-sandal movies and dramas at Universal in the early 1950s, just about the time Budd showed up at that lot. In a 1991 *Movieline* interview with Stephen Rebello, Hunter said Columbia signed him to a contract in 1943 at a salary of $1500 a week, but that seems unlikely to me, given he was a newcomer to films. He said he made 20 pictures for the studio, but the real number is closer to ten, and most are C-level mediocrities. When Cohn dropped Hunter in 1945, he felt a "terrible, terrible shock, because when you're big in this town, you're huge, whether or not you deserve it. The minute you're out, every door in town slams in your face." He said actress Ann Sheridan suggested that he study film production, and he did, and by 1952 he was working at Universal (where Sheridan had a multi-picture deal, by the way). Within a few years he was successfully producing such big-budget dramas as *All I Desire* and *Magnificent Obsession*, as well as the family-friendly comedies *Tammy and the Bachelor* and *Pillow Talk*. He remained with Universal until 1970, with his last big hit being *Airport*. "I don't want to hold a mirror up to life as it is," he once said. "I just want to show the part that is attractive." That he did. He died in 1996.

Hunter's *Guy, a Gal and a Pal* co-star Lynn Merrick didn't last much longer at Columbia either, once the war came to an end. The Texas native, named as a "baby star" by the Motion Pictures Publicists' Association in 1940, was with Republic from 1941 to 1943. There she made over 20 movies, 16 of which starred Don "Red" Barry. At Columbia she appeared in several of the studio's "series" movies involving the likes of Boston Blackie, Crime Doctor and the Whistler. She racked up 45 film credits before retiring from films in the late 1940s. Two marriages, one to actor Conrad Nagel (20 years older than she was), caused her nothing but grief. She made the headlines in March 1950 when she took an overdose of sleeping pills in an act that was seen as either a serious suicide attempt or a cry for help. She survived, fading into obscurity and dying in March 2007 at her West Palm Beach, Florida, home. "She wasn't a great thespian, but she was good enough, and that's all it took in those B Westerns," Western film author and historian Boyd Magers said at the time of her death.

As you might imagine, the likes of the *New York Times* and *The Nation* were unlikely to send a critic to see *A Guy, a Gal and a Pal*. But the trade publications liked the movie. "Situation farce strictly patterned for laughs," said the *Variety* reviewer (March 9, 1945). Boetticher, the reviewer wrote, "always keeps an eye open to comedic possibilities." *The Hollywood Reporter*'s same-day review called the film "a pleasant, expertly produced and well-played little comedy." I can't disagree. Not quite as snappy as 1944's *One Mysterious Night*, this comedy is head and shoulders above almost everything else Budd made in the 1940s.

But you cannot please everyone. Clive Hirschhorn in *The Columbia Story* said, "Monte Brice's screenplay … was, like Boetticher's soporific direction, of no consequence whatsoever. The same could be said of Wallace MacDonald's instantly evaporating production."

Assigned to Danger (An Arc Production, 66 minutes, released through Eagle-Lion, in May 1948) Director: Oscar Boetticher. Producer-Screenwriter: Eugene Ling. Cinematographer: Lewis W. O'Connell. With Gene Raymond (Dan Sullivan), Noreen Nash (Bonnie Powers), Robert Bice (Frankie Mantell), Martin Kosleck (Louie Volkes), Mary Meade (Eva), Ralf Harolde (Matty Farmer) and Gene Evans (Joey)

Synopsis: Insurance investigator Dan Sullivan goes undercover as a doctor to ferret out a band of robbers hiding in a remote rest home.

After a three-year absence from filmmaking because of his military service and a year doing nothing at the Hal Roach Studio, Budd Boetticher made two films at the fledging Eagle-Lion Studios for producer Eugene Ling. But whereas Anthony Mann, a Boetticher peer, struck cinematic gold with some taut low-budget noirs at the studio, Budd floundered with his two pictures, partially because he had lost his rhythm as a filmmaker. And unlike Mann, Budd didn't get to work with sharp scripts at the studio.

Eagle-Lion endured a brief, rocky tenure and was one of several efforts to start a so-called "independent" movie studio in the postwar years. American railroad magnate Robert R. Young and J. Arthur Rank of British motion picture production fame founded Eagle-Lion in the summer of 1946. The deal was to make and distribute pictures in both the United States and Great Britain. It was a good idea, but it was a dream that didn't last long.

"Eagle-Lion attempted to do the impossible: break into the majors. It failed for two reasons, the company could not gain access to stars or first-run theaters," wrote Tino Balio in his excellent *United Artists: The Company That Changed the Film Industry* (The University of Wisconsin Press, 1987).

Young had bought PRC (Producers Releasing Corporation, but known inside the industry as "pretty rotten crap") in 1943 and let it stay PRC until about 1947. In the food chain of movie studios, PRC was at the bottom. If Monogram had Johnny Mack Brown, the Bowery Boys and Charlie Chan on hand to entertain patrons, PRC had Lash LaRue and… well, come to think of it, just Lash LaRue. Eagle-Lion used the old PRC studios and spent a million bucks to upgrade it for Eagle-Lion product.

Young hired Bryan Foy, an old hand at turning out B productions at an assembly line pace for other studios—Warner Bros. and 20th Century Fox, for instance—to run Eagle-Lion. Arthur Krim, an entertainment attorney who would help spearhead United Artists in the early 1950s, was hired as president of joint operations. So far, so good.

The studio set about hiring so-called stars to headline its pictures, but it was a line-up that didn't exactly excite viewers: Louis Hayward, George Brent and Gene Raymond were among the veterans, while up-and-comers Scott Brady, Richard Basehart and Richard Carlson represented the younger "name" performers. Young invested $12 million in Eagle-Lion and said each film would cost about a million dollars. Actually the studio invested about half that much into each production, firmly identifying itself as a solid B film production entity.

Among Eagle-Lion's initial productions were *It's a Joke Son, The Adventures of Casanova, Out of the Blue* and *Red Stallion*. With titles like that and stars like Louis Hayward and Robert

Rolf Harolde (left) gives the menacing eye to hero Gene Raymond (center) and heroine Noreen Nash who find themselves mixed up in a den of iniquity in Budd Boetticher's melodrama *Assigned to Danger* (1948)—one of his worst films (Photofest).

Paige, it's no wonder the studio posted losses of over $2 million in 1947. Krim later said one mistake the studio made was in hiring actors who the public didn't care about.

PRC quietly faded away by the end of 1947 as Eagle-Lion slowly emerged in its place. Foy became an independent producer for the company with Krim in charge by the end of that year. A new belt-tightening policy took place and, in its own way, brought creative inspiration to a series of now well-regarded film noirs: *Raw Deal* and *T-Men* (Anthony Mann again) and *Canon City* (Crane Wilbur). The latter production cost about $424,000 to make and took in $1.2 million, and the Mann films did well, too.

"Cost-cutting became something of an art," Balio wrote. Maybe so, but the company was in trouble. In 1947–48 it produced 14 films. Five earned a profit and two broke even, which means, at best, it was running at 50–50 gambling odds. Two films in that period showed substantial losses, though Balio, in his history, doesn't say which two those were. I wonder if Budd directed either or both of them.

Eagle-Lion shut down by the end of 1948, though it still released some Rank product like *The Red Shoes* and the independent contemporary Western *Tulsa*. It merged with Film Classics after a title change to Eagle-Lion Classics had no impact. Film Classics didn't last long either, and they weren't classics anyway. In 1950, Krim resigned while Young launched an unsuccessful $15 million antitrust lawsuit against Loew's and RKO, saying that they were refusing to show his movies in New York City and other big markets. He lost. Eagle-Lion and its somewhat related successors were gone by 1951.

Budd shot his first picture for the studio in two weeks in December 1947, about three years after he had completed his last assignment for Columbia. *Assigned to Danger* opens with slam-bang action, making a Boetticher fan hopeful. Alas, after the five-minute mark, the movie descends into a cinematic mire, putting its main character into one unrealistic situation after another and taxing the viewer's patience.

Acme Insurance Agency investigator Dan Sullivan (Gene Raymond) is assigned to figure out who pulled off a daring armed robbery that leads to a brief street shoot-out. One gang member gets killed during the melee, resulting in this memorable exchange of dialogue:

THUG 1: Where's Nip?
THUG 2: He ain't!

On a tip, our hero travels to the small rural town of Alaza, where people go for their health, but it's not very healthy for him: Soon he's trapped in a remote lodge housing the gangsters, including wounded ringleader Frankie Powers (Robert Bice). Frankie's sister Bonnie (Noreen Nash), who is not directly involved in her brother's nefarious activities, runs the joint.

Dan stops by the office of the local doctor, who sends him up to the lodge with a handful of his business cards, urging Dan to hand them out to the clientele there. In a sequence right out of a Three Stooges short, the bad guys find the cards, assume Dan is a doctor and force him to pull the slug out of Frankie's body. Dan does this without even a double take and no explanation as to how an insurance investigator could easily remove a bullet from a bleeding man.

Maintaining his guise as a doctor, Dan does little to get out of his predicament, other than to wander around the house like a sleepwalker. His one clever escape routine consists of throwing a magazine at two armed thugs to distract them, and it doesn't work. Later, desperate to find a gun, Dan inexplicably looks under the cushions and pillows of a couch! This is one hero who deserves to get offed.

Unlike *Behind Locked Doors*, which at least maintains a sense of minimal tension, *Assigned to Danger* quickly falls apart. It is left to character actor Martin Kosleck to provide what kinetic energy it has, and when his character is killed off near the 50-minute mark, you get the sense that things are quickly going to deteriorate. And they do.

The climactic gun duel is unexciting. At one point, Raymond's character, attempting to get the drop on an armed bad guy, enters a parked car through one and springs out the other side—a clumsy and noisy effort that wouldn't fool a five-year-old playing cops-and-robbers in the backyard.

Budd Boetticher: "I made *Assigned to Danger* with Gene Raymond and I met probably the most beautiful woman I ever met in my life—Gene had me to dinner and I met his wife, Jeanette MacDonald. I always though she couldn't look like she did in the movies, but she did."

Raymond never was much of a leading man, though he enjoyed a limited period of screen stardom in the mid–1930s when he was under contract to RKO. Tom Kemper, in his intriguing study *Hidden Talent: The Emergence of Hollywood Agents* (University of California Press, 2010), devotes several pages to Raymond's career in reference to his agent at that time, Charles Feldman: "Raymond, who had arrived in Hollywood in the early 1930s, sold himself as an all–American leading man after a string of fairly successful seasons on Broadway. His first few films failed to draw attention to these qualities, and some critics found Raymond's mail-order handsomeness to be rather bland." At that time, Raymond was complaining that Feldman wasn't doing enough to further his career or ensure he got top billing. But, Kemper notes, Feldman stuck with him and Raymond kept working, eventually seguing into character roles on television in the 1950s. *Assigned to Danger* was one of his last starring roles in a theatrical release.

Leading lady Noreen Nash never quite got the breaks she should have, despite being put under contract to both Paramount and MGM in the early to mid–1940s. Among her pre–*Assigned to Danger* jobs was a modeling gig with a young Marilyn Monroe in which the two cuties playfully pose with some young puppies. She later worked in a lot of B Westerns and ended up in the campy *Phantom from Space* (1953) before winning some prize money on a game show and writing the historical romance novel *By Love Fulfilled* (1980). Nash married 20th Century–Fox's main medical director, Lee Siegel, who tended to Monroe during the actress' contract days to that studio. Noreen Nash told me:

> I enjoyed *Assigned to Danger*. Budd was the best director I ever worked with, that's for sure. He was so helpful in maintaining the tension of the piece. I remember a scene where we were hiding outside behind some bushes and he came over and talked to us, trying to explain what we should be feeling. He gave us some idea about what he wanted us to think and convey. More than any other director I worked with, Budd talked with us [as actors].
>
> I don't smoke, and I don't remember if it was his idea or my idea, but I smoked throughout the whole movie! And I did it badly! I was under contract to Eagle-Lion at the time, the studio used to be PRC. Gene Raymond was easy to work with, affable, a dear man.

I told Noreen that the film was shot in 12 days and asked if that surprised her.

> Oh, that's the way it was in the old days. They made 'em really fast, particularly at the smaller studios.

Assigned to Danger remains one of Budd's weakest pictures. *Variety's* reviewer called it "an entertaining low-budgeter, [with] plenty of pistol play mixed up with enough love interest to bring about the happy medium for keeping patrons satisfied."

Behind Locked Doors (Arc Production, 62 minutes, released by Eagle-Lion in September 1948) Director: Oscar Boetticher. Producer: Eugene Ling. Screenplay: Malvin Wald and Eugene Ling. Cinematographer: Guy Roe. With Lucille Bremer (Kathy Lawrence), Richard Carlson (Ross Stewart), Douglas Fowley (Larson), Ralf Harolde (Fred Hopps), Tom Browne Henry (Dr. Clifford Porter), Herbert Heyes (Judge Finlay Drake), Gwen Donovan (Madge Bennett), Kathleen Freeman, Dick Moore, Wally Vernon and Tor Johnson.

Synopsis: Private investigator Ross Stewart gets himself committed to an insane asylum to find a wanted man he thinks is hiding there. He soon realizes nearly everyone in the joint, including the employees, are nuts.

An adequate entry in the film noir canon, *Behind Locked Doors* uses a familiar plot device and a claustrophobic setting to create and sustain tension in the tight running time of about 62 minutes. Not one of us would like to be stuck in a prison-type insane asylum whether we were crazy or not, and the picture does a fair job of portraying a potentially horrifying scenario in having an average guy slowly realize just what he is up against in crooked management, sadistic wardens and a frightening ex-boxer (Ed Wood, Jr., perennial Tor Johnson) who is willing to kill at the sound of a bell.

Lucille Bremer, who was having a heck of a time trying to re-establish her career after the 1946 failure *Yolanda and the Thief*, was one of several MGM contract players ere sent over to Eagle-Lion to play out their contract time. She plays yet another somewhat unethical reporter who has plenty of time on her hands and no hesitation about breaking legal and moral codes to get her story. She approaches Richard Carlson's novice investigator Ross Stewart (who hasn't had a client yet) with the far-fetched idea of marrying him—or pretending to marry him—and then committing him to the La Siesta Sanitarium where he can then deduce whether judge-on-the-run Drake (Herbert Heyes) is hiding there from the law. Drake's not-too-bright mistress, Madge (Gwen Donovan), rather carelessly pays nocturnal visits to the judge and is easily spotted by Stewart. After casually leafing through a book on mental illnesses, Stewart comes across a description of manic-depressive and decides that's just the ailment for him. He pretty much slouches in his chair, keeps his hat tipped over his face and murmurs one-syllable responses to anyone who questions him to prove he's a nut case, and voila!—he's in.

Once inside, he quickly realizes his mistake. "You came here to be cured," one of his roommates tells him. "You're more likely to be killed." Among Stewart's challenges is sadistic bespectacled staffer Douglas Fowley, who likes to use a ring of heavy keys to swat prisoners on the knuckles (it plays well and looks painful), and a patient who is a firebug anxious to get his mitts on some matches. Carlson, an actor who had a steady if unexceptional career, does all right as a man who realizes he has stepped into a hell-on-earth situation and wants out. And once the picture moves into the so-called "rest home," it maintains interest as Stewart discovers that things are not quite as they seem. He is immediately aided by both a chatty roommate and a sympathetic asylum aide named Hopps (played by an agreeable Ralf Harolde) who, in a coincidental turn, has a disabled son (Dickie Moore) among the patients. The best sequence involves a slap-happy ex-pugilist, played by Tor Johnson, going batty at the ring of a bell and pummeling a helpless Carlson in a one-sided boxing match in a cell. Johnson's grunting character later breaks free of his prison and takes his revenge on the sadistic Fowley character in a very satisfying turn of events.

Budd appeared to be at home in the world of film noir, successfully capturing the claustrophobic confines of an asylum. He didn't care for the picture. In *Film Noir Reader 3, First Limelight Edition* (2002), he said, "I did some pictures, some 12-day pictures, like *Behind Locked Doors*, that I am not particularly proud of. I don't know if any of those were film noir but whatever you call them, I don't think they were any good.... They gave me a job to do, and I did it."

Aside from Johnson and Moore—whose stock had fallen since his days as a leading player in the Our Gang comedies—the cast includes a pre–Jerry Lewis Kathleen Freeman, cast as a chatty nurse, and the striking but hardly charismatic Bremer. In *The Golden Era: The MGM Stock Company* (Bonanza Books, 1972), James Robert Parish and Ronald L. Bowers have this to say about her: "One of the most spectacular cases of whatever-happened-to-what's-her-name is Lucille Bremer.... Three years after joining MGM she was off the lot, a year hence she had retired from the screen, and by the 1960s she was just a vague memory of things past." Bremer appeared in just eight

Richard Carlson wonders what former MGM star Lucille Bremer plans to do with that revolver she is holding in *Behind Locked Doors*, made at the short-lived Eagle-Lion Studios.

movies, five for MGM (she played the older sister in the holiday favorite *Meet Me in St. Louis*) and three at Eagle-Lion, all on loan from an unhappy MGM. Her misfortune, it seems, was to have appeared in a rare Fred Astaire flop, *Yolanda and the Thief*, and her guest appearances in all-star MGM musicals like *Till the Clouds Roll By* and *Ziegfeld Follies* didn't help. The New York native was finished with movies by age 25 and later ran a children's dress shop in La Jolla, California.

Carlson, on the other hand, had plenty of time and plenty of breaks to make it big, but he didn't. His pre–*Behind Locked Doors* career includes relatively straightforward turns in supporting parts in films like *The Ghost Breakers*, *Hold That Ghost*, *The Little Foxes* and *White Cargo*. World War II interrupted his career, and he had a hard time resuming it after the war and had to accept low-budget melodramas like *Behind Locked Doors*. In his book *The Creature Chronicles: Exploring the Black Lagoon* (McFarland, 2014), Tom Weaver quotes actor Richard Stapley, a friend of Carlson's, as saying, "Carlson was a really terrific actor. I don't think he ever got the break he should have gotten…but Carlson drank a lot. I don't think he ever drank [while working], he was very, very strict with himself. But I think he was kind of disappointed with his career. He started off much higher, then he didn't become a star." In that same book, actress Martha Hunt summed up Carlson's screen appeal perfectly: "He was sort of like the detached scientist…. Richard didn't have warmth personally."

Carlson moved into the science fiction genre in the 1950s, most notably in 1954's *Creature from the Black Lagoon*, and handled himself competently as a director of a couple of Rory Calhoun Westerns, though that branch-out of his career didn't help him much. He died at age 65 in 1977.

In his autobiography, Boetticher called Carlson "as fine an actor as I thought he would be" and says that every day on the set was a pleasure. "But these, again, were black-and-white fillers and my career wasn't going anywhere."

Variety (September, 3, 1948): "Oscar Boetticher's direction points up the action nicely… [A] fast, suspenseful little action meller." *The Hollywood Reporter* (September 3, 1948) called it an exploitation film that "definitely isn't for children."

Black Midnight (Monogram, 66 minutes, released in November 1949) Director: Oscar Boetticher. Producer: Lindsley Parsons. Screenplay: Clinton Johnson and Erna Lazarus. Story: Clinton Johnson. Cinematographer: William Sickner. With Roddy McDowall (Scott Jordon), Damian O'Flynn (Bill Jordan), Rand Brooks (Daniel Jordan), Lyn Thomas (Cindy Baxter), Gordon Jones (Roy) and Kirby Grant (Sheriff Chuck Gilbert).

Synopsis: Naïve ranch hand Scott Jordan tries to help the mustang Black Midnight, who is abused, framed for murder and then attacked by a mountain lion.

---

*If you could make pictures for Monogram, you could make pictures for anybody.—Steve Broidy, president of Monogram–Allied Artists (*King of the Bs*, by Todd McCarthy and Charles Flynn, E.P. Dutton and Company, 1975)*

For someone like Budd Boetticher, the experience of working at Monogram must have been akin to having his car break down outside a roadhouse where the food would be inedible, a fight would break out and nobody would give a damn. The three Monogram films he made in 1949 and 1950 represent the nadir of his career, and it is amazing that he pulled himself out of the rut.

Producer Lindsley Parsons, known for his economic ways with B Westerns, hired Budd to make three pictures, two for "associate producer" Roddy McDowall. Parsons, the executive in charge of Monogram productions from about 1940 to 1944, started with the studio in the early 1930s, penning B pictures starring John Wayne and others. He stuck with Monogram after it morphed into Allied Artists and all told, he is credited with producing about 75 movies for the studio between 1938 and 1958. (His best B Western may be 1953's *Jack Slade,* an uncompromisingly violent picture that should be better known.)

If you were making a Western in 1949, would you cast an English-American and Irish-American in two of the lead roles? Maybe if you were making it at Monogram, you would. Here Roddy McDowall (left) and Damian O'Flynn examine the body of Gordon Jones in *Black Midnight*, Boetticher's first Western.

Budd recalled the films as 18-day shoots, but 18-day shoots were a rare treat at Monogram. The American Film Institute catalogue reports that *Black Midnight* was shot in three weeks, but notes that the ensuing two Monogram films Budd directed were shot in two. That may be why the first of his three Monograms boasts decent production values and some fine location shooting at Lone Pine, California.

But Monogram was a clearinghouse for fading careers like Kay Francis, and maybe—just maybe—a real talent like Don Siegel might be found there. For the most part, the studio's pictures showed a profit of no more than a few thousand dollars each.

While the screenplays for Monogram pictures were uniformly wretched, the studio productions and those of its independent producers usually called upon experienced directors such as Spencer Gordon Bennet, Howard Bretherton, *William Beaudine and Jean Yarbrough, who often managed to get credible films out of shabby material.—Gene Fernett in* American Film Studios *(McFarland, 1988)*

Roddy McDowall, in a 1994 Directors Guild presentation of Budd's work, said the films were shot in 12 to 18 days. "And then we all went to the hospital," he joked. "The schedules were absolutely frightening." Of producer Parsons, McDowall said, "Lindsley—art he didn't want. He just wanted it tomorrow. Or yesterday." But Budd, according to McDowall, "was wonderful. He was like a great big kid but very shrewd...and he really knew what he was doing."

Maybe so, but to describe the three films Budd made for Monogram—*Black Midnight*, *The Wolf Hunters* and *Killer Shark*—in the vernacular of *The Grinch Who Stole Christmas*, they "stink, stank, stunk." Of the three, it is

Rand Brooks is about to let Roddy McDowall have it in one of the few exciting moments from *Black Midnight*.

possible that *Black Midnight* stinks, stanks and stunks the least.

Black Midnight was released around the same time as a slew of pictures that follow the same boy-and-his-horse or man-and-his-horse plotline, in which the horse is usually treated badly by some human beings and then ends up getting attacked by a cougar or, in the bizarre case of *Red Stallion in the Rockies*, by an angry moose. The audience for these pictures was probably young boys in the age range of four to eight, and maybe a few girls. It's of interest because it is the first Budd Boetticher film to be shot in Lone Pine, and because it features a slightly likable villain (played by Rand Brooks) who is more interesting than the hero. Shades of things to come in the Randolph Scott pictures.

McDowall exudes a confident humor, which helps, because he spends a lot of time slipping, falling and being pushed into messy situations. His girlfriend sneaks up behind him and scares him, so he falls into a duck pond, pulling her in with him. At a barn dance, he missteps and tumbles into a punchbowl full of lemonade. On the ranch, he trips and does an Oliver Hardy–like dive into a basket of waiting eggs, receiving a facial omelet. He jumps on a horse to show off his equestrian skill and gets dumped in a muddy river. All these antics diminish his potential for Western heroism, and you've got to wonder what woman would fall for an inept idiot like him.

Worse yet, early in the film McDowall's character spends several minutes of screen time dusting, sweeping and scrubbing walls to get the ranch house ready for visitors. Watching McDowall and actor Damian O'Flynn (playing his uncle Bill) fastidiously clean may make you wish Randolph Scott would show up to run them out of town. We don't hear about "Blacky," an old horse of McDowall's, until the 13-minute mark. We do know that McDowall's Scott Jordan has a long-missing cousin named Daniel (Rand Brooks, who unlike McDowall does not sport a British accent) who may be involved in criminal hijinks. "You never talked about Daniel. Why did he leave?" one character asks Uncle Bill.

"I don't want to talk about it," Bill responds.

Black Midnight shows up and Scott buys him and trains him to be nice, but Daniel and his brutish sidekick Ron (Gordon Jones) abuse the horse for reasons that are unclear. A black cougar roaming the hills also takes after Black Midnight, but the horse proves himself in an off-camera slugfest.

Budd gets to play with the twisting ravines of Lone Pine for the first time as he puts his villain, rifle in hand, up in the rocks to draw a bead on the clueless sheriff (Kirby Grant) before Scott stops him. Here the director, let loose on the prairie for the first time in his career, shows he is engaged: Brooks and McDowall get into a good fistfight, and there's one terrific bit when McDowall leans back against a big rock and the camera tilts up to show us an angry cougar sitting on a rocky ledge just above his head.

McDowall was a credible if gawky teen performer and out of his league in a Western setting. Just a few years before he had been a major child star, appearing in such prestigious films as *My Friend Flicka*, *How Green Was My Valley* and *The Keys to the Kingdom*. Age did what it usually does to child stars: It made them grow up and left them floundering around at smaller studios. A few made the transition to character actor. Others moved into related fields. Many retired early or had tragedy befall them (Carl "Alfalfa" Switzer comes to mind). McDowall was somewhat lucky: He recovered and turned into a dependable character actor in the 1960s. He kept working until his death in the late 1990s. But he was struggling when he agreed to act as associate producer for a handful of Monogram cheapies for Parsons, two of which Budd directed.

Rand Brooks, a friend of Boetticher's, probably never got a larger part in his life than in *Black Midnight*. Gordon Jones was the Green Hornet in a Universal serial just a decade back and couldn't even hold on to leading man status on that level. Kirby Grant, who fared just a little bit better in Budd's subsequent Monogram offering *The Wolf Hunters*, had been ejected from Universal and was looking for a safety net. Lyn Thomas had promise but spent most of her early career trying to avoid going to bed with the likes of Harry Cohn and Louis B. Mayer. Producer Hal Wallis put her under contract and also chased her around the desk. She stopped off for six months at 20th Century–Fox, where apparently nobody chased her, and by 1948— less than a year after MGM had signed her with the hope of turning her into a star—she found herself at Monogram playing the ingénue in *Black Midnight*. "Oh, Roddy and Budd. We had so much fun on locations. But Budd's just got a deal with ego," Thomas told Michael G. Fitzgerald and Boyd Magers in *Ladies of the Western* (McFarland, 2002).

Thomas said the wranglers on the set taught her to ride. "God, I'm used to hoisting a highball glass, not putting my leg over a horse," she jokingly told Fitzgerald and Magers. "Horses and I have never gotten along real well." Her double, Ann Robinson, did a lot of the riding and apparently fell for Budd, then still married to Emily Cook. "Budd fell in love with her and they had a big romance," Thomas said. "How long can they romance for 12 days? She was rooming with me and she said, 'Oh, we're going to get married.' And I said, 'Boy, if you believe all that, you are a sorry little girl.'"

Robinson clearly was enamored with Budd and his directing, even some 60 years later when I interviewed her. "Budd and Roddy were in close communication all the time," she said.

> I didn't have to do anything else but ride a horse—ride it fast and look the other way so I would look like Lyn Thomas. One day Budd said, "She's been hiding her face so let's give her a close-up," and he gave me a close-up in the barn dance scene, where I'm watching the dance and clapping a little too exuberantly.
>
> Budd was eccentric and a little full of himself. He was a good person, very self-confident. I don't know how "crazy" he might have been, but anybody who gets in front of a bull was bound

to be a little crazy. I remember him reading the entire script for *Bullfighter and the Lady* to me at actor Richard Carlson's house in Malibu. He was so excited. I always blamed Budd for sidetracking my career with bullfighting. Warner Bros. was so interested in signing me to a contract but I fell in love with a bullfighter—Jaime Bravo—and ran away. I like to joke that I traded my career for a good marriage and two wonderful sons. It couldn't be better.

Robinson said producer Parsons interviewed her and hired her for the job, and that none of the sequences in the film were shot at the Monogram lot. Lone Pine, she said, was a lonely outpost with a hotel, restaurant and bar. "I hired someone to teach me how to play pool in the bar," she said. "There was not much to do in Lone Pine in those days."

"Budd was good," Lyn Thomas said. "I like Budd, but he was temperamental and egotistical and boy, you do what he said, so I said, later, Charlie." (And, apparently, "Hello again, Charlie," because Thomas worked with Budd again in his television production of *The Three Musketeers*.) She recalled producer Parsons as "wonderful, adorable, sweet man…just a doll."

Rand Brooks told me, "Budd gave me some jobs when I needed them. I worked for him when he needed me. He lived in my guesthouse for quite a while. He made a story very interesting. He could twist it a little bit but he was terribly talented. He had the ability on the set to keep everybody alive and happy."

Brooks and Boetticher had a falling out of some kind in the mid–1940s, and then Budd called up Brooks to say, "I know you're mad at me but remember, there's two sides to every story. I need you for a picture." The picture was *Black Midnight*. Why did Budd need Brooks? "Because he put me on a horse that was famous for going backwards. I could ride, drive, use whips, do things that most actors couldn't," Brooks said. Maybe, but I didn't see any horse going backwards in *Black Midnight*.

Budd shot the film in the early summer of 1949. Not one of the cast members ever changes clothes.

Variety (November 21, 1949): "The film is loaded with poorly framed fistfights and mighty tame wild horses." The reviewer called Budd's direction "spasmodic." On that same date, *The Hollywood Reporter* found it to be a "fast-moving outdoor drama. The plot has a few holes in it, but director Oscar Boetticher keeps the actors moving at such a rapid pace that they are not noticeable." How, then, did the reviewer notice them to start with? *The Hollywood Reporter* said that Brooks "almost steals the acting honors."

As poor as *Black Midnight* is, worse was to come in the form of *The Wolf Hunters* and *Killer Shark*. But at least, at Monogram, Budd could hire his friends.

The Wolf Hunters (Monogram, 69 minutes, released in October 1949) Director: Oscar Boetticher. Producer: Lindsley Parsons. Screenplay: W. Scott Darling. Cinematographer: William Sickner. With Kirby Grant (Corp. Rod Webb), Jan Clayton (Renee), Edward Norris (Paul), Helen Parrish (Marcia Cameron), Charles Lang (McTavish), Ted Hecht (Musoka), Elizabeth Root (Minnetaki), Luther Crockett (Edward Cameron) and Chinook the Wonder Dog.

Synopsis: Mountie hero Rod Webb and his dog Chinook investigate skullduggery at a remote Canadian river outpost.

"Hollywood never did right by the Mounties," wrote Don Miller in his affectionate homage to B Westerns, *Hollywood Corral* (Big Apple Film Series, 1976). "Generally," he added, "the Mounties got their men on quickie schedules."

Miller ain't kidding. Shot in Cedar Lake, California, *The Wolf Hunters* is a two-week cheapie that shows almost no sign of having been directed by our man Boetticher. Except for an exciting climactic fistfight between good guy Kirby Grant and bad guy Charles Lang, it is a long, dull Mountie opus that bears almost no resemblance to its source material, James Oliver Curwood's 1908 novel *The Wolf Hunters*.

Monogram seemed to like producing films about the Mounties, starting with 1931's *In the Line of Duty* and including a series of Renfrew of the Royal Mounted films in the late 1930s. In 1949, Monogram decided to try again with a series of ten cheapies starring former bandleader and light leading man Kirby Grant. Screenwriter Edmund Hartmann, who knew Grant at Universal in the mid–1940s, told me

Kirby Grant and Chinook the Wonder Dog examine an early victim of an unknown murderer in Boetticher's second Western, *The Wolf Hunters*.

Grant was an affable guy with a nice voice and just enough acting talent to get along, and that about sums it up. Universal tried Grant out in a short-lived series of B Westerns in the mid–1940s before the studio gave him the boot. "Grant appeared slightly uncomfortable at first but soon loosened up and became a pleasantly acceptable lead," Miller writes of the star's work in the Universal Bs of 1945 and 1946.

Curwood's novel focused on the friendship between the brave Indian warrior Wabi and his loyal white friend Roderick—shades of James Fenimore Cooper's work, but a lot less fun to read. The novel is taken up with mystery, skeletons in caves, a rival Indian gang called the Woongas and lots of wolf attacks on humans. Just one character from the novel, Minnetaki, ends up in this movie, though perhaps Grant's Corp. Rod Webb is a grown-up version of Roderick in the novel. The plot has nothing to do with Curwood's novel otherwise, and seems like a leftover Charlie Chan script hastily rewritten to accommodate a north-of-the-border setting.

Webb, who had already been introduced in Monogram's initial entry in the series *Trail of the Yukon*, is out to learn who is killing fur trappers. Our hero doesn't show up with his faithful dog Chinook until the 12-minute mark, and when he does, he's caught in the embarrassing position of having to carry his canoe over his head on land. Chinook is a good looking "White Fang" type of dog, but his array of tricks is limited to fetching firewood (a stick, in other words, which all dogs like to fetch), fetching water (he brings the canteen down to the river and drops it in, but we don't see him bring it back) and attacking bad guys.

The bad guy, McTavish (Charles Lang), comes up with nefarious schemes to steal other trappers' wares and tries to seduce the innocent Renee (Jan Clayton), who is engaged to the happy-go-lucky Pierre (Edward Norris).

"Dullsville, with a dirgelike pace and all that nice talent hanging around with little to do," Miller wrote of the film. I'm not so sure the talent is nice. Clayton does give off the sense that she was a natural actress, until the script gives her some ridiculous emoting to do when she stupidly thinks that Chinook has eaten her baby! Norris is agreeable enough as the happy Pierre, who doesn't let a bullet in his shoulder stop him from trying to romance Renee. Lang was a bland secondary lead and one can see why he did not rise through the ranks of Hollywood players to ever land an A film. He and Boetticher remained friends and Lang wrote both *Decision at Sundown* and at least the first draft of *Buchanan Rides Alone* for Boetticher. Elizabeth Root, as Minnetaki, is pretty darn hot, particularly in the opening shot that captures her from behind with an off-the-shoulder blouse pin-up look. But she is hampered with simple-minded dialogue and hasn't got much to do, only managing to run away at one point with Renee's baby in her arms, which causes lots of grief for Chinook. One wonders if there was anything personal going on between Budd and Root, for though her film career pretty much stalled by 1950, he gave her small, non-speaking parts in *The Cimarron Kid* (1951) and *City Beneath the Sea* (1953).

Helen Parrish was an almost-star of the 1930s. Her film career was petering out by the time she made this stinker. She was married to Lang, so one wonders if he got her the job or she got him the job on this one. Regardless, they both probably later regretted it.

Grant had a pleasant baritone voice and the film gives him and Clayton the chance to perform a lullaby for the baby. The infant yawns and falls asleep around the 40-minute mark, but the viewer has to stick it out for another half hour or so.

Edward Norris, Jan Clayton and a dubious-looking Elizabeth Root tend to a baby in *The Wolf Hunters*. Later, Clayton will accuse Chinook the Wonder dog of eating the infant!

The best bit of dialogue is exchanged between two villains:

Villain 1: Things are bad!
Villain 2: "They aren't good!"

The most memorable thing about *The Wolf Hunters* is a sex joke that somehow got past the censors. In one scene, Chinook is seen flirting with a comely female wolf. After Grant's Corp. Webb has caught the culprit and is leading his man back to town, Chinook sneaks off to see his love up in a cave in the hills. When he gets there, he finds her nursing a litter of wolf cubs while a male wolf guards over her, growling threateningly at the poor canine cuckold. The look of surprise on Chinook's face is hilarious; then he takes off, realizing he lost his gal to a rival. My question is, since all the action of *The Wolf Hunters* takes place within a few days (unity of time, action, place—you know, true Greek drama stuff), was Chinook courting an already-pregnant wolf or was he the daddy? And why would the screenwriter try to pull off a gag like that, knowing the target audience for the film—eight-year-olds—probably wouldn't get it?

That joke aside, *The Wolf Hunters* is not nearly as enjoyable as the unintentionally funny *Killer Shark* that followed it.

Budd Boetticher (*Filmfax* magazine): "*Wolf Hunters* was interesting because all of my friends were out of work, and they are all in the picture." Budd went on to say that the picture was "just awful." He was right.

Grant appeared in eight more Mountie films, finishing with 1954's *Yukon Gold*, before he achieved television stardom with the popular series *Sky King*. He died in a car crash in 1985.

Budd may have first met actor Charles Lang, who plays the head bad guy, on the set of this film. The Brooklyn-born Lang reportedly tried out to be a pitcher for the Brooklyn Dodgers, drove a milk truck and sold insurance before studying acting for a year at New York City's American Academy of Dramatic Arts. He somehow landed a part in playwright Victor Wolfson's 1939 *Pastoral* ("a bucolic version of *You Can't Take It with You*," one underwhelmed critic wrote of the play). Newspaper articles at the time said RKO, MGM, Warner Bros., 20th Century Fox and Universal were all waving studio contracts at Lang as a result. Given he ended up working as an actor for most of those studios in the next decade, that may not be an exaggeration. RKO cast him in supporting roles in a couple of one-hour programmers in 1940, and then Universal kept him busy in roles that kept getting smaller and smaller during the war years in such pictures as *Six Lessons from Madame La Zonga*, *Where Did You Get That Girl?* and *Keep 'Em Flying*. By the late 1940s, Lang was reduced to even smaller roles at smaller studios, so a chance to upgrade to a leading villain in a Monogram B could not have looked all that bad. He married actress Helen Parrish in 1942 and they divorced in the mid–1950s. Lang quit acting in 1950 and turned to writing teleplays and screenplays, the best of which are Budd Boetticher films: *The Magnificent Matador*, *Decision at Sundown* and *Buchanan Rides Alone*. He and Budd remained friends for at least a decade, though by the time of his death in 2004 Lang harbored some resentment at Budd's public criticism of Lang's script for *Buchanan Rides Alone*.

Variety (January 10, 1950): "An OK reception as a dualer... [A]long standard commercial lines...with direction of Oscar Boetticher adequate." A January 24, 1950, review by Ed Thomas in the clippings file of the Margaret Herrick Library does not cite a publication source, but Thomas said Budd's direction was "brisk and effective."

Many film critics praised the dog. According to Western film historian Boyd Magers, Chinook was an all-white, 140-pound, two-year-old thoroughbred German Shepherd who often had to be muzzled on the set if strangers came around. "Although trained not to bite flesh, every now and then Chinook would get carried away," Magers wrote in *B-Western Movie Reviews, Volume 2*. "Chinook's salary rose from $150 a week to $1250 per week over the five years the ten films were produced. There were no doubles for Chinook."

Killer Shark (Monogram, 1950, 76 minutes, released in March 1950) Director: Oscar Boetticher. Producer: Lindsley Parsons. Screenplay: Charles Lang. Cinematographer: William Sickner. With Roddy McDowall (Ted White), Laurette Luez, (Maria), Roland Winters (Capt. Jeffrey White), Edward Norris (Ramon), Rick Vallin (Agapito), Douglas Fowley (Bracado), Dick Moore (Jonesy), Nacho Galindo (The Maestro) and Charles Lang (McCann)

Synopsis: Shark hunter Jeffrey White has not seen his adult son Ted for 12 years. When Ted unexpectedly shows up at the wharf, Dad discovers that the boy is an effete dandy prone to gumming the works up.

"Come on aboard—I'll show you the new refrigerator!" This line of cheery welcome, uttered by Capt. Jeffrey White to a visitor to his two-bit shark-hunting vessel, ushers in the most exciting moment in the first five minutes of *Killer Shark*, a poorly titled stinker that is the only Boetticher film that you might mistake for an Ed Wood, Jr., production.

The film's title suggests a pre–*Jaws* horror epic. But *Killer Shark*—which could have been subtitled *An Idiot's Fable*—has no killer shark, though a shark does bite off a few legs along the way. Capt. White and his crew use tuna as bait to catch the sharks, which were (and still are) valued for their livers, which contain Vitamin A. The picture is about Ted's efforts to prove himself in the eyes of his father and his cynical crew members—all of whom sport such colorful but somewhat unrealistic names as Bracado, Jonesy and The Maestro.

McDowall's entrance is a hoot: He shows up sporting a goofy captain's cap, a pair of white shorts and a white T-shirt. "I don't think you'll get the chance to play very much tennis until we get back," his father sadly comments. When Ted gets seasick and prepares to vomit, a crew member deadpans, "I don't think he's very happy."

The kid is pretty useless on a shark hunt, and his ineptitude leads some sharks to tear off the legs of both Ted's dad and another hapless crew member. "You don't know how awful I feel," Ted tells his dad in the form of apology.

Douglas Fowley threatens a naïve Roddy McDowall in *Killer Shark*, probably the nadir of Boetticher's career. And maybe McDowall's too, come to think of it.

The climactic bar brawl in *Killer Shark* is one of the worst cinematic action sequences Boetticher ever choreographed. Here Nacho Galindo (center, as the Maestro) attempts to fend off Douglas Fowley (right) and his henchman Ken Terrell. The unidentified actors at left and in the background look unimpressed, as well they should be.

"Ah, cut it out. It's not your fault," the captain responds. Rather than expressing either pain or resentment at their situation, the two legless patients mostly act as if someone told them that their newspaper subscription had been cancelled. A visitor to the convalescence ward tactlessly asks Capt. Winter, "How's the leg?"

Given the minuscule budget and not-very-good cast, it is easy to see why Boetticher made no impression with these Monogram Bs. Here, because of a limited budget and mediocre script, he could not convey a sense of the scope of the ocean around the men—no watery Line Pine to highlight their isolation and loneliness. Scenes of hooking, killing and gutting sharks are far from the tense gun duels and fast-paced Indian battles of the later Westerns. And as much as you may fear sharks, watching the men make mincemeat out of them isn't much fun. The film ends with a weakly scripted barroom brawl with Ted leading his father's crew members against a rival shark-hunting gang. Poor Dickie Moore, whose career would soon end, is reduced to a bit part with nary a line of dialogue until the one-hour mark.

For male viewers (and women who like this sort of thing), the sight of bikini-clad Hawaiian beauty Laurette Luez, as McDowall's love interest, stimulates amorous interest. Oddly enough, in his autobiography Boetticher describes her as possessing "the body of a hippo." He said he took her aside to give her some direction, which included, "Remember to hold in your stomach."

She did, according to Boetticher, but as an actress she was easily distracted, and so shot after shot was wasted as she took her focus off of McDowall (hardly the Errol Flynn type) to watch a seagull fly overhead, a bus pull up to the pier, a fishing boat sail by, and so on. Boetticher took her aside again and told her the most important thing in film acting is to "learn to listen."

"Forget that you've read the script and know the next line your fellow actor is about to deliver. Look into his eyes when he speaks. That will be the very first time you've ever heard what he is saying. Listen to Roddy, sweetheart, listen to him."

After this impassioned plea, all Luez could think of to say was, "But you told me to hold my stomach in."

It's a good story, but given that around this time *Esquire* magazine released Luez's measurements as 34-24-35 (va va va voom!), it doesn't quite make sense. Luez briefly hit the A ranks when she got a role in MGM's 1951 film version of Rudyard Kipling's *Kim* (opposite Errol Flynn) but then it was back to the dreck with such films as *Prehistoric Women, African Treasure* and *Jungle Gents*.

Boetticher knew his film career was stalling but recalled the three Monogram films as fun, saying McDowall was one of his favorite actors. In later interviews he insisted that he helped arrange for McDowall, who was no longer the prim and proper carefully chaperoned star of MGM, to lose his virginity. (Boetticher doesn't say where he found the woman to accomplish this, but you've got to wonder if money exchanged hands.) The director praised producer Parsons as pleasant and hard-working. "Now, you must remember, on these little two-week shows, you weren't making *Gone with the Wind*," he accurately pointed out.

He wasn't kidding. It's particularly painful to sit through the farewells Ted and his dad exchange near the end.

TED: Let's not wait another 12 years before we see each other again.
JEFF: Getting to know you is worth losing two legs!

Amazingly, in the late 1980s, Budd told film historian Ronald Davis, "I made better pictures at Monogram than I made at Columbia, but there's no comparison between the two studios…. Me, as a D director making D pictures instead of a B picture with a little money, at Columbia." He also told Davis that one day, when the crew was shooting at sea, actor Douglas Fowley vomited up his false teeth, which disappeared into the deep dark waters below. Since Budd had only shot one scene of Fowley up to that point, they reshot that bit—without the teeth—and "that became the great Douglas Fowley character that was in a million pictures after that, without the teeth." Fowley went on to appear in a much better role in a much better film, MGM's 1952 musical *Singin' in the Rain,* and continued to work for another 30 years beyond that in character roles, so maybe Budd is on to something.

Andrew McLaglen, who later worked with Boetticher on both *Bullfighter and the Lady* and *Seven Men from Now*, was as uncredited second assistant director on this film, which was shot late in 1949.

Variety (April 12, 1950): "The story is a weak one that unfolds leisurely." *The Hollywood Reporter* (March 27, 1950): "[*Killer Shark* is] acceptable as secondary fare… [T]he direction of Oscar Boetticher smartly plays up the action values." *The Motion Picture Guide*: "About the only thing exciting here is the film's title."

Both actress Lyn Thomas and screenwriter Kirk Ellis, who knew and worked with Budd in his later years, said Roddy McDowall loved working with Budd. But when McDowall died in 1998, Thomas said she called Budd to urge him to attend the funeral and Budd said he couldn't because he was working on a new project. "I said, 'Damn, he hasn't changed a bit, he's still full of himself,'" recalled Thomas.

Bullfighter and the Lady (Republic, 124 minutes, released in May 1951) Director: Budd Boetticher. Producer: John Wayne. Screenplay: James Edward Grant. Story: Budd Boetticher and Ray Nazarro. Cinematographer: Jack Draper. With Robert Stack (Johnny Regan), Joy Page (Anita de la Vega), Gilbert Roland (Manolo Estrada), Virginia Grey (Lisabeth Flood), John Hubbard (Barney Flood), Katy Jurado (Chelo Estrada) and Paul Fix (Joseph Jameson). With special appearances by real-life matadors Luis and Felix Briones, Luis Castro "El Soldado," Ricardo Torres, Alfonso Ramirez

Though two out of three of Boetticher's bullfighting films provide excitement, the publicity stills that went along with those movies often did not. Case in point: this static still of a pensive Virginia Grey, a tie-tying Robert Stack (center) and a somber John Hubbard in *Bullfighter and the Lady*. All three actors give convincing performances in this, Budd's breakout film.

"Calesero," Andres Blando, Antonio Velazquez, Arturo Alvarez "El Vizcaino," Juan Estrada and Manuel Jimenez.

Synopsis: Hot-shot American Johnny Regan learns the hard way that becoming a matador is a deadly business.

Bullfighter and the Lady is a pretty limp title for a pretty exciting movie. Budd's original title was *Torero!* and it was apparently released in Mexico under that title, based on Mexican cinema lobby displays that I've seen advertising the picture. The film captures the mystique of men who need to prove themselves by facing death on a weekly basis and the rush of glory that overcomes them when they best a bull. With footage of real bullfighters fighting real bulls and a minimum of background music (the roars of the crowd suffice as the soundtrack), the picture captures the fear that takes hold in the ring. It also gives substance and weight to the story of the women who wait for their men to come home from the arena—assuming they do come home. "Somehow I think that Sunday afternoons are more difficult for women who bring us home than the men who face death," says Gilbert Roland's matador.

In essence, it is Budd Boetticher's own story, and along with *Arruza* and *My Kingdom For...* it reflects his personality more than any other picture he directed. Shooting far from home and away from the prying eyes of Hollywood executives down in Mexico (and with a major star backing the production), Budd was able to do what he pleased, especially with a cadre of lower-echelon actors who were eager to impress. In later interviews it is easy to see Budd's excitement growing as he discusses *Bullfighter* and everything that came after it—including the Universal films—and it's also clear he didn't think much of any of the ten feature films he made before this film.

It's a little tough to figure out when Budd started dreaming up *Bullfighter* as a movie. In some interviews he claimed he first told the story in the mid-1940s to fellow Columbia director Ray Nazarro, who then went and filed the story idea with the Writers Guild of America under his name and Budd's. But Andrew McLaglen, who worked without credit with Budd on *Killer Shark*, says Budd first told him the story of an American sportsman who goes to Mexico and becomes fascinated by bullfighting—the story of Budd Boetticher, in other words—during the shooting of that picture. McLaglen told writer C. Courtney Joyner that Budd asked him how he could get the film made, adding, "And I know you're a friend of John Wayne's." McLaglen said he would show the story to Wayne in return for a job as first assistant director and a credit as associate producer. (He didn't get the latter wish.) In another version of the story, Budd said McLaglen actually gave the story to screenwriter James Edward Grant, who then tipped off Wayne about its potential.

In *When in Disgrace*, Budd wrote, "Over the distant hill rode the Duke to rescue me from all the Indians…. I was finally able to make *Bullfighter and the Lady*—thanks, almost completely to John Wayne." Wayne, then under contract to Republic, asked his pal Grant to write a screenplay based on Budd's story and then set up a meeting with Budd, Wayne and Herbert J. Yates, the head of Republic.

What followed was an unintentionally comic bit of financial byplay as Wayne and Yates bickered about the quality of the story and the proposed budget and the casting of the lead (Yates wanted either Wayne or Forrest Tucker—imagine either one of them as a matador!). When Wayne told Yates that the producer owned him a percentage of the profits for both *Angel and the Badman* (1947) and *Sands of Iwo Jima* (1949), Yates agreed to a $250,000 budget. Wayne finally got him to up that amount to $350,000, but when Wayne started arguing for another $50,000, Boetticher—never known to be a compromiser—kicked Wayne in the leg under the table to urge him to take the deal. By his own account, Wayne put in the other $50,000 with the goal of making it a "John Wayne Production." For all that, Budd told me, "Duke and I fought all the time. I loved him but there were times when I hated his guts." Budd told film historian Ronald Davis, "[Wayne] was a bastard on one side and a wonderful guy on the other side, according to what his attitude was that day and whom he liked."

Budd hated what Grant did to his story, later saying the alcoholic writer may as well have been writing about tennis. He claimed he didn't use one word of Grant's script, creating his own screenplay out of his story outline instead. Grant, Budd liked to say, became the head of the Los Angeles branch of Alcoholics Anonymous—"and you have to be a pretty big drunk to do that!" Once, while Wayne and his wife Chata were visiting Mexico and joined Budd at a bullfight, Grant showed up—having disappeared in some sort of drunken, sex-driven haze—with ten prostitutes in tow. Chata turned toward Wayne and said, "If you even smile at one of those women, I'm going to slap you." Wayne remained immobile and kept his gaze fixed on the action in the arena below.

When Budd cabled Grant his thoughts on the script in April 1950 ("excited about some, disappointed about some else"), Grant fired off an angry reply saying he was delighted if Budd was upset and said Budd probably wrote the initial cable because "guess who was looking over your shoulder and you were anxious to act like John Ford whom thank God you ain't." Budd probably wanted to haul off and hit Grant, but his professional sense kept his temper in check.

Filming began in the spring of 1950. Boetticher found a role for his old pal John Hubbard and cast Virginia Grey in a relatively shallow supporting part. He chose Gilbert Roland as the famous matador for a number of reasons, including the fact that Roland's father had been a matador in Spain. Joy Page, a decent actress who was Jack Warner's daughter-in-law, secured a contract ensuring that no one else in the cast would have their names in larger or more prominent type in ads for the movie.

Bullfighter and the Lady (1951) revived Budd Boetticher's career after a long string of mediocrities.

Budd liked Robert Stack and brought him down to Mexico for a vacation where, as Stack recalled in his autobiography *Straight Shooting* (Macmillan, 1980), it turned into a "really unique audition," one in which Stack was expected to prove his mettle by stepping into the ring with a bull-bred cow. The feisty calf repeatedly knocked down Stack as Boetticher, Wayne and McLaglen roared with laughter from the sidelines. "They must have thought my performance was the funniest thing since Laurel and Hardy," Stack wrote. The actor eventually bulldogged the animal and tied her up with his cape to make good his escape.

A few days later, Budd called Stack to say he had cast him as the lead. "You've just seen the cows," an excited Boetticher told a startled Stack. "Wait till you see the bulls!" (Production notes indicate that Budd first offered the role of the Mexican matador to actor Ricardo Montalban, who turned it down in hopes of acting in director John Huston's unrealized bullfighting film *Matador*.)

Boetticher turned Stack over to a number of experienced *toreros* in Mexico. He would be doubled by matador Luis Briones, who had recently been gored by a bull in the head. "Every pass with the cape requires constant practice, just as a virtuoso musician or star athlete perfects the most difficult moves and makes them look easy," Stack wrote. "A pass can look flashy in front of a mirror and yet not work with a bull." Stack had to learn to handle both the cape and the *muleta* (a red cape attached to a stick to guide the bull) for medium and long shots. In his autobiography, Stack did a beautiful job relating the rigor of training for bullfighters and the elaborate and sometimes theatrical process behind the actual sport in his book. "Bullfighters lead an exaggerated, fast-paced life," he wrote. "Many of them seem larger than life; they live for the excitement and thrill."

Budd fit right into the madness, as Stack related: "Boetticher is a man with insane kind of charm, a sort of Pied Piper of Pamplona." Budd got Stack on horseback and the two of them rode into a pen of bulls, with Boetticher goading them on until they turned and charged the horses, prompting the two men to gallop away. Stack realized Budd was testing the bulls for bravery: They, too, had to audition for the film.

Wayne showed up for a few days of shooting and threw a big party while he was there. On the set, he annoyed Boetticher by stepping in to direct a scene featuring Stack, Hubbard and Grey. Wayne wanted Stack to play John Wayne, Boetticher maintained. In some accounts, Budd said Wayne did this three times before he stepped in; in other accounts, he said Wayne did it five times. Finally Budd pulled Wayne aside and asked if he thought he could direct the picture better than Boetticher. "One of us has got to go home," Boetticher told his producer.

Wayne then did something that impressed Boetticher. He assembled the cast and crew and said, "I've made a very big mistake. My director, in whom I have implicit faith, tells me that I'm interfering with him. It's his story and his picture and I'm going home and I'll be back at the end of the show." Wayne held true to his word, which Budd always appreciated.

There were other troubles on the set when it came to bribing local government officials to gain access to Mexican sound stages and film crews. Stack said that after a Republic executive told him the studio wouldn't stoop to such a low, the actor watched as that same man paid out $10,000 (after some cheerful chitchat about the weather) to grease the wheels of progress.

Other challenges surfaced when both the

A double for Robert Stack shows how easy it is in this action scene from *Bullfighter and the Lady*, the film that made Budd Boetticher's reputation in 1951.

American Humane Association and Production Code Administration (the Breen Office, which oversaw censorship in films) weighed in with their concerns. Breen wanted the production to eliminate the potentially offensive word *cabron* (goat) from the script, which makes sense, and expressed serious concern about a scene set in a steam bath involving Roland, Stack and other male characters. "No offending outlined contours," the office pleaded, suggesting that the producers send in some photos of what the men might look like in their towels and shorts in the scene so they could assess the situation!

Mel Morse, Western Regional Director of the American Human Association, wrote Breen in June to say that Republic and Boetticher were "going against our advice that animals should not be sacrificed for the sake of a Motion Picture" and charging that Republic had purchased 12 bulls specifically to photograph them dying in the ring. According to Morse, Budd "cannot understand any limitations that anyone would place upon this 'sport.'" Morse asked Breen to talk to Yates about this situation.

Yates talked to Wayne, who fired off a cable on June 26: "We stuck to the letter of the law and the Humane Office ruled [sic] concerning not killing the bulls." He said one bull was fought off-camera for the pleasure of the crowd as a reward but still it was not killed. "I do not know where the Humane Society gathers its information," Wayne said, adding that a Humane Association officer, identified as a Mr. Jacko, had been on hand all during the filming to ensure that no animals were hurt during production. When the film opened the following spring, Morse said he saw the film and "to the best of my knowledge the bulls were not killed for the sake of the picture."

Well, maybe. Morse likely saw the much-truncated 87-minute version that John Ford edited against Boetticher's wishes, and not the full 124-minute version screened in the mid–1980s and later released on video and DVD, which includes at least one violent scene in which a bull charges a horse and a sequence in which a clearly dead bull is dragged out of the ring. Decades later, Stack told one interviewer that at least one man was killed in the ring during the making of the film, and two others were gored badly.

Budd told me the only two actors he disliked were Gilbert Roland and Ray Danton, because both men had huge egos and were difficult on the set. In *Bullfighter*, Roland's character gets gored and quickly dies after stepping in the ring to save arrogant Stack's life. (Sorry to give the ending away, but Budd already did that a thousand times in various interviews over the years.) Roland came forth with a three-page soliloquy for his character to recite before expiring. "If I had actually filmed it as he suggested, it would have made Greta Garbo's demise in *Camille* look like a walk-on," Budd said in his autobiography. He said he and cinematographer Jack Draper shot it the way Roland wanted, except they didn't roll the camera. As a result, it's an incredibly powerful depiction of the reality of death—and very quiet. In Don Miller's book *Hollywood Corral*, he wrote that Roland was credited with "additional dialogue" for several cheap Cisco Kid pictures that the star made for Monogram in the late 1940s. "It was a simple matter to spot the scenes," Miller wrote. "Everything stopped while Roland would declaim lyrically about the beauty of woman, or nature, or both, or some such flowery verbiage."

Wayne's end-of-shoot cast party got out of control with locals who played extras firing off real guns with real bullets and shooting bullets into the windows of anyone who did not wish to attend the fiesta—like Page. Wayne got drunk and flipped off a veranda into some bushes below, and Boetticher downed too much tequila and passed out, leading a Mexican doctor to declare him dead on the spot. "But nobody cried," Boetticher recalled. "Now that's one hell of a way to die." Some of the partygoers decided to do the right thing and pick up his body—but only to move it out of sight so they could continue to celebrate without feeling guilty. Budd survived, of course.

He almost didn't survive what John Ford and Republic did to him later. Ford called Boetticher and said he wanted to see the film, and then, after viewing it and declaring it magnificent, he asked to edit it. Ford promised Boetticher he would win an Academy Award for it under Ford's editing touch. Boetticher relented—this was John Ford, after all—and later regretted his decision.

"Two men can't love one another without being fags," Ford told Boetticher. Boetticher countered that men could love one another without it being physical, but Ford didn't buy it and cut out over a half-hour of what he called "chi-chi shit" between Roland and Stack as well as a number of other bits: close-ups of real-life matadors that Budd had shot to give the film authenticity, bits of Mexican children watching in awe as the bullfighters practice, a roughly five-minute scene involving actor Paul Fix as an American writer working on a book about bullfighting, and more. Boetticher claimed to be heartbroken when he saw the altered 87-minute cut, which Republic released in the spring of 1951 to an overwhelmingly positive critical reception and decent box office. A few years later, Ford ran into Budd on the RKO lot and told him that he had no choice: Republic and Wayne had asked him to step in or they were not going to release the picture at all. And in those days, no director really had approval of the final cut.

Wayne clearly had something to do with that decision, for apparently he did not think much of Budd's direction, according to material found in Scott Eyman's excellent *John Wayne: The Life and Legend*. Eyman writes that Wayne told Herbert Yates that he, Wayne, had brought in "the best director in the business" (John Ford) to fix what Wayne called "a bad job of direction" (on Budd's part). Ford's cuts probably helped the film at the time, but today, Budd's cut is the stronger version, though it *could* use some editing. And Wayne clearly saw talent in Budd, or he wouldn't have reached out to him again to ask him to direct *Seven Men from Now* a few years later.

Time (April 23, 1951) called *Bullfighter and the Lady* "a modest movie with an uncritically simple story. Yet it is a picture that shows more pointedly and dramatically what bullfighting is like and its place in Latin life." That review noted that Ford had edited the film without credit and compared it to Robert Rossen's then-topical bullfighting picture *The Brave Bulls*, saying the bullfighting sequences in Budd's film "outdo Rossen's in style and grace and violent excitement."

Darr Smith of the *Los Angeles Daily News* wrote that *Bullfighter* was "an exciting and authentic essay into the pageantry of bullfighting." *The Saturday Review of Literature* weighed on May 5, 1951, calling the picture "a mighty tasty dish.... Budd Boetticher...deserves special commendation not only for turning out a superior picture on a low budget but also for the first time revealing Robert Stack as an interesting young actor." The *New York Times*' Bosley Crowther gave *Bullfighter* a mixed critique, panning Stack's character for his mythological status and devil-may-care attitude:

> [Boetticher] did the same thing for his picture that Mr. Rossen did for *The Brave Bulls*. He took his cameras and cast to Mexico and shot a great deal of footage there—in the bullrings, with actual bullfights happening, and on the interesting bull-breeding farms. Further, he documented, to a certain informative extent, the methods of training bullfighters, from the earliest drills with the cape right into the ring. He captured a measure of the flavor and excitement of a *corrida*, and he used good toreadors for "doubles" in the critical bullfight scenes. The consequence is some intriguing background and bullring sequences, marred only by the intrusion of the fantastic story and the cast.

The film made Boetticher's reputation and still packs a punch, but it has just enough flaws to keep it a notch away from being considered great. First of all, little explanation is given as to how a Broadway theater producer (Stack) and his pals (Hubbard and Grey) could hang out in Mexico for so long with seemingly nothing to do but go to the arena. The Paul Fix scene is unnecessary and should have stayed out of the final cut—his character basically says he'll never publish his book on why men fight bulls because he doesn't know why men fight bulls. And one character, a Dr. Sierra who oversees the arenas, shows up out of left field late in the film to serve as a catalyst for Johnny's re-entry into the ring following his friend's death.

But Boetticher got amazing real-life footage of matadors being gored, knocked down and flipped—including Stack, who immediately curls up into a ball of fear at one point, adding realism to the scene. The performances, if not always sterling, never disappoint. Grey always provided bounce to the lowest C-level production (*Unknown Island*, *Desert Pursuit*) and Hubbard is naturally appealing as her tolerant husband. Jurado, on the cusp of greater stardom for her work in *High Noon* (1952), adds a sense of nobility and forgiveness to the role of Roland's quietly suffering wife. And Stack is good, making one wish he hadn't returned to B-level potboilers like *Bwana Devil* (1952) and *War Paint* (1953). Budd liked to say that his films helped make stars out of a lot of actors, including Stack, but Stack didn't quite pull it off, despite an impressive Oscar-nominated turn in 1956's *Written on the Wind*. But he worked continually, was well regarded within the industry and eventually became a major television star via *The Untouchables* and *Unsolved Mysteries*. His autobiography is worth seeking out. *Bullfighter* didn't really help Joy Page's career much; she drifted out of the business by the end of the 1950s. Both Budd and Stack later said she had no real drive to be an actress and felt no regret when she left the business.

In the mid-1980s, Budd and Stack worked with the Museum of Modern Art in New York City and the University of California–Los Angeles (UCLA) film and video archives to restore *Bullfighter* to its original form.

Budd and John Wayne wouldn't run into one another or talk again until the spring of 1955, when Wayne asked Budd to direct Burt Kennedy's script for *Seven Men from Now*. After that, there would be more drinking, and at least one occasion where Wayne tried to hit Budd and missed, smashing his hand into Budd's fridge instead. (Actor Walter Reed inherited the second-hand appliance and loved showing off the dent in the fridge to visitors.) But for the time being, Budd hated Wayne, Ford and Republic. He would never go to work for that studio again. And, for what it's worth, Wayne, unhappy with Yates' cheap tastes and refusal to make a film version of the siege of the Alamo with Wayne, left the studio early in 1952 to freelance. Republic would stagger on until the end of the decade, turning out cheaper and cheaper oaters and melodramas until it closed in the middle of 1958.

Budd was aware of what Wayne had done for him. "I've always remembered that if Duke hadn't produced *Bullfighter and the Lady* and *Seven Men from Now* I might still very well be a B director by the name of Oscar Boetticher, Jr.," he said.

This film marks the first time Boetticher used his nickname "Budd"—or "Bood," as John Wayne liked to call him—on his directorial credit. Many interviewers, including me, asked him why. "Because it was the first film I really directed," or, "It was the first time I felt I was a director," became his stock answers.

It's unfortunate that after making a near-classic that spoke to the kind of man he was, Budd once again signed with a studio to make assembly-line features. None of his next nine films represent him at his best, but they kept him busy until he could reteam with Wayne for his next semi-classic, *Seven Men from Now*.

The Cimarron Kid (Universal, 84 minutes, released in January 1952) Director: Budd Boetticher. Producer: Ted Richmond. Screenplay: Louis Stevens. Story: Stevens and Kay Lenard. Cinematographer: Charles P. Boyle. With Audie Murphy (Bill Doolin, a.k.a. The Cimarron Kid), Beverly Tyler (Carrie Roberts), James Best (Bitter Creek), Yvette Dugay (Cimarron Rose), Hugh O'Brian (Red Buck), Leif Erickson (Marshal John Sutton), Noah Beery, Jr. (Bob Dalton), John Hudson (Dynamite Dick), William Reynolds (Will Dalton), Roy Roberts (Pat Roberts), David Wolfe (Sam Swanson), John Hubbard (George Weber), Palmer Lee [Gregg Palmer] (Grat Dalton), Frank Silvera (Stacy), Richard Garland (Jim Moore), Rand Brooks (Emmett Dalton) and John Bromfield (Tulsa Jack).

Synopsis: Bill Doolin (Audie Murphy) wants to go straight after his parole, but fate and his ex-partners—including members of the Dalton Gang—foil his plans, leading to a lot of shooting and dying.

The Cimarron Kid

> *I am not faithful to history when it risks making a mess of the film."*—Budd Boetticher, Cahiers du Cinéma, 1965

Budd Boetticher signed his one-year contract with Universal on May 7, 1951. Ten days later, he was at work on the first of the nine features he made for the studio in just two years: *The Cimarron Kid*, based on the exploits of Bill Doolin, a Dalton Gang member who later helped form the infamous Wild Bunch. Budd shot the film between May 17 and June 15 in the Sonora area and the Universal back lot for less than a half-million dollars—about the price of a good Budd Boetticher-Burt Kennedy-Randolph Scott movie of the late 1950s.

Budd claimed that he went up to Coffeyville, Kansas—site of the infamous 1892 Dalton Gang robbery of two banks—to interview old-timers there about the events surrounding that botched criminal deed. "I met seven or eight old guys in the old folks' home that said they'd been there when the Daltons rode into town. I finally came back with all this wonderful information because this was one of my first Westerns and I was going to do it right." He told *Cahiers du Cinéma* in 1965, "[Coffeyville] awarded me a medal for having so faithfully respected the historical truth." It must have been the kind of medal that the Wizard of Oz handed out so readily at the end of the 1939 film, because Budd's depiction of the Coffeyville raid is chock full of historical errors and problems.

For one thing, there is nothing in the Universal studio files, housed in the University of Southern California library archives, to suggest that between May 7, when he signed his contract, and May 17, when filming began,

Director Boetticher (with foot on box) watches Audie Murphy (on ladder) and Beverly Tyler play out a scene from the Universal Western *The Cimarron Kid*, Budd's first film for Universal.

War-hero turned actor Audie Murphy fires away during an exciting scene from *The Cimarron Kid*. Though Murphy and Boetticher made two films together, neither is among either man's best work.

Budd traveled to Kansas. Most historians agree that Bill Doolin was not part of the five-member gang that attempted to rob two banks at once in Coffeyville on that fateful morning of October 5, 1892. Yet in the film, Doolin (Murphy) is there and escapes with Bitter Creek (played by James Best) as townsfolk shoot and kill four Dalton gang members, including Emmett (Rand Brooks). In real life, Emmett survived and was sent to prison. And history has never suggested that anyone involved in the raid set fire to a hay wagon in town, which in turn obscured the few survivors' escape from Coffeyville, as is depicted in the movie. It's an exciting sequence in the movie all the same, with Murphy and Best hightailing it under cover of the smoke.

Western novelist and historian Johnny D. Boggs, author of McFarland's *Billy the Kid in Film* and *Jesse James in Film*, doesn't believe Budd's claim: "If Budd Boetticher talked to old-timers about the Coffeyville raid and that's what he put on film, they were either pulling his leg or he wasn't listening," Boggs said. He continued:

> The movie sends Bill Doolin and George "Bitter Creek" Newcomb into town with brothers Bob, Grat and Emmett Dalton. Some historians say that Doolin was part of the original plan but that his horse went lame or he chickened out, although Emmett Dalton—who, unlike in *The Cimarron Kid*, wasn't killed in the raid but survived wounds and 15 years in prison—said Bob did not let the "reckless" Doolin ride with them to Kansas. Others suggest that the "sixth man" was Newcomb who, in one theory, rode in from the south for additional support. In any event, neither Doolin nor Newcomb made it inside either bank—and certainly didn't escape town under a hail of gunfire.

Boggs added, "Otherwise, *The Cimarron Kid* manages to whitewash most of its history," noting that many of the characters depicted did not die the way that the film indicates.

Those legitimate gripes aside, *The Cimarron Kid* is fast-paced matinee fun, and probably the best of the first five Westerns that Audie

Murphy made for Universal between 1949 and 1952. In his autobiography, Don Siegel said his main job on 1952's *The Duel at Silver Creek* was to give Murphy confidence, but something about *The Cimarron Kid* (including the fact that Murphy had just come off working for John Huston in his artistic misfire *The Red Badge of Courage*), indicates that Boetticher also imbued Murphy with a confidence that comes through in every scene.

"I loved Audie Murphy, he was great," Boetticher told David Schwartz. "He didn't drink, he didn't smoke, he didn't womanize but he gambled about everything. Two crows on a fence, he'd bet you a thousand dollars that the one on the left would fly out first." Budd said he lost a lot of money to Murphy during the film.

Boetticher told me of Murphy, "He was a damn good actor, a really good actor. John Huston knew he was a good actor or he wouldn't have gotten into his pictures. I've said so many times in the last couple of years, 'What do you do as an encore after you've got the Congressional Medal of Honor and you are 18 years old?' You're going to be bored."

Murphy had earned over 30 military medals for bravery after his World War II exploits, which included killing some 240 German soldiers and taking part in military campaigns in France, Italy and Germany. He was just 21 when the government told him, "Great job, thanks, here's your medals," and he probably had no clue what was in store for him next. Actor James Cagney saw Murphy's image on the cover of *Life* magazine and invited him to Hollywood. "I figured that a guy with drive enough to take him that far in the war had drive enough to become a star," Cagney said.

Cagney was right—assuming you accept that some actors are destined to be B-level stars, and there's a lot of those types who are much less interesting than Audie Murphy. Murphy had killed people and, in the movies, it shows in the "death stare" look you often see in his eyes as he blasts away with a prop six-gun or rifle. Interestingly, in an effort to make his *Cimarron Kid* character sympathetic, he only wounds other characters, leaving the door open (in the movie) for his redemption and a happy ending.

Budd, who had faced death in the bullring, connected with Murphy. "I think everything that you think is good in life, Audie believed in," Budd told me. "He was a very good man." This very good man did tend to sometimes pursue a lot of women other than his wives, and he shot up hotel rooms attempting to kill German soldiers who were coming after him in his nightmares. The Universal executives, Budd said, "were terrified of him. Nobody was gonna argue with him…. Audie's eyes would turn absolutely gray right in front of you. He got mad at me a lot of times. But he had respect for me because of my background."

Budd said that an actor on the film—who later became a big star in television—began messing around with his prop pistol and gave other performers on the set some "hot foots"—and Audie got mad. Murphy went into his trailer and then came out with a .45 pistol stuck in his belt. "And he walked up to this guy and Audie stuck his gun in this guy's stomach and he said, 'You've kidded around with me for the last time.' And the prop man behind this actor shot off a blank shot and this guy went to the toilet."

Universal studio archives indicate that actor Hugh O'Brian began playing around with his prop pistol, accidentally shooting off a shot that scared the horse carrying actress Yvette Dugay's in one scene. Murphy and co-star James Best managed to pull Dugay away from the bucking bronco before she got hurt. But Budd said the actor who pulled the hotfoot gags was not O' Brian.

William Reynolds, who played one of the Dalton Brothers in the film, said, "Audie had a reputation, that with Audie Murphy pictures, if you spent $750,000 on it, you could make a profit. Everything you spent over $750,000 was money that you were throwing away, because they thought he had a very finite audience. In a sense, he did. He didn't like it." Reynolds said Audie was

> a much better actor than most people gave him credit for. Audie instinctively knew the right tone, the right element that was necessary…his

instincts were probably always good, probably came from his life experiences. He understood life. He didn't have anything to prove. He didn't have to play macho. Obviously he was heroic. He didn't have to develop an identity that would speak for him."

Reynolds recalled that a bookie came on the set to collect some money (probably from Murphy, a life-long gambler) and Murphy ran off the lot.

Actor Gregg Palmer—known as Palmer Lee in this film—said Murphy was both underrated and well-regarded by Universal. "Audie didn't act," Palmer said. Instead, he *reacted*. Palmer said Murphy's eyes were "steely ... had a lot behind them. God knows what was going on in there."

One day on the set (May 24), Palmer watched as stuntman Dave Sharpe, doubling for actor John Hudson, fell off a horse and down an embankment near the classic Universal waterfall for a chase scene:

> And off the horse fell Davy and down the bank he rolled and into the rocks and off into the waterfall—a 40-foot fall easily. Davy goes under the water and, jeesh, Davy doesn't come up. We wait a few minutes and finally Budd jumped up and dived into the water and pulled Davy up. Dave said, "I'm all right, I'd like to do it again. I just stayed down long enough for you to get your whole shot. I just didn't like how I came off that one rock there. I'd like to do it again." And so, they did it again.

For Boetticher, his first Universal production was a step up from Eagle-Lion, Monogram and Republic. And how did he respond? Well, Boetticher told Sean Axmaker that he threw a Universal executive named Jack Grossman off the set for challenging Boetticher's direction. "I grabbed the son of a bitch by the seat of his pants and I threw him out." He said studio executives checked with assistant director Joseph Kenny to get his side of the story, and when he backed Boetticher, they let the whole thing go. "That's the last problem I ever had at Universal," Budd later said.

As for the film itself, well, throw out the historical inaccuracies and you have a B picture that does exactly what it sets out to do, entertain you for less than 90 minutes. If there is not a lot of real sexual chemistry between Murphy and Beverly Tyler, it may because our star had just married Pamela Archer and was intent on giving all of his loving to her. Actor Rand Brooks, who appears in the film, said that one scene called for the ensemble, as outlaws, to ride out of town fast with bags of money in their hands and that Boetticher insisted the actors fill up their money bags so that they looked and felt heavy. "To mount horses quickly with a heavy bag is not too much fun," Brooks said (*The Films of Audie Murphy*, Bob Larkins and Boyd Magers, McFarland, 2004). Brooks also recalled that in a scene in which the gang members flee from town following a robbery, Murphy's body caught a lighting scaffolding just off-camera and he got hurt. "He wouldn't acknowledge he was hurt. I don't know how badly but he just wouldn't mention it. I could see he had a little limp."

The action scenes are really well defined, including the Coffeyville raid, a shoot-out in a downtown rail yard and a lengthy and elaborate train robbery sequence. That said, the Dalton Gang members are awfully well-dressed and clean-shaven and joke around like the Bowery Boys out west. Only Hugh O'Brian, as the passionate and angry Red Buck, really registers as a realistic Old West character. Larkins and Magers' *The Films of Audie Murphy* is right when it reports that Murphy "tended to get lost in the somewhat overpopulated shuffle of supporting characters, many of them played by members of Universal's talent school."

Budd's old buddy John Hubbard shows up as an oily double-dealing railroad man—practicing for his larger turn as a similar character in 1957's *The Tall T.* Budd also used Ann Robinson, a paramour from his Monogram days, in a bit role. James Best later showed up in Budd's *Ride Lonesome*. The rest of the cast is made up of people who would become television stars—like O'Brian—or leads in grade-Z films (Gregg Palmer in *Zombies of Mora Tau* and John Bromfield in *Curucu, Beast of the Amazon*). But for a few good years, they were under contract to Universal, and probably all hoped that they would develop into major stars like Murphy, Tony Curtis, Jeff Chandler and Rock Hudson.

Audie Murphy would never be Randolph Scott, but he lasted longer than anyone in the cast in terms of stardom, and he hired Budd to direct his abortive comeback effort, *A Time for Dying*, in 1969. Budd said of Murphy, "I think [Universal] took advantage of his Medal of Honor, that's all there was. They used it up, like all studios do, and got rid of him."

William Reynolds said Budd was "very macho, Sammy Fullierish in some ways. He was a former bullfighter and a boxer and he was a tough guy. He wasn't afraid to throw his troops into action."

Budd never thought much of his Universal pictures. In the late 1980s, he told Ronald L. Davis, "Universal made a picture, and they knew before computers were invented that this picture in Dubuque, Iowa, was going to make X number of dollars, whether it was good or bad...and nobody cared, nobody cared."

In his book *Western Films—A Complete Guide*, Brian Garfield said of *The Cimarron Kid*, "Unexceptional oater is nowhere near as solid a job as the movies Boetticher directed with Randolph Scott later in the decade."

Bronco Buster (Universal, 80 minutes, released in May 1952) Director: Budd Boetticher. Producer: Ted Richmond. Screenplay by Horace McCoy and Lillie Hayward, based on a story by Peter B. Kyne. Cinematographer: Clifford Stine. With John Lund (Tom Moody), Scott Brady (Bart Eaton), Joyce Holden (Judy Bream), Chill Wills (Dan Bream), Don Haggerty (Dobie Carson), Walter Reed (Fred Wharton) and real-life rodeo stars Casey Tibbs, Bill Williams, Pete Crump, Manuel Enos and Jerry Ambler as themselves.

Synopsis: This human drama, one part *Bullfighter and the Lady* and one part *All About Eve*, is about a veteran rodeo rider who takes a brash young hothead under his wing and comes to regret it.

Bronco Buster is arguably Boetticher's all-around best Western film outside of the string of superior Burt Kennedy–scripted films he made with Randolph Scott (and it's certainly better than 1959's *Westbound*). It predates some of the recurring themes of those Kennedy-Boetticher-Scott films in following the efforts of an experienced Westerner trying to set a moral example for younger hellions who believe they can act outside convention and the law. *Bronco Buster* also reaches back to Boetticher's *Bullfighter and the Lady* in capturing the grit, fear and excitement of a different kind of arena—the rodeo—chock full of the same kind of animals and challenges that bullfighters contend with. Given Budd's penchant for drawing good performances out of not-quite-good actors, it's not surprising that the three leads—none of whom would ever gain top-line stardom—provided insightfully shaded performances. The picture includes a beautifully played night-time love sequence between John Lund and Joyce Holden's characters in which she lays out her frustrations at his love affair with the rodeo, which leaves her waiting at home for him for extended periods of time, wondering if he'll ever marry her.

> TOM: I love you. You love me. We're gonna get married. Period.
> [*Long pause*]
> TOM: Mad?
> JUDY: No.
> TOM: What are you thinking about?
> JUDY: Nothing. [*Pause*] Period.

The script by Horace McCoy and Lillie Hayward (he would go on to write *They Shoot Horses, Don't They?* while she would later pen *The Shaggy Dog*) makes it clear that Tom and Judy are lovers, and that maybe Bart and Judy are lovers too, making Holden's character surprisingly open-minded for the time period. There's a wonderful bit where both Lund and Brady's eyes move over Holden's curvaceous figure as she performs an impromptu shimmy in a diner. And then the two men's eyes meet and they both understand what they are up against in their desire to win the woman—another common theme of the Boetticher-Kennedy-Scott films.

Bronco Buster is helped (and hurt to some degree) by the use of real-life rodeo stars competing in real-life rodeos. If a rodeo rider got thrown on-camera, Boetticher and cine-

There was lots of bronco-busting in Budd Boetticher's 1952 Western *Bronco Buster*—his best Western at Universal.

matographer Clifford Stine caught it on film. The picture provides an honest look at how these rodeo cowboys drive by night, live in trailers, compete for peanuts and eat in greasy spoon diners all for the love of the game. They bask in almost as much celebrity glow as the matadors of Budd's bullrings. *Bronco Buster* expertly evokes that brief rush of power and joy that comes with being a champion—even if for just one day. Only near the film's end does the real-life footage intrude, taking all the momentum out of the narrative that has been building around it.

Bart Eaton's confident arrogance—"It's kind of nice to know where you want to go, and I want to go to the top," he tells his mentor Tom—may be seen as an on-screen metaphor for Budd's own ego-driven personality. But despite the later potshots Boetticher took at Universal, it's clear he learned how to cooperate with producers, handle contract players and work with fairly tight B+ budgets in the $500,000 to $800,000 price range. The direction, script and work of Brady—a surly sort of actor who never quite seemed at home in the Western genre, though he appeared in a lot of oaters—really captures the slow evolution of Eaton from a humble rodeo rookie to an egotistical media star, particularly in an amusing sequence where, given the chance to appear for a moment on a local live television program, he hogs the camera and brags about his accomplishments while dressed in flashy, matador-style attire.

Here again is where Budd's ability to work with actors pays off: He makes you realize that at one time John Lund and Scott Brady had the potential to be good actors. Lund was downright hilarious in a long-forgotten Paramount comedy called *Miss Tatlock's Millions* (1948) and he actually out-goofs Dean Martin and Jerry Lewis in both of the *My Friend Irma* films of that period. Unhappy with his lot at Paramount, he left the studio shortly before the filming of *Bronco Buster* began in August 1951, signing a multi-picture deal with Universal that, with the exception of *Bronco Buster*, kept him in the same sort of staid, dull character parts he often played at Paramount. In August 1951, Lund rather honestly told Hollywood columnist Bob Thomas, "Now I'm a limited kind of actor; there are only a few roles I can do. The one thing I can't do is the thing [Paramount] had me doing most—the 'square John' type who holds the heroine's hand and says, 'There, there.'" After his brief stay at Universal, Lund ended up in even less interesting roles in less interesting films like *Dakota* (1956) and *Five Guns West* (1955) or throwaway parts in quality pictures like *High Society* (1956). His career pretty much ended soon after.

Brady would out-last Lund, working as a character actor up until his death in the mid–1980s. But after leaving Universal around the time *Bronco Buster* was released in the spring of 1952, he bounced from lower-grade studio to lower-grade studio, making a series of "gets-increasingly-worse" movies through the 1950s and 1960s—with 1954's *Johnny Guitar* proving to be the one exception to that rule. It's not quite clear why Brady left Universal, though one brief memo in the *Bronco Buster* files indicate he "flatly refused" to agree to do a five-minute radio interview to help promote the film because he was mad at Universal's marketing department for not granting him a personal favor. So maybe he was, for lack of a better term, "difficult."

Joyce Holden was a gifted actress whose career also ended by the end of the 1950s, though that seems to be a matter of personal choice

Universal targeted *Bronco Buster* (1952) to the rodeo crowd at a time when rodeo was one of the most popular sports in the country. The film didn't click with audiences, however, and remains one of Budd Boetticher's most obscure efforts.

as she became a Jehovah's Witness and actually partook in the old door-to-door campaign of passing out literature and trying to attract spiritual converts. A couple of decent roles in Universal films got her nowhere, and within a few years she was gracing Bowery Boys comedies (*Private Eyes*) and appearing in Grade-C horror films (*The Werewolf*). Budd, in later years, would sometimes confuse her with actress Jennifer Holden (no relation), who played a small role for him in 1958's *Buchanan Rides Alone*.

As for Chill Wills, he is more subdued than usual in this film and plays the role of the rodeo clown as if he's the most important part of the show, which rodeo clowns often were. On the set, he managed to ad-lib a line about a mule his character encounters and turn it into an inside-joke reference to Universal's popular Francis the Talking Mule series, for which Wills provided the voice of the mule. Today the joke is innocuous and of no value to anyone who doesn't know anything about the Francis films. I wonder if, at the time, the bit drew laughs or groans (or both) from audiences.

Universal had the story outline for *Bronco Buster* set to go by December 1950, months before Budd signed up with the studio and before his *Bullfighter and the Lady* was released, making one wonder if the similarities in the two stories are nothing more than coincidental. In the early 1950s, the rodeo was one of America's most popular sporting attractions, and several studios all decided at once to make a movie about the subject. Screenwriter McCoy actually worked on RKO's superior *The Lusty Men* before abandoning it to go to work on *Bronco Buster* while MGM began preparing *Arena*, which follows much of the same storyline of all three films (arrogant young rodeo rider causes grief for those around him). Even low-budget Monogram got into the act with *Rodeo* (1952).

Budd was aware of the pressure to get his film out of the chute first. In an August 7, 1951, letter to producer Ted Richmond, he outlined some concerns he had about the script and said his hopes for an "exceptional" motion picture were being compromised by "direct competition with several other major companies." The letter goes on to make some character-change suggestions for the three leads, at least one of which—downplaying Tom's interest in other women early in the picture—seems to have been adopted. Budd suggests that Judy may be using Bart to get to Tom, and there are hints of that in the final film. "This certainly should not be a girl who wants to settle down on a small ranch in the San Fernando Valley and cut up puppies," Budd wrote. "She would much rather have Tom win the championship and end up having lunch at 21."

Budd also wisely warned Richmond,

> We can bore the devil out of the audience if we use too much [real-life rodeo footage] in the wrong places. This is not a documentary on rodeos. This is the story of people and what these people stand for... [A]bove all else, from the opening scene we must fear these animals; respect these men and smell the sweat and dust of the rodeo circuit.

Budd was right about the over-use of footage and many audience members and theater owners complained of this in preview cards and letters to the studio.

Boetticher's letter to Richmond is one of only two samples in the Universal files of our director offering suggestions in advance to improve the script. There is no record of a response to Budd's ideas, making me think he was ignored.

Universal thought it had a huge hit on its hands. And it should have been a huge hit. After the studio gave an audience a "sneak-peek" at *Bronco Buster* in November 1951, all but about 25 of a crowd of 314 cinema patrons rated the film "good" to "outstanding" and raved about the acting and script. Many, however, said "too much rodeo" and one viewer rather snidely wrote, "This picture is just what my 5th grade class would enjoy!" (I doubt it—it's pretty adult in nature.) Another preview patron wrote, "I would like to re-write the last scene. I know nothing about writing."

But patrons and theater exhibitors really gave it to Universal when it came to the name of the film. "The title...was very poor," one exhibitor wrote Universal, saying the latest *Ma and Pa Kettle* film was doing better business than *Bronco Buster* because the public knew exactly what to expect with that comedy's title. He went on to say that *Bronco Buster* is the sort of title he would expect to find on a "Rocky Lane or Charles Starrett picture."

And it didn't help the studio that natural disasters, Humphrey Bogart and Katharine Hepburn got in the way. In mid–April, Lund, Wills and Holden traveled to Omaha for the world premiere. Instead of plugging the film there, they ended up touring the waterlogged defense lines set up by some 8000 workers who were trying to stem the flow of the terrible Missouri River flood that hit the city just as they arrived. Universal marketing executives and Omaha's leaders and citizens praised the trio of actors for pitching in wherever they could, even to the extent of running canteen lines to those fighting the flood. The film's April 18 premiere at the Orpheum Theater turned into a benefit for the flood victims, but unfortunately for Universal, nobody in Omaha was too interested in seeing a movie while the city was under threat of watery destruction. The actors all agreed to tape public service announcements and help the Red Cross in its efforts during their brief stay there, which bought Universal an incredible amount of good will.

But the next stop, Des Moines, wasn't Omaha, and it wasn't underwater, so Universal expected something of a comeback for *Bronco Buster*. No such luck. Though 40,000 plus people showed up for a rodeo parade featuring the stars before the film's premiere in that city, and 3000 people showed up for the 8:15 star showcase that night, only 50 to 75 people actually bought tickets to see the film. "As a matter of fact, a great many more of them went next door to the De Moines Theatre to see *The African Queen*," a studio marketing staffer wrote. Universal's chiefs considered the twice-over failure to attract audiences early on "a shocker" that would hurt the film's chances down the line.

The title seemed to do the film in everywhere, and by late April Universal was fielding calls and letters from theater exhibitors everywhere saying business was bad—"less than 50 percent of average," one wrote—and urging the studio to change the name. Studio executives fired back that the few attempts to pull a film in, change its title and re-release it under another name met with very limited success, and in the end Universal let *Bronco Buster* stand as it was. It died a quiet death at the box office and pretty much disappeared from view for decades after. (I had to search far and wide to find a decent DVD copy of it. The print I saw features the musical overture from Abbott and Costello's 1942 comedy *Ride 'Em Cowboy!*, which doesn't fit the dramatic tone of *Bronco Buster* at all.)

Not that Universal's marketing department was all that smart in advertising the picture to begin with. The idea to let Casey Tibbs do newspaper interviews in which he talked about the rodeo being very similar to moviemaking in terms of "show business" and rattle on about the daily life of a bronco buster on the circuit was pretty shrewd, but it's hard to suppress a chuckle at the notion of "cooking up a story saying that Scott Brady plans on entering the Salinas Rodeo (or some such rodeo) after learning how to ride bucking broncs in *Bronco Buster*. The studio could intervene at the last moment to save him from this." There's a comedy somewhere in that idea, that's for sure. Imagine the studio *not* intervening at the last minute and Brady really getting on all those bulls and horses.

The film ran into less trouble with both the Breen Office and the American Humane Association than *Bullfighter and the Lady*, though apparently an early line in the script—"you no-good s— — — —"—was deemed unacceptable. The American Humane Association, which kept a close eye on rodeos but seemed to understand they were physical in nature, simply asked the studio to ensure that there was no cruelty to animals in the making of the film. (England's censors snipped about 75 feet out of the film—mostly violent rodeo action involving horses and bulls.)

But based on studio files, only the actors took a beating in this one, and not just the stars. Cowboy Bill Williams was thrown from a bull and ended up in the hospital to get his lip stitched up, and a bull knocked an extra down, resulting in a kidney contusion and a trip to the hospital.

Like most of the Universal films of the time, everyone involved pretty much started working around 8 a.m. and quit around 6 p.m. Monday through Saturday. Here's a fun bit of trivia: For a shot of Lund's character mounting and riding a bucking horse, it took the crew 19 minutes to set the shot up, 12 minutes to line up the horse, and three minutes to actually get the scene on camera.

Bronco Buster was shot between August 21 and September 13, 1951, on a budget of about $590,000. Screenwriter McCoy was paid an extra $1000 for being available in mid–June for potential rewrites. Real-life rodeo star Tibbs played himself and doubled Lund for an additional $55 per day while Wayne Burson doubled Brady for $55 a day. The Universal files indicate that Audie Murphy swung by the set to act as unofficial technical advisor.

The production notes, as well as existing still photos, prove that Boetticher did take a cape and, on the last day of shooting, goad a bull out of its chute to get it to charge the camera for a shot in the film, as Budd said in his memoir. Camera operators Eddie Coleman and technical assistant Paul Uhl dug a hole in the ground to put the camera in. Boetticher told the press, "There was always the chance that if I did it earlier [in the production shoot] I'd have been too crippled to finish." In his autobiography, Budd wrote that the bull actually broke through the chute to get at the director: "It was just wonderful! I felt like Lee Marvin after he'd just shot his brother in *Cat Ballou*. Everything I'd believed in worked! ...[I]t was so perfect that I continued to 'play' him after the filming was complete."

Then, Budd wrote, the bull escaped the studio pen and took off down the hill toward the set of a "Tits and Sand" picture being directed by an effeminate director. Three of the rodeo riders working on *Bronco Buster* chased the errant bull, whose snort-charging flight sent extras clad in harem pants and such running here and there. The director, who Budd does not name, screamed at him, "Goodness gracious! If you insist on playing these silly games, you could at least let me know. I could have been squashed."

That's another good Budd Boetticher story. But is it true? I would think that Universal, which kept detailed daily production logs of every movie it shot, would have made note of these hijinks. But there is no reference to this incident in those logs.

Already Budd was earning a reputation as a "wild man" (a term both Brady and L.Q. Jones would use about him, as well as numerous others who worked with him). Lund said that one day Budd invited him to watch some of the real-life rodeo cowboys bulldog, making it clear he expected Lund to at least do his own stunt for that competition. And Lund did—that's clearly him riding hellbent-for-glory on a horse before jumping from it to bring down a dodging and angry calf. Brady agreed to perform an unnerving action stunt in which his character is tricked into trying to stay in the saddle of a mechanical contraption that spins him around like an out-of-control merry-go-round. The actor's facial expression of physical sickness is no performance, and that's him falling from the saddle and being dragged around the arena by the still-moving machine. He wrenched his back in the process and had to be "taped up" for future filming. "The words 'stunt men' are not in Boetticher's language," Brady told the press.

Lund told interviewer Ronald L. Davis that one day Brady—who Lund called "an amusing fellow"—came up to him to say of Boetticher, "You know, this guy says, 'I don't ask anybody to do anything I wouldn't do myself.' I thought that was fair enough. And then I realized this son-of-a-bitch'll do anything!"

Years later, Lund was visiting Paris when the words on a marquee of one of the cinemas on the Champs Elysses caught his eye. It simply read, "Budd Boetticher Westerns."

Robert Hinkle, in *Call Me Lucky—A Texan in Hollywood* (University of Oklahoma Press, 2009), recalled working in the Pendleton, Oregon, rodeo when Budd and company showed

Chill Wills not only brought laughs to *Bronco Buster* (1952), he also played up the rodeo clown's importance to the sport.

up to shoot footage. "I was the general size of one of the stars, so they dressed me in western clothes to match the character's wardrobe in the movie. All I had to do for my $300 a day was what I was doing anyway—ride rodeo." Some time later, Budd gave Hinkle a small role in *Wings of the Hawk*, in which he was mowed down by a machine-gun. "My mother cried later when she saw me die in my first movie," Hinkle said, but that job helped Hinkle establish a foothold in Hollywood, where he worked steadily for some time as a bit player, extra and actor.

Variety (April 16, 1952): "A lot of actual rodeo footage is used…to bolster authenticity and add interest to the development of what actually is a routine plot… [E]xcellent scripting and direction, however, gloss over and enliven the stock plot."

The Hollywood Reporter (April 11, 1952) called the film "a lively, action-packed saga.

Lund turns in a nice, likable, virile performance as the rodeo champ. Brady is almost too-convincing as the smart-alecky heel." Denver's *Rocky Mountain News* (June 13, 1952), said the film was "full of honest drama," but the *Denver Post* (June 16, 1952) called the plot "slight, offering no real suspense."

Red Ball Express (Universal, 83 minutes, released in May 1952) Director: Budd Boetticher. Producer: Aaron Rosenberg. Screenplay: Billy Grady, Jr., John Michael Hayes, Marcy Klauber. Cinematographer: Maury Gertsman. With Jeff Chandler (Lt. Chick Campbell), Alex Nicol (Sgt. Kallek), Charles Drake (Pvt. Ronald Partridge), Judith Braun (Joyce McClellan), Sidney Poitier (Corp. Andrew Robertson), Jacqueline Duval (Antoinette Dubois), Hugh O'Brian (Pvt. Wilson), Frank Chase (Pvt. Higgins), Cindy Garner (Kitty) and Palmer Lee [Gregg Palmer] (Tank Lieutenant)

Synopsis: In the wake of the successful Allied invasion of Normandy in the summer of 1944, Gen. George Patton leads a charge into

France that outpaces his supply troops. So a convoy of supply trucks known as the Red Ball Express run round-the-clock to catch up to the advancing military forces.

Red Ball Express is a frustratingly disappointing film. Not only does it blow the opportunity to explore race relations in the military, but it comes off as no more than the standard, stereotypical Hollywood war film—almost entirely devoid of reality—with its melodramatic script. It's the age-old story of a band of "goldbricks, trouble-makers and misfits," as one character puts it, who somehow bond quickly to pull off a successful mission, despite an over-abundance of forced internal conflict among some of the men. Boetticher said years later that he only made one war film because he hated the genre because it involved a group of men and not the individual. And in watching *Red Ball Express*, you can suddenly see that one theme running throughout most of Budd's post–1940s Columbia pictures is that of a lone man who has a job to do and who gets it done. (That's even true of the three shoddy Monogram pictures of the late 1940s.)

Red Ball Express is a Boetticher picture that curried controversy, though most of that happened before Budd came aboard to direct in the autumn of 1951 (shooting began on Halloween). Both the Universal studio files and an excellent 2013 article by University of Maryland professor and lecturer Robert K. Chester ("We Feel the Wound Is Closed: *Red Ball Express* (1952), the Department of Defense Pictorial Division and the Reluctant Embrace of Postwar Integration") make it clear that the studio really had no idea what it was doing or how insensitive its approach to the subject matter was. In reality, some 75 percent of the transportation drivers who took part in the roughly 100-day-long Red Ball Express convoys were African-American. But an early draft outline of the story put the emphasis on Italian-American drivers, a move that angered many African-American newspapers, including the *California Eagle*. In a May 10, 1951, front-page story, that newspaper reported that Universal was deliberately trying to "build a plot structure with Italian instead of Negroes as the heroes…" William Grady, who provided the original story to Universal, told the *Eagle* that, based on his knowledge, at least 60 percent of the Red Ball Express participants were African-American, but "just how far the studio wants to go, I don't know. They will have to use some negroes to make it authentic." Grady went on to tell the *Eagle* that the story was "mostly a Western with trucks," and said his 58-page treatment had "a few negroes in the story but they weren't important."

In the Universal archives file at the University of Southern California is a copy of the *California Eagle* story with a handwritten note, penned by some unknown Universal ally, to the studio's marketing department saying the *Eagle* editor wanted to get a comment from Universal and to be wary because the editor is a "Red" who wants to stir up trouble. Remember, in the spring of 1951 the House Committee on Un-American Activities was holding Congressional hearings about Communists in Hollywood.

So what Universal did—and this is still before Boetticher got involved—was rework the story to include three somewhat substantial African-American roles and integrate them into an otherwise mostly white unit of military men. One of the three African-Americans, played by musical artist Bubber Johnson, tells his fellow African-American military buddies that he likes everyone in the unit "even though half of them are white," but it's hard to spot more than a handful of black servicemen in the entire movie. When Universal did try to inject some racial undertones (or overtones), as Chester points out in his article, the Department of Defense and its federal allies pressured the studio to downplay that angle for fear Americans might think the military was racist. (Keep in mind that for the most part African-Americans and white soldiers served in segregated units during World War II.)

So Universal's *Red Ball Express* tries in vain to show an integrated unit, mostly made up of whites with only one overt racist (played by Hugh O'Brian), and keeps the racial divide to a minimum. It is left to actor Sidney Poitier, playing what he does best—Sidney Poitier—to articulate the angry, defensive feeling of being on the receiving end of racial slurs in a brief but effective scene in which he asks commanding officer Jeff Chandler for a transfer following a physical altercation with O'Brian. "The punches I can take," Poitier's character says, and the line has a rare weight that most of the film's other dialogue doesn't come close to hefting. Universal had to walk a fine line until October 26, 1951—just five days before the start of production—until the Department of Defense agreed to give its approval, as well as trucks and drivers to the studio for use in the project.

Whether Boetticher was aware of any or much of this is not documented, though in his typical fashion he said, decades later, that he went to the military archives in Washington, D.C., before filming began (perhaps—it was at least close to Fort Eustes in Virginia) to review military documents on the Express drivers. "The top brass didn't want people to know that these were kamikaze pilots," Boetticher told one journalist. "They got the black kids who were just 17, 18, 19 years old and they taught them to drive the trucks forward. They didn't give a damn if they were killed. They wanted to get the gasoline and ammunition to Patton and his troops."

There is considerable truth to that statement, but it's also valid to say, based on a review of research papers and interviews with former Red Ball Express drivers, that the Red Ball Express drivers often put themselves in danger, pushing on through the night and exceeding pre-set speeds of 25 or 35 miles per hour (accounts vary) to get to the next point on time. "The real story of the Red Ball Express was often more like a free-for-all at a stock car race," historian David P. Colley wrote in *On the Road to Victory: The Red Ball Express*. One element that Boetticher's film does effectively capture is the pure exhaustion of men who were supposed to drive non-stop in shifts but who nonetheless could often only

Jeff Chandler kicks a German soldier (actor unidentified) in Boetticher's misfire *Red Ball Express*.

find time to sleep while at the wheel, which led to a lot of accidents.

Filming took place mostly on location near Fort Eustis, Virginia, which gives the picture a more authentic look than the usual Universal back lot production. Media reports indicate that the African-American and white actors and the African-American and white servicemen from the area were kept in segregated areas during the filming, which could not have helped ease racial tensions. Budd later said that the black actors had to go to a segregated part of the nearby "Nigger Town" to eat, and that he couldn't visit them there. "So I didn't see the people I really cared about," he said. "I mean, those were the days, boy."

The Universal archives indicate that once filming began, it went pretty smoothly. Perhaps being away from the usual array of Universal studio executives who were likely to poke their noses into any director's business allowed everyone to relax and stay on track. Filming continued until December 6, 1951, on a budget of about $680,000 (Budd brought this one in under budget by about $3000). Travel time—45 minutes to and from location—was included in the daily production log. There are no reports of accidents, delays, personality problems or military intrusion in those logs.

In his autobiography *This Life* (Alfred A. Knopf, 1980), Poitier does not comment on the racial strife surrounding the film or Boetticher's talent (or lack of) as a director. He mentions the picture almost in passing, noting that being on the set refueled his desire to be a film actor: "Off to Hollywood I went for the second time. As unbelievable as it seemed to me, there was no escaping the fact that I was even more excited the second time around." When, on the first day of shooting, Poitier heard the first assistant director call for quiet, the actor reflected,

> I became suddenly aware of something very special happening inside of me. It seemed as if an unknown value had opened up somewhere in my gut, sending juices rushing to my brain and from there filling my whole body with an exhilaration that somehow appeared to be completely in sync with the gentle humming sound coming from the activated camera. Before the morning was over, I realized how much I had missed acting in the movies; I was hooked deeper than I had allowed myself to admit.

Aram Goudsouzian, in his 2004 biography *Sidney Poitier: Man, Actor, Icon* (University of North Carolina Press), wrote of the film, "Black soldiers comprised about 70 percent of this Red Ball Express, fighting both the Germans and the racism of their fellow soldiers." He said the truckers rank among the most significant African-American contributors to the Allied victory. "Hollywood, however, nearly omitted the African-Americans" from the story. He said the film version "is no penetrating examination of race regulations" and said the three black characters most prominently featured are "oversimplified, historically suspect characterizations of race relations." It's hard to disagree with that assessment.

Red Ball Express has a lot more problems that go far beyond the question of race. Almost all of the characters are played as types: the tough sergeant with an axe to grind (Alex Nicol), the edgy racist (O'Brian), the goofball (Frank Chase, whose hijinks get very annoying) and the woman-chasing braggart (Charles Drake, who gives a very good performance). Throw in the troubled but understanding commanding (Chandler), a Patton-type martinet (nicely played by Howard Petrie) and the trio of African-American characters, all of whom vie to show off a little individuality, and you've got quite the Mulligan's Stew of characters.

The narrative also makes room for a couple of hot-looking Red Cross girls who seem to have just come out of the spa even when they show up on mud-covered roads on a cool autumn day. And the business of Drake's carrying on with a young French girl, who always seems to show up on her bicycle at just the time when the convoy has left him behind, gets tiresome. But in that romantic subplot, Drake does pull off a fine bit of acting: Upon being invited to the girl's home for dinner, he discovers her poor family is giving him everything to eat, leaving nothing for themselves.

Does this look like a racially integrated military unit? That's part of the big problem with *Red Ball Express*. Alex Nicol (center left, front) didn't like working for Budd. Star Jeff Chandler (right) must have, because he returned for Budd's juvenile adventure story *East of Sumatra* the following year.

The small perks—including Boetticher's handling of the action sequences—are offset by the mostly one-note look at a culturally challenging issue. *Red Ball Express* moves at about 25 miles per hour with just enough momentum to carry you along. For what it's worth, Budd's claims he shamed Chandler into doing his own driving through a flaming town and that seems to be the case: The actor actually looks nervous as he navigates the vehicle through a road of torched buildings.

Budd, in typical bragging form, liked to say how he helped discover a number of stars, including Poitier. But it's not clear that he had much to do with the casting of these pictures during the Universal days, when the studio was doing its best to showcase its contract players such as Palmer Lee—later to be known as Gregg Palmer—who had small roles in two Boetticher films, including *Red Ball Express*.

"You would maybe have a featured role in a picture, maybe we would star, maybe we would do a little cameo, but we were working," Palmer told renowned film historian and author Tom Weaver. Budd once said that Poitier thanked him for the role because up to that point he had been cast in roles requiring him to wear tribal attire with a spear in his hand and a nose in his bone, but that is absurd. Poitier had already scored big in a role as a black doctor asked to attend to racist victims in 1950's *No Way Out*, and he also featured prominently in 1951's *Cry, the Beloved Country*. *Red Ball Express* didn't exactly jump-start his career, either: He was still three years away from a sympathetic supporting role in MGM's *Blackboard Jungle* and six more years away from true stardom with 1958's *The Defiant Ones*.

Author Louis L'Amour, best known for his Western stories, wrote in his autobiography

Education of a Wandering Man that he was sitting in a Hollywood nightclub one evening, telling some World War II stories related to his own experiences, that included some references to the Red Ball Express. He was dismayed to come across the film, "with my role, much exaggerated, played by Jeff Chandler." That didn't stop L'Amour from selling one of his stories, which later became *East of Sumatra*, to Universal for Budd to direct.

The *New York Times*' May 30, 1952, review of the film hit the problematic nail on the head and hammered it deep by calling the film a

> completely stereotypical and shoddy war picture... [W]hy, oh why did the creators of this fraud feel they had to re-heat that ancient device of having the lead an officer who is hated by his men.... The cast, in the tradition of his brand of fake, is made up of various "types." But since most of the soldiers in the real Red Ball Express were Negro Quartermasters troops led by white officers, the authors had to pay lip service to better race relations and did it in a patronizing and superficial fashion.

The *New York Herald Tribune*'s same-day review tried to say something nice about the movie, "highlighting a problem which has more or less been taboo." The *Los Angeles Examiner* (May 26, 1952) liked the movie but not its "contrived injection of a race prejudice problem," saying it was "equally unnecessary and unfair to both races." The *Los Angeles Times* said the film reinforces the idea that "there is no question of overall courage involved and Negro as well as white soldier acquit themselves in individual acts of heroism."

Many media outlets did not mention the subject of race at all, with the industry-friendly *Variety*, in its April 30, 1952, review, calling Boetticher's direction "realistic" and praising Chandler's "strong, straightforward performance."

The picture raked in $1.5 million in its initial release. In some cases it was paired with Budd's *Bronco Buster* for a double-bill of Boetticher. Actor Gregg Palmer told me that Budd's direction was "ballsy" and said he liked to encourage actors to get physical, as is evident in a couple of brawling sequences. Palmer—a really nice guy who worked forever, never became a star and never seemed to display any bitterness about a career that did not take off—told journalist Jeremy Roberts in 2013, "Universal put me under contract in 1951, and I stayed there for about five years." He said he and other studio players took acting, diction and even ballet classes on the lot. (Imagine Audie Murphy and Jeff Chandler doing that!) He died in 2015.

Alex Nicol, in a 1996 interview with Wheeler Winston Dixon, said Budd was "the only director in my career who I couldn't get along with. He had a very big ego.... Boetticher like to have all the actors be his audience. Budd was treating everyone like they were boys and girls." According to Nicol, Budd would sit at the head of the dinner table and talk to everyone as if he were the king—a trait he would maintain to his last days.

Budd would get rankled when, decades later, people (including me) typed him as a Western film director:

> Let me tell you something. I don't make Westerns. I make movies. That's just laziness on the part of all those critics! I've made 52 pictures, counting the one that I made for the war for the Navy [*The Fleet That Came to Stay*] and out of that, I've made 12 Westerns and they say, "He's a Western director." ...So it's a lot of nonsense. I'm a director, I don't make westerns.

I will give Budd—who is no longer alive to punch me in the nose—a little grief on this statement. He worked on not quite 20 films at the Hal Roach lot in various capacities from 1940 to 1942, served on a few Columbia pictures as an assistant director of some sort and gave technical bullfighting advice to the makers of 1941's *Blood and Sand*. He also made not quite 20 television shows. So all told it's fair to say he worked on 50-some movies and some 20 television shows. But as a director, he has 33 credits. Two of them are documentaries, and of the remaining 31 features, 16 are Westerns—more than 50 percent of his total output. That's about the same ratio of Westerns directed by Sam Peckinpah, who made a total of 14 films, seven of which are Westerns. Compare those percentages to the filmography of

Anthony Mann, who directed not quite 40 feature films—12 of which are Westerns—or to John Ford, who directed about 60 sound feature films (1929-1966), of which about 15 are Westerns. So you can see why both Boetticher and Peckinpah got typed as Western film directors. And, in both men's cases, unlike Ford and Mann, most of their really good work was about the West.

With his next picture, Budd Boetticher would return to that genre.

Horizons West (Universal, 83 minutes, released in October 1952) Director: Budd Boetticher. Producer: Albert J. Cohen. Screenplay: Louis Stevens. Cinematographer: Charles P. Boyle. With Robert Ryan (Dan Hammond), Julie Adams (Lorna Hardin), Rock Hudson (Neal Hammdon), Judith Braun (Sally Eaton), John McIntire (Ira Hammond), Raymond Burr (Cord Hardin), James Arness (Tiny McGilligan), Dennis Weaver (Dandy Taylor), Frances Bavier (Martha Hammond), Tom Powers (Frank Tarleton) and John Hubbard (Sam Hunter)

Synopsis: Civil War veteran Dan Hammond returns to Texas with the goal of ruling it. It's up to his brother Neal and father Ira to stop him.

Perhaps the best place to start with any *Horizons West* write-up is with a list of the 105 possible titles initially considered by Universal. They include *Cattle King*, *A New Life*, *Give Me Your Gun*, *Empire to the Son*, *Storm Over Texas*, *Texas Fury*, *Texas Man* and *Vengeance Valley*. The full list of titles has a pencil checkmark by *Horizons West*. Who chose it, or why, remains unclear, but it does suggest that the studio did not quite understand the material at hand. Writer Jim Kitses appropriated the film's title for his seminal 1969 look at the most famous directors of Westerns reaching back to John Ford and up to Clint Eastwood—and including Budd Boetticher.

Here's what *Horizons West* does well: It hints at the post-traumatic stress disorder affecting so many military veterans lives in the post–World War II (and, by the time the film was made, Korean War) era. It offers hope for reconciliation—a big theme in Westerns during the Korean War era—in its look at how both the North and South came together again to work for both good and evil in the post–Civil War years. Louis Stevens' script moves the Western a small step forward in the world of psychological "adult" Westerns by presenting a bad good guy as its hero and pushing the limits of familial loyalty and conflict. The Western was maturing in 1951, when Budd Boetticher directed this, but it was often stumbling about like an awkward adolescent, and *Horizons West* is typical of that uncertain evolution. It doesn't seem to know whether it's another 80-some-minute B oater off the Universal assembly line or a more ambitious in-depth analysis of the flawed Western hero—a man who doesn't realize that his individuality and sense of self-righteousness is killing him and everyone around him. Regardless, it's a mostly engaging study of a megalomaniac misfit (Ryan) who wants to create and run an empire for no other reason than this: It's better than dying.

If, for Boetticher, this is a lesser effort that doesn't even reach the bottom step of the "A-plus" work he did with Harry Joe Brown, Burt Kennedy and Randolph Scott, then for screenwriter Stevens and producer Albert J. Cohen it was probably a masterpiece.

For Budd, it must have been a more personal product than most of the Universal films he directed, because as with *Bronco Buster*, he interjected his thoughts on the script to producer Cohen and production manager James Pratt, kicking off his suggestions with a critical, "For once I would like to start a picture with a shooting script to be shot." That suggests that his previous three films were all given to him with an uncompleted script, though the Universal archives don't suggest that.

His suggestions in that January 9, 1952, memo include eliminating any discussion of the parents of the Hammond brothers (Ryan and Hudson) in the initial scene and building up a poker sequence involving Ryan and Raymond Burr's characters. Of Lorna's character, Budd suggested the producers and screenwriter build her up "in every scene she is in." He calls her a woman who "enjoys life, has plenty of guts of her own and now aside from the power, prestige and wealth, has love and sex for the first time."

Lorna was played by Julie Adams, best known for the 1954 sci-fi classic *Creature from the Black Lagoon*, but she was also a damn good natural actress and the object of Budd's affection. He would tell many journalists—including me—that he fell in love with her. They worked together on a total of three films. Adams was too much of a lady to comment on any of that in her autobiography, *The Lucky Southern Star: Reflections from the Black Lagoon* (Hollywood Adventures Publishing, 2011), but she describes Budd as "a director with a great flair for action" and writes that Burr, who played her abusive husband, played it "very well." Of co-star Ryan, she recalls a man interested in supporting efforts to help the schools, and she tells a story of having some difficulties with riding side-saddle on a sorrel who reared up "so high I thought I was going to slide off his backside." Budd said he was so smitten with Adams that he had to leave the studio and America to get away from her—one reason he left Universal to go shoot the ill-fated *The Americano* in Brazil in another year or so.

Did the producers accommodate Budd's request or respond to his suggestions in writing? There's nothing in the Universal archives to suggest they did, but he may have been able to work with Adams to create a more sensual, progressive female character. In an early scene in which Dan Hammond and Lorna Hardin first interact, Hammond spots the high-class woman sitting in a waiting carriage. Not knowing she is married, he initiates a flirtatious give-and-take dialogue with her, obviously hoping she is available. She becomes the aggressor fast. "I'm beginning to wonder what

Power-mad Robert Ryan (center) tries to convince Raymond Greenleaf (with Ryan) that everything is just Jim Dandy in a quieter moment from *Horizons West*, an interesting misfire that is still worth seeking out.

you look like with a shave," she says, seconds before running her eyes up and down his body and adding, "And some up-to-date clothes." Her eyes, however, say "*no* clothes." It's an amazing moment.

Interfamilial relationships play a big role. Dan's father Ira and brother Neal want to go back to the simple life of ranching, despite the hard chores and financial challenges. Dan has gone beyond that. "It seems kind of quiet around here," he tells his dad shortly after returning from fighting a lost cause. Ryan uses minimal facial expressions to convey the pain of a combat veteran well aware that he cannot separate his current life from his violent past. Late in the film, you can feel that it wants to delve a little deeper and make its audience uncomfortable with some decidedly unpleasant plot turns—maybe Dad will kill his son, or one brother will kill another, or visa versa. But this Western isn't quite ready to go there.

Around the same time that Budd made this film, George Stevens was shooting *Shane* and Stanley Kramer was filming *High Noon*. All three focused on "a man alone" who has to do a job that nobody else wants to do.

The problem with *Horizons West* is that the script gives Ryan's character little motivation—beyond possible combat stress—to work with when it comes to his Napoleonic desires to rule Austin. It's a film that doesn't ask you to pull for Dan Hammond but to understand and forgive him, and that's tough to do once his character becomes a hair-trigger killer. Late in the film, Boetticher's direction and the work of the players have to make some big leaps in narrative gaps to overcome scripting deficiencies in the development of Ryan's character. He quickly turns into an out-of-control despot whose sole purpose is to create and run an empire and let others do the fighting for him. In short, he turns psycho fast,

Universal played up the romance between anti-hero Robert Ryan and Julie (billed as Julia) Adams in marketing 1952's *Horizons West*.

wantonly threatening and killing people when reason—combined with the power he has amassed—may have done the job better.

Here and there the film attempts to address the issue that even the experts couldn't address: What to do with kill-crazy war veterans who didn't know how to harness the skills they perfected in the war. "Something happened to you," one character says to Ryan's Dan Hammond. Hammond agrees but can't say what it is: "I'm not quite certain.... I don't know how to do it any other way." And then his character kills the other guy, because he doesn't know what else to do. It's likely that in 1951 no combat veteran knew what to do when life seemed out of control and they wanted to reach for a gun to put things in order.

Horizons West is full of problems and potholes. A shoot-out in and around a corral is sloppily filmed, devoid of the usual detail-oriented care Boetticher gave to such set pieces. In one scene, a lynch mob takes up a battering ram to knock down the front door to the jail to get to their intended victim. But do the mob leaders send even one member of their group around the back to check out the alternative exit lest their prey get away? Nope. And so the intended victim hightails it out the back door.

But maybe Universal knew what it was doing. *Horizons West* features up-and-coming stars (Hudson), guys who were kind-of-stars but not really (Ryan) and lots of action. The idea of warring brothers had already developed in Anthony Mann's 1950 Western *Winchester '73*, but a year or two later the studio wasn't quite ready to take the idea into deep dark territory mined by the likes of *Gunman's Walk* and *Saddle the Wind* later in the decade. There's lots of riding and shooting and a pretty woman and some good acting, so who cares, once it's over, if it really motivated you to give additional thought to the personal problems of its main characters.

Horizons West, initially budgeted at about $630,000, was shot between mid–February and mid–March. Newcomer James Arness received $750 a week. In his 2001 autobiography, he said little about the film other than this:

> Sometimes I had a little too much fun on the set, and there were times when directors weren't too pleased with my shenanigans. I remember in *Horizons West* … we had some scenes at a Thanksgiving family gathering in a ranch house. Rock Hudson, who was just a kid at the time, and I started laughing about something and couldn't stop. The more we tried to get ourselves under control, the worse it got. They had to stop the filming several times, which interrupted the shooting schedule and cost money, and we rightfully got a thorough chewing out by the director. I guess in some ways I was still the mischievous boy back in Minnesota, staring out the classroom window waiting to hop a freight.

Coincidentally, future screenwriter Burt Kennedy worked two days on the film as an extra in crowd scenes late in the movie. I couldn't spot him despite repeated viewings, but he's there on the daily production log sheets, referred to as Bert Kennedy but signing

Director Budd Boetticher (right) strolls along the *Horizons West* **(1952) set with stars Rock Hudson and Judith Braun (Photofest).**

his payroll card Burt Kennedy. Universal paid him $55 a day for the two days, February 22 and 25. A few years later, when Kennedy and Boetticher met to talk about Budd directing Burt's script for *Seven Men from Now*, producer John Wayne began introducing Burt when Budd cut in and said he recalled meeting Burt on *Horizons West*. Burt said he thought it was *Man from the Alamo*, but Budd was right. "I think Budd has always had me mixed up with a good actor, which I wasn't, but I was in the picture and I did do something," Kennedy told Sean Axmaker for the story "Burt Kennedy: Writing Broadway in Arizona." He continued:

> I had some lines, because I remember it was at Universal and I was trying to be a writer and I was dealing with a fellow over there who was the head of wardrobe. I'm trying to make a deal with the head of wardrobe to write, you know, and he's trying to be a producer, and I would go in the morning as a writer and then in the afternoon I would go in the back gate as the actor. I worked a couple of days on the picture, that's where I first met Budd.

The production logs indicate that Budd was late a few minutes on the set a couple of times, that Raymond Burr missed one day of work because of illness, and that cloudy skies slowed down filming now and then. On March 8, Budd decided to change the way a scene was shot at the last minute, causing some delays. Between weather conflicts and an extra day of work because of the need to call back Burr, McIntire, Hubbard and Douglas Fowley, the budget jumped toward the $640,000 mark.

Universal "sneaked" the film on June 20, 1952, at the Cornell Theatre in Burbank. Of the 116 preview cards turned in, all but 13 found the film to be "good" to "outstanding." Universal's publicity department went mad trying to play up the 35th anniversary of the studio's Western film set, which was created for a 1917 Hoot Gibson oater. Robert Ryan did his best to promote the film, telling Hollywood columnists that he enjoyed making Westerns because "you take off your dinner jacket or lounging suit and slip into a pair of Levis, a ten-gallon hat and a gun belt and all of a sudden you feel as though you could lick the world." That's how most of us playing cowboy—if any of us still play cowboy, that is—feel.

Horizons West received mixed reviews, which it probably deserved. The *Los Angeles Examiner's* Lynn Bowers wrote, "The action is fast and violent, Budd Boetticher's direction keeps the pace clipping along" (October 23, 1952). The *New York Times* reviewer said that while Boetticher "does keep the revolvers smoking and the citizens cringing, the cast is left to dodge bullets more or less on its own resources.... *Horizons West* bites the dust before anybody in it."

Budd told film historian and author Ronald Davis that he didn't think much of the film:

> They were trying to make a Western star out of Rock, and you know nothing happened with Rock until he met Doris Day.... He was very serious and very frustrated and it was years after the world began to realize he had a problem that I discovered it. I never had any indication of it. He was a wonderful fellow to work with.

Most sources list the film as running 83 minutes but the print I saw was closer to 88 minutes.

Seminole (Universal, 87 minutes, released in February 1953) Director: Budd Boetticher. Producer: Howard Christie. Story and Screenplay: Charles K. Peck, Jr. Cinematographer: Russell Metty. With Rock Hudson (Lt. Lance Caldwell), Barbara Hale (Revere Muldoon), Anthony Quinn (Osceola), Richard Carlson (Major Harlan Degan), Hugh O'Brian (Kajeck), Russell Johnson (Lt. Hamilton), Lee Marvin (Sgt. McGruder), Ralph Moody (Kulak), Fay Roope (Zachary Taylor) and James Best (Corp. Gerad)

Synopsis: Lt. Lane Caldwell, friend of the half-breed Seminole leader Osceola, tries to salvage a peace treaty between the Seminoles and the U.S. government. But an ambitious and meddlesome superior officer mucks things up good.

"Vengeance was their cry! Courage their weapon! Glory their reward!" That sounds like something the Texans looking for retribution against Gen. Santa Ana might say following the Mexican assault on the Alamo. But in fact these are the tag lines—coming from the Native American point of view—that Universal used to promote *Seminole*, an adequate actioner that vaguely follows historical guidelines.

There really was a half-breed Seminole chief named Osceola, and he dressed quite colorfully, as Anthony Quinn does in portraying him in this film. He was born Billy Powell in Alabama in 1804 and moved with his mixed-race mother to Florida about ten years later. By the time of the second Seminole War (1835–1842), Osceola had become leader of the swamp-living tribe. Osceola and other chiefs refused to give in to President Andrew Jackson's demand that they move west and cede their territory to the United States. So Jackson ordered troops to force the Seminole out. But in this case, the U.S. Army found it very difficult to navigate the jungle-like terrain of the Florida swamps, which led to a lengthy conflict with no real winners. *Seminole* captures the hellish conditions under which the Army fought and the frustrating challenges of overcoming an enemy that could not be found. "How do you fight a swamp!" Major Harlan Degan (Richard Carlson) screams out in despair as he flails around in the mud, still far from his objective of launching a surprise attack on Osceola.

The middle sequence of the film, in which the glory-seeking Degan and the Seminole-sympathetic Lt. Caldwell (Rock Hudson) lead two dozen men into the swamp to wage war, is the movie's highlight. But it makes little sense to me how a career-savvy military officer could believe that just 25 men lugging one cannon would overcome hundreds of defenders in an unfamiliar environment. When Carlson tells Hudson, "Indians in the swamp are no different than Indians in the woods," you

Hugh O'Brian inexplicably sports a Mohawk hairstyle for the Florida-set *Seminole*. Rock Hudson, center, looks perplexed, since the story concerns the Seminole nation of Florida. Fay Roope is at right.

get the sense that the handful of 1950s "Westerns" featuring the Seminoles really weren't that much different from the traditional cowboys-vs.-Indians stories set out west. Florida just gave producers the chance to throw in a few novel elements that you wouldn't find in Arizona or New Mexico: alligators, quicksand and jungle fever, for example. And why is actor Hugh O'Brian, as the warlike Seminole named Kajeck, sporting a Mohawk hair style? According to Barbara Hale, O'Brian called her up one day before shooting began and said, "Guess what I did? I shaved my head!" While O'Brian was proud of his handiwork, Hale was right when she said, "Of course, it looked terrible."

Another scripting problem surfaces as Hudson's character, via flashbacks, recalls the events leading up to his court martial. It's one thing for him to tell his version of the story from first-hand experience, but his testimony includes a lot of scenes and dialogue from sequences in which his character doesn't even appear, which is just ridiculous.

Carlson plays Hudson's somewhat demented superior as if he had just finished memorizing the Capt. Queeg role in Herman Wouk's 1951 novel *The Caine Mutiny* (which would be adapted for the stage in 1953 and for film the following year). If it is a one-note turn, Carlson adds a tone of politeness to his mostly harsh martinet, and unlike his work in Budd's 1948 noir *Behind Locked Doors,* he is forceful and lively.

Quinn and Hudson have little screen time to share, making it difficult for them to project either the bonds of friendship or build any protagonist-antagonist conflict. It doesn't help that Quinn's part is written and played as a passive, sorrowful soul. He mostly stands around making pained faces and spouting forgettable dialogue. He is barely seen in the tense battle sequence, in which Seminole warriors ambush the Army soldiers deep in the swamp, killing all but a few in a violent, frightening encounter.

But *Seminole* moves along at a snappy pace, and Russell Metty's cinematography is beautiful. Two of the supporting characters, played by Lee Marvin and James Best, get some brief moments to shine. It's sort of sad to see Best, billed tenth in one of his last Universal movies after a promising start at the studio, reduced to uttering a few lines of dialogue and mostly acting terrified and/or ill with malaria. By his own account, he began shacking up with "the wrong woman" and thus got the boot from Universal just about the time this picture was being made. "The wrong woman," to me, sounds like the wife or girlfriend of a bigwig movie executive rather than a tramp from the poor side of town. In his autobiography *Best in Hollywood* (BearManor Media, 2009), Best said the woman in question was a Miss Universe contestant who was also dating a Universal executive who was none too pleased with the set-up.

The bit where Best's character, lying wounded on a raft carrying the cannon, slowly sinks into the swampy quicksand, is terrifying. Budd being Budd, he insisted on shaming his actors into doing the stunt by first performing it himself. Studio technicians fixed up a hydraulic lift about seven feet under the water and slowly lowered the raft into the muck-filled studio tank.

In his autobiography, Best paints a rather frightening picture of a stunt that could have gone wrong. "Budd was nicknamed 'the bloody director' because he loved to create drama by showing blood on camera and he did not care how he went about getting it," Best wrote. The first time he went underwater with the raft, Best was equipped with a hose with which to breathe air. It didn't work, so he raised his hand out of the swampy mire and the crew had to set the sequence up again with an aqualung below Best.

That idea didn't work either and Best, panicked over not getting enough air, once again stopped the shot. "Budd was tearing out what hair he had left," Best wrote. For take three, Best drew in a mouthful of cork which made him have to remove the hose, spit out the cork, and put the hose back in again. He thought everything was going fine until he encountered crew members sloshing into the water to rescue him. Budd began screaming at the actor, "Your ass was sticking out of the damn water about three feet!" It turns out the aqualung, full of air, pushed his body above the surface, ruining the shot.

The fourth shot was mucked up when Hudson, fishing around in the murky water to find Best, inadvertently grabbed his private parts, leading Best to bust out laughing as he broke the surface. Budd, none too pleased, let the actor have it again before they finally got the sequence on the next take. Best encountered similar life-threatening stunts when he worked with Budd again on *Ride Lonesome*.

So no wonder that swamp fight looks realistic: A lot of people got hurt doing it. Carlson got a cut on the nose, actor Frank Chase suffered a scalp wound and stuntman David Sharpe hurt himself falling from a tree during the fracas.

Budd shot *Seminole* in about 30 days in the summer of 1952 on a budget of about $638,000. Here's an amusing tidbit: On July 17, Hudson and Quinn came back from lunch about a half hour late. Later that day, the two of them kept fluffing their lines in a rewritten sequence, forcing the company to finish around 6:30 p.m. without getting the scene in the can. I wonder if the duo imbibed a bit too much during one of those three-martini lunches.

Universal strove for some authenticity by asking the U.S. Army for some technical advice. But when Col. Paul R. Davison responded, the studio probably wished he hadn't bothered. He called the script "far-fetched" and said it was full of errors in "matters military, tactics, commands, general dialogue, nomenclature, procedures and detail." He went on to say that the script "could stand major surgery" and predicted that the audience wouldn't swallow a scene where a Seminole climbs a stockade wall. ("I won't say it can't be done," he noted.) He said many of the terms used in the script, including "liaison" and "calculated risk," came into use after 1835, when the picture was set. But, he said, much of the film was at least faithful to the time period, though he warned the studio about using "too much shooting without reloading. I had this problem to solve in *The Red Badge of Courage* (1951)." A look at the final film indicates that Universal cottoned to some of his ideas and ignored some others.

Hudson had other problems to deal with, according to Hale. She told Western film historian and author Boyd Magers,

> He lived in a house on the side of a hill, with stilts. There was a terrible earthquake and Rock came running out of that house and refused to ever go in again. Later, I went to his dressing room to run over our lines. Then the trailer started going back and forth, back and forth. We thought it was another earthquake. Rock jumped 30 feet out of the door. It turned out to be the crew, rocking the trailer as a practical joke.

When it came to promoting the film, Universal went all-out. Some of their ideas may seem politically incorrect today. For one thing, they hired eight Seminole Indians to go on a tour of Florida with the movie, paying them $10 per day plus expenses, though their leader netted $100 per week plus expenses for keeping them out of trouble. The studio made up 300 to 500 sets of alligator teeth ("the good luck charm for the Seminoles," one marketing staffer explained) in the form of a key chain as the "ideal gimmick to send to press people!" The marketing department suggested that the studio convince the Seminoles to give away bottled water from St. Augustine's Fountain of Youth to attract patrons into the theater. In return, the studio would do what it could to help Seminole residents of Florida get a special Seminole tag added to their license plates. Not surprisingly, the film did great business in Florida, outgrossing bigger-budgeted studio films released around the same time. The studio held the world premiere in Miami on January 19, 1953, and made about 1600 pens with the Red Feather symbol of Osceola imprinted on them along with the words "Universal-International's Seminole." They cost $1.05 each but the penny-pinching studio took note that it cost 4 cents to ship each one out. The studio ran out of them fast and had to write a lot of apology letters to patrons and theater owners who wanted more. I'd like to have one of them now just to see if it still works.

Award-winning Western author and Seminole expert Lucia St. Clair Robson told me the film is somewhat realistic:

> The scenes of the soldiers slogging through the swamps with their weapons over their heads is exactly as described in sources I've read. Also, the clothes the Seminole extras wore are the real deal. No mistaking them for Plains Indians. The filmmakers made clear early on that Osceola had Anglo heritage and wanted peace. A Lt. John Graham did befriend him, and the Army at that time did have its share of sadistic, sociopathic and incompetent officers.

But, she added, the screenplay "threw history under the bus. The most glaring example, other than the silly Hollywood romance between Osceola and the woman settler (Hale), was that Osceola died in prison in South Carolina.... Kajek's feather roach headdress was accurate but worn mostly pre–1800."

The Hollywood Reporter review of February 19, 1953, summed up the film in a few words: "Acceptable screen fare for the action market [with a] rather hackneyed script."

City Beneath the Sea (Universal, 87 minutes, released in March 1953) Director: Budd Boetticher. Producer: Albert J. Cohen. Screenplay: Jack Harvey and Ramon Romero. Story: Harry E. Rieseberg. Cinematographer: Charles P. Boyle. With Robert Ryan (Brad Carlton), Mala Powers (Terry McBride), Anthony Quinn (Tony Bartlett), Suzan Ball (Venita), George Mathews (Capt. Meade), Karel Stepanek (Dwight Trevor), Lalo Rios (Calypso) and Woody Strode (Dijon).

Synopsis: Deep-sea treasure hunters Brad Carlton and Tony Bartlett dive for a lost treasure reportedly hidden somewhere in the famed "City Beneath the Sea."

City Beneath the Sea is a soggy, convoluted and silly tale that makes little sense. It's arguably Budd's worst Universal film and, along with *Westbound*, his weakest post-1950 offering. He probably saw it as a fun lark, as he would later say, but there's barely a personal Boetticher touch in the picture to indicate he was behind the curtain moving all the machinery around. It rises above the ludicrous mediocrity of *Killer Shark* only because it has higher production values and a good cast.

But don't let my opinion dissuade you from watching it. Audiences loved the picture when it was released in 1953, based on both the preview card responses and the box office results. Universal bought television commercial time (one of the first instances that the studio did this) and it paid off, with cinema exhibitors praising Universal for giving them a hit. The manager of the RKO Palace in Cleveland said *City Beneath the Sea* scored the biggest opening since the 1952 Joan Crawford melodrama *Sudden Fear*. Another Ohio–based theater owner wrote Universal to say that he tracked his opening weekend grosses back to July 1950 and could not find another title that had "even approached" the money he was making off *City Beneath the Sea*. In no time at all, *City Beneath the Sea* was out-grossing the following Universal titles: *Battle at Apache Pass*, *Take Me to Town*, *Up Front*, *The Stand at Apache River* and *Lost in Alaska*. Now, it turns out I have seen all those other films, and I gotta tell you, there's not one that is really better than *City Beneath the Sea*, so take that for what it's worth. But when some 300 preview-screening patrons label the film as "good" to "outstanding" and write such comments as "I lost three fingernails" (a nail-biter, we assume), you know the picture must have caught fire with a nation still enthralled by the notion of sunken cities and long-lost treasures.

I can't help but think the movie would have been helped immensely had some unknown threat come out of that mysterious sea. This is a picture that needed a Creature from the Black Lagoon or a Beast from 20,000 Fathoms or even the underwater Zombies of Mora Tau to threaten our heroes and liven things up. The biggest underwater challenge our two protagonists face—in separate occasions—is to have their air lines clogged, which leads the other partner to heroically dive down and rescue him. (It seems to me that would take a long time and probably not be successful.) Ryan and Quinn both look uncomfortable in the heavy diving equipment—they had to be rolled onto the set in wheelchairs when they were in those suits—and the best either man can do when they are walking the ocean floor looking for treasure is make the sort of expressions that Victor Mature might call "Biblical faces." And script-wise, it's really tough to figure out what's going on, but after the initial, boring set-up of our boys working together in a vain effort find a $5,000,000 stash in a sunken galleon, it's something like this: Two rival treasure seekers, both crooks, individually hire Ryan and Quinn to find the treasure. Along the way, both of our heroes get romantically involved with women. Ryan's character gravitates towards the comely Mala Powers, while Quinn falls for young, vivacious nightclub singer Suzan Ball.

I like Ryan but here he is miscast as a two-fisted playboy with a yen for adventure and romance. In real life, Quinn and Ball started a passionate affair which he recalls in his memoir *One Man Tango*. Though Quinn was pushing 40 and Ball was barely 20, they generate heat and both actors inject a sincere and sensuous energy into the proceedings. Incidentally, Budd wanted Katy Jurado, who had worked so well with him in *Bullfighter and the Lady*, for Ball's part. Universal suggested Shelley Winters for the Mala Powers role.

Leave it to Powers to steal the show in a brief eye-popping sequence that somehow got past the censors. She and Ryan are lounging on a ship out at sea in bathing suits—hers is a one-piece gold affair. She dives in the water and Budd and cinematographer Charles P. Boyle then let the viewer delight in following her body as she climbs up the ladder to the deck of the ship, the suit clinging a little too fastidiously to the contours of her bottom. You get to see a lot. And then what happens next? She dives in the water a second time and repeats the show. It really is a kick for voyeurs to see, but it also speaks to the likelihood that Budd was bored on the film and couldn't figure out what to do to make it exciting. Early in the proceedings, a saloon brawl is handled pretty haphazardly, and there's not much any director could do with footage of a couple of

Anthony Quinn (right) lets loose with some fists of fury on an unidentified foe in a brawling sequence from *City Beneath the Sea*. Little else in the film measures up to this bit of fun.

guys in clunky diving suits stumbling around the ocean floor and spouting such dialogue as, "I found a miniature Atlantis!" or "It must have been something I ate!"

Midway through the film, things heat up a bit when Ryan, Powers and a character named Calypso stumble upon a voodoo ceremony and are surrounded by the revelers, whose faces are hidden by masks and hoods. But even this scene is mucked up when the imposing-looking voodoo leader, speaking in the somewhat reassuring tone of a radio announcer, simply points his finger at the trio and says, "You must stay away from the sunken city. Let the dead stay dead!" Again, an appearance from a few zombies could have spiced things up.

When it came time for the studio to publicize the picture, one marketing executive asked if they could hire an "authentic technical advisor for the voodoo drums and native chants… [H]e should be good for a wire story comparing modern music with the primitive."

Production began late in March 1952 on a 31-day schedule. Universal's technicians turned the studio's identifiable Western street into a seaside waterfront. The underwater scenes were shot on a dry set with the camera speeded up, with 60-pound blocks of metaldehyde forming the walls of the undersea kingdom. The studio inserted some dynamite sticks in those walls to bring the whole thing tumbling down for an okay climactic bit of tension. Some work was done in the studio's big water tank, 16 feet deep and 25 feet in diameter and holding about 40,000 gallons.

Deep-sea diving expeditions were in the news a lot those days, thanks to the work of real-life adventurer and author Harry E. Rieseberg, who had discovered the lost city of Port Royal—which toppled into the sea following an earthquake and hurricane and God-knows-what-else, way back in 1692. The "lost city" has almost nothing to do with the plot of this movie other than to serve as a backdrop for where the sunken galleon of gold is supposedly located. Rieseberg wrote a piece on treasure hunting for *The American Weekly* in the summer of 1952, and the studio kept track of all the magazines and publications—26 in all—that had run articles on Port Royal between July 1940 and January 1953.

Budd liked to say he knew he was in trouble when he read the script and then turned to his wife to say, "I just know an octopus is going to show up on page 100… It actually showed up on page 87." Maybe that's true in an earlier version of the script, but there's no octopus in the final screenplay or in the film. But there should have been.

The two leading ladies bore their share of misfortune on the film. Shortly after filming began, Powers got ill. A studio doctor concluded that despite the fact that she had a temperature of 102, she could keep working. By mid–April she was visiting the doctor more than the set, and by April 17 she was in the hospital for blood tests. On April 18, the studio insiders were reporting that her condition was "more serious than first thought"—especially after she collapsed on the set. After she missed about five straight days of work, a doctor told Universal she could not return to the set any time soon as she had some sort of blood infection. Some on-the-set rewriting then took place, which may explain some of the hard-to-swallow plot points that follow. Given that her character—a former Naval officer—is very formidable and demanding in the early scenes, I have to wonder if her illness and disappearance from the set resulted in a watering-down of her character (no pun intended). She becomes a quiet, obsequious camp follower of Ryan's by film's end.

Regarding her illness, Powers told interviewer Tom Weaver:

> I was entertaining troops in Korea and I came down with a virus of some kind, and they gave me a drug called chloromycetin when I got back home. But I was allergic to chloromycetin, it destroyed a great part of the bone marrow, and I sort of stopped producing blood. I had a great many transfusions, and the doctors really didn't hold out a lot of hope for me as far as living was concerned.

Ball had it worse. Cancer in the teenager's knee forced doctors to amputate it. Too late: The cancer took her life in 1955. In Quinn's memoir he calls her "the true love of my life!

(From left) Robert Ryan, Mala Powers and Lalo Rios do not seem particularly concerned with these voodoo-worshiping warriors in a strangely dull moment from *City Beneath the Sea*.

Ah, what a vacuum she has left in me... [S]he would have been one of the great ones, no question. There was a radiance about her, a magic." He goes on to say how he set her up in an apartment near Universal so he could carry on his affair with her away from the prying eyes of the Hollywood gossip columnists and his wife Katherine DeMille. "When she spoke, the rest of the world fell silent," Quinn wrote of Ball. When cancer swept over her body, he recalled, "Her decline was swift. The laughter stopped."

Ball married actor Richard Long. A Hollywood urban legend has it that as she took her final breath, she uttered her last word: "Tony." If true, no wonder Long took to the bottle to die the slow death of an alcoholic.

The ladies do get the final jabs in on-camera, and while it is an amusing bit to end this mediocrity, it seems like business pulled out of an Abbott and Costello movie. The final shot sees our two boys, with their respective ladies on their arms, on board a ship that is going to take them away from Port Royal and all their troubles. The ship's captain is ready to perform the double marriage ceremony so they can all go off to their cabins and consummate their union. Suddenly, Calypso shows up to tell the boys that they can take another crack at diving for more treasure if they hightail it back into town on the double. What do our virile symbols of masculinity do? They dump their hot honeys and rush down the gangplank to follow Calypso on yet another undersea jaunt. Powers gives Ball an exasperated look and asks, "Think we'll ever have a honeymoon?"

"Sure we'll have it," Ball responds. "But it looks like it will be underwater."

Fade out.

Universal wanted to authenticate the offerings with some real-life camera footage of Jamaica. The studio's timing was terrible: A hurricane had just hit Jamaica and wiped out the slums, the sugar cane fields and the banana plantations. That notion was scrapped.

Once filming was completed, the studio rented a treasure chest from a Frank Fish (no joke) of Van Nuys to use on promotional gigs. The studio ended up paying Fish an extra $50 for damages theatergoers perpetrated upon the chest on the tour.

After the film was released, Budd said "every screwball" in the country began writing him letters courtesy of Universal, pitching him equally nutty ideas for movie stories, including one about a boy and girl who grow up on the same cloud but are separated by a thunderstorm, and a more ominous piece about puppets on a television show who come to life and step out of the TV set to cause chaos. Budd could discount those hair-brained schemes all he wanted to, but I bet either one would have made a better movie than *City Beneath the Sea*.

In one latter-day interview, Budd said that once he read the script, he called some authorities at California Tech and asked, "If there's a sunken city not too far from land and there's an earthquake, what would remain of the city?" They said, "Nothing. Water's thicker than air. Nothing's left at all." I said, "That's what I want to know." That's what we did. And it kind of saved the picture." Budget: About $710,000.

The *New York Times* (March 12, 1953): "The entire enterprise, including a fairly ambitious finale, gives the impression of having been slung together during lunch time." The *New York Daily Mirror* (March 12, 1953): "A lusty, adventurous tale of deep sea divers." The *New York Herald Tribune:* (March 12, 1953): "The undersea mixture as concocted many times before with no extra seasoning to set it off from the commonplace."

The Man from the Alamo (Universal, 79 minutes, released in August 1953) Director: Budd Boetticher. Producer: Aaron Rosenberg. Screenplay: Steve Fisher and D.D. Beauchamp. Story: Niven Busch. Cinematographer: Russell Metty. With Glenn Ford (John Stroud), Julie Adams (Beth Anders), Chill Wills (John Gage), Hugh O'Brian (Lt. Lamar), Victor Jory (Jess Wade), Neville Brand (Dawes), John Day (Cavish), Myra Marsh (Ma Anders), Mark Cavell (Carlos) and Jeanne Cooper (Kate Lamar).

Synopsis: Alamo defender John Stroud reluctantly agrees to leave the mission in the heat of battle to save some of the families of his fellow Texan combatants. Later, mistakenly branded a coward, he works to redeem himself and avenge the death of his family while guiding a small wagon train to safety.

The Man from the Alamo, which many consider to be Budd's best pre–Randolph Scott Western, fortunately kicks up a lot of dust to obscure its many faults. Unlike the other Boetticher Universal films, the script mirrors the fear and uncertainty gripping many Americans at the height of both the Cold War and the Red Scare, what with its protagonist being a man falsely accused of a deed he did not do. (In 1952, Republicans took control of both the White House and Congress, and Hollywood was ridding itself of anyone even remotely connected with a leftist cause.) The picture is not afraid to suggest that not all Americans are good and not all Mexicans bad—this about a decade after the infamous Zoot Suit riots of Los Angeles and years of anti–Mexican sentiment in California—and it offers a protagonist who would fit right into the Western world of Anthony Mann. It also predates the Randolph Scott series with the introduction of a Western hero (Glenn Ford) seeking revenge for the death of his family and disregarding the welfare of everyone else around him in the process.

Budd was invested in the action scenes. They have a fiery verve to them that suggests he was standing just off-camera, urging the actors and stuntmen on with a "Come on, fellows, you can do better than that. It's just a staged fight. Swing a little closer to each other's chins; don't be afraid to get a little dirt on you."

And the acting, overall, is pretty good, right down to bit players Walter Reed (as a scared Alamo defender) and newcomer Guy Williams (as an exhausted relay rider). Actor Arthur Space would not have been my first choice to play William Travis, and the brief bit between him and actor Stuart Randall, as Jim Bowie, in which they jest with each other about cutting out of the Alamo before the Mexicans arrive, is pretty weak. But Space brings a gravitas to the role.

Ford is just about perfect as a man trying to reclaim his reputation and dead set on killing the men who murdered his wife. Julie Adams brings a spark to the role of one of the few people with faith in Ford's character. And I like that the film doesn't try to throw heartbroken and recent widower Ford into her arms for a happy ending.

The picture's depiction of Anglo-Mexican relations and the toll that war takes on families is beautifully played up in a brief interchange between Ford and Chill Wills' one-armed, cynical newsman: The latter tells Ford he won't take a Mexican boy on a wagon train to safety because he's, well, Mexican. "Don't you know we're at war with Mexico?" Wills asks.

"I didn't know we were at war with kids," Ford replies.

Finally, in a feminist-tinged finale, the women of the wagon train take up arms to blow away some mounted renegades out to rob the wagon train in a satisfying but somewhat unbelievable wrap-up.

A serious-minded effort, *The Man from the Alamo* does not forget that its main purpose is to entertain, and so for nearly 80 minutes you get caught up in the intrigue and action of the story, even if the script slowly begins to sink under all the weight it's trying to carry. The first third is really strong. The second third is an acceptable variation of the "go undercover and pretend to be a bad guy to infiltrate the outlaw gang" routine. And then the last third segues into the land of mediocrity with some really dumb plot points to accept. When Victor Jory's outlaw gang gets the upper hand over the wagon train (which is carrying bank money that the bad guys covet), the bandit king inexplicably calls off the attack after just a couple of minutes of shooting. "Come on, we're getting out of here," he tells a cohort.

"Let's go after them," the underling suggests.

"We'll go after them later!"

And that's that.

Part of the problem is that *The Man from the Alamo* required serious rewriting while its

Glenn Ford in the title role of *The Man from the Alamo*, a film beset by problems.

star, Glenn Ford, recovered from a bad accident on the set. The accident occurred around 2:45 p.m. on September 15, 1952, at Pollard Lake when Ford and his horse ran into a tree during a fast-paced riding scene. The company was dismissed and the production remained closed until October 20, when filming resumed with a much-bruised Ford back on the lot. Ford broke three ribs. Penny-conscious Universal estimated the shutdown to cost $48,441.61. Yup, they figured it down to the last cent.

In Peter Ford's biography of his father, he wrote that the accident occurred during a riding sequence between Ford and Victor Jory for the climax, which is accurate. "Glenn was galloping at a good clip when two other riders veered sharply into Glenn's mount and forced him straight into a tree at high speed." Julie Adams said, "It was a terrible thing to see.

Glenn was a very good rider and with Budd's encouragement he was really riding hard that day. The horse lots its footing and Glenn got slammed."

Several actors who I interviewed said that Budd pushed his cast members to perform their own stunts. On the back lot of Universal, some took to calling the energetic director "Bat-out-of-Hell Budd" and "Wild-man Boetticher." Budd admitted in a 1952 interview that he sort of shamed John Lund and Scott Brady into performing some of their own *Bronco Buster* stunts. "[Actors] all have egos," he said. "I say, 'Let's do it this way,' then I go ahead and do it. After that, their pride won't let them back down."

Actors do have egos, and I suspect the men who worked with Budd admired his gutsy approach and felt they had to prove their mettle to him. (Ford should have known better; after all, just a decade before, Budd had thrown a chair and hit the actor during the filming of a bar fight for *The Desperadoes*.) Ford told the press that the riding sequence had been well-rehearsed but it didn't go as planned: "It was just a tough-luck situation."

Maybe not. A lot of people got hurt on the set. On August 9, stuntmen Roydon Clark and Jack Carry were treated at the studio hospital for injuries related to some horse-jumping action. That same day, stuntman Fred Carson inadvertently fell from his horse and fractured a foot. On August 30, bit player Dan Poole was "shaken up" during a fight scene and sent to the studio hospital. On September 2, extra Marion Meade injured her knee getting down from a wagon. On September 9, Julie Adams suffered a nosebleed that halted filming. On September 13, another bit player suffered a hand injury during an action scene. On October 22—after shooting resumed followed Ford's absence and recuperation—stuntman Dave Sharpe received facial burns and abrasions following a powder explosion in the Alamo battle. Another bit player in that scene was also singed. And on and on...

While Ford was out, some rewriting had to be done. For example, the film opens with a bunch of Texans—including Sam Houston—sitting around a table talking about the war with Mexico, which provides a touch of historical clarity to the battle. More scripting and footage was suddenly allotted to the Alamo battle scenes—shot after Ford returned to the set—including the poorly staged banter between Travis and Bowie. A new scene in which Julie Adams' Beth Anders asks Ford's John Stroud why he stays with the wagon train—totally unnecessary to the plot—was added to buy a still-battered looking Ford time to recover. The scene before that, featuring Ford's Stroud awakening after being wounded, reflects the actor's real-life pain and gave audiences members a reason to understand why he was moving slowly. And take a look at the double playing John Stroud in the Alamo scenes. He doesn't look like Ford, he doesn't jump with the grace of Ford, and his face is carefully hidden from the camera. He bounces around like an ape, in fact.

Budd's description of the accident puts the blame on the actor. "My problem with Glenn is he's so ballsy that if I were going to make a long shot of covered wagons, like in *The Man from the Alamo*, I'd have to find Glenn and make him sit down next to me because he'd be out there where I couldn't see him, leading the pack, and if he falls, the picture's over. He broke his shoulder and some ribs the last day of filming *The Man from the Alamo*." Budd added that Ford's *Alamo* mishap led to the studio casting Van Heflin instead of Ford in Budd's next movie, *Wings of the Hawk*.

In Adams' autobiography, she recalled the shooting this way: "Early calls, long days ... temperatures would be above 100 degrees almost every day. So be it, we went to work." She wrote that the nosebleed occurred because of the searing, dry heat. "Makeup tended to it and we got the shot. Ah, what a glamorous profession. But of course I loved it." Ford, she wrote, "gave a masterful performance. He revealed enough to show that he was a good man, while never giving away why he had actually left the Alamo." She recalls talking with actor Neville Brand, a highly decorated combat soldier in World War II, about his bravery in action. Brand downplayed his role in taking a German pillbox full of machine-gunning Nazis, claiming he blacked out after seeing a buddy killed and woke up to discover all the German soldiers dead at his feet. "So much for bravery," he said. *The Man from the Alamo* builds Neville's secondary villain character up nicely in the beginning, then unfortunately forgets about him along the way. It looks like he did not return to the lot after Ford recovered and shooting resumed—perhaps because Brand was working on another project—and so his character just disappears.

Walter Reed told me that Budd was "one of the finest directors who ever lived, but his own worst enemy sometimes. Budd wanted it done his way. He was impatient with some of his producers. "

Producer Aaron Rosenberg told the press that it was "a proven fact of history" that one man did escape the actual Alamo siege. James Donovan, author of *The Blood of Heroes: The 13-Day Struggle for the Alamo and the Sacrifice That Forged a Nation*, has this to say about that idea:

> One intriguing element is the film's premise—that one man escaped from the Alamo just before the final assault on the morning of March 6. Stroud has different reasons for leaving, but a defender did depart the mission-turned-fortress the night before, or the previous night. His name was Louis "Moses" Rose, and he left, as he told people later, "By God, I wasn't ready to die." … Unlike John Stroud, Rose never found vindication. He lived another 16 years, mostly in western Louisiana, until he died in his sixties—still branded as "the coward of the Alamo."

Donovan said that the film, while not great, includes a "surprisingly accurate" depiction of the siege of the Alamo.

Budd later called Rosenberg his

> favorite producer of all time.... I'm not sure he liked me at the end, but I just loved him. He was a wonderful, kind, very physical All-American football player from Southern Cal who worked his way up. He was, I guess, my favorite producer of all time because he was so damn honest.... I was trying to make better pictures because I was never satisfied with what I had an opportunity to do, and we both really believed what we were doing.

Budd Boetticher seems to be enjoying himself as he directs a stuntman on the set of *The Man from the Alamo* while Julie Adams looks on.

Add up Budd's respect for Rosenberg, his desire to work with Ford (his first big "star" at Universal) and his admiration for Julie Adams, and one can see why he was more enthused than usual on the *Man from the Alamo* set.

The picture cost a little over $800,000, with Ford earning a fee of $62,500 plus 15 percent of the gross. Budd finished filming on November 4, which was four days over schedule not including all the time that the set was shut down.

Universal released the film in August 1953, a year after filming began and a few months after Budd had left the studio for Brazil to shoot *The Americano* with Glenn Ford. Once again the Universal publicity department came up with some hare-brained schemes, including encouraging the state of Texas to hire "a tall Texas beauty" to transport some actual Alamo artifacts (which would be insured by Lloyd's of London) to Hollywood for use in the film. The studio also suggested getting the word out that Chill Wills wanted Francis the Talking Mule to play a bit part in *The Man from the Alamo*. (So where would Donald O'Connor be in that scenario? Hiding under the bed in a back room of the Alamo?) Wills agreed to go on publicity junkets for the movie, along with Hugh O'Brian and Julie Adams, and he was apparently quite successful at convincing patrons to buy tickets to the movie wherever he appeared. In Houston, he waylaid patrons planning to see the adult comedy *The Moon Is Blue* and convinced them to go see his movie instead—an act that may not have been so difficult given that *The Moon Is Blue* was controversial.

The Man from the Alamo was based on a story by Niven Busch. When *Variety* announced the sale of that story to Universal, John Ford and John Wayne stepped in to say they had copyrighted the word "Alamo" for their own production and Universal should change the title. That led to arbitration and ended with Ford and Wayne rather sheepishly admitting they had no right to copyright it. Their action suggests that, as of 1951, Wayne was hoping Ford would direct his long-planned movie on the Alamo at Republic. Republic head Herbert Yates wouldn't ante up the money, which is one reason Wayne left that studio in the spring of 1952. In 1955, Republic produced the story under the title *The Last Command*. Wayne's big-budgeted *The Alamo* came out in 1960.

In *The Man from the Alamo*, the Travis character, after contemplating a Mexican offer to surrender, calmly sets a match to a waiting cannon fuse to offer his response: a resounding "no" punctuated by cannon fire. This same bit shows up in John Wayne's version, with actor Laurence Harvey, as Travis, doing the same thing.

Glenn Ford (fourth from right, in white hat, his arm around Mark Cavell) brought some much-needed star power to Universal's *Man from the Alamo* (1953), which co-starred Julie (billed as Julia) Adams (center), Chill Wills (to the right of Adams) and Hugh O'Brian (to the right of Wills), all of whom appear in this lobby card featuring one of the less exciting moments of the film.

Universal had another hit on its hands. The *Los Angeles Times* (August 8, 1953) called it "excellent entertainment for devotees of outdoor film fare," and the *New York Times* said it "generally makes a dogged, straight-faced try for authenticity," but gave the filmmakers grief for not letting Ford's character explain himself until almost the end of the picture. The *Los Angeles Examiner's* reviewer (August 8, 1953) agreed: "The strange part of it all is that the people in the picture are so blind to [Ford's] virtues for so long when we in the audience can see it all at first glance."

Budd professed to like the film and over the years many western film historians have considered it one of his best works. "A superior B Western," wrote Phil Hardy in *The Overlook Film Encyclopedia*, going on to say that the wagon train attack is among "the most impressive Boetticher has ever filmed." In his *Western Films: A Complete Guide* (Rawson Associates, 1982), Brian Garfield says it is "well directed and well played but it's tedious and virtually without action." In *The Western* (Grossman, 1973), George N. Fenin and William K. Everson call the film "intelligent and above average."

Glenn Ford (to C. Courtney Joyner):

> I was always drawn to characters who were complex or multi-dimensional but I think as an actor you should be prepared to take on any role. [Regarding his on-set accident:] I was filming a chase scene. The scene called for me to ride a horse standing in the stirrups. My horse ran right into a tree and everyone thought I had been killed.

Screenwriter Niven Busch, to Patrick McGilligan, in *Backstory 1: Interviews with Screenwriters of Hollywood's Golden Era*:

> I never tried to inject a Freudian context into any of those films. My objective was to make the people real and to give them three dimensions in terms of modern culture. People in Westerns weren't often like that. And maybe some of my characters are more modern in psychological terms than people of that period really were. Certainly their actions were self-revealing. But the Freudian element is one we impose, like a surface coating. It was not my intention. It came from the eyes of the viewers. And the movies that had this were *Pursued*, *The Furies*, *The Captive* and *The Man from the Alamo*. Now, of course, let's face it; I'd had some psychoanalysis—not a huge amount, but some. So I may have been influenced, I don't know. Really and truly, if you look at any of the masterpieces of literature, not that I'm putting myself in that class, there's a Freudian level. You could say that Shakespeare and Dostoyevsky prefigure Freud and Wagner—even Balzac and Stendahl. So if I'm accused of imitating the Freudian picture—it's a good label, but it wasn't intentional.

East of Sumatra (Universal, 82 minutes, released in September 1953) Director: Budd Boetticher. Producer: Albert J. Cohen. Screenplay: Frank Gill, Jr. Story: Louis L'Amour and Jack Natteford. Cinematographer: Clifford Stine. With Jeff Chandler (Duke Mullane), Marilyn Maxwell (Lory Hale), Anthony Quinn (Kiang), Suzan Ball (Minyora), John Sutton (Daniel Catlin), Jay C. Flippen (Mac), Scatman Crothers (Baltimore), Aram Katcher (Atib), Anthony Eustrel (Clyde), Gene Iglesias (Paulo), Peter Graves (Cowboy) and Earl Holliman (Cupid).

Synopsis: Mining engineer Duke Mullane leads his crew to the remote isle of Tunga, east of Sumatra, to mine tin. But he doesn't count on running into ex-lover Lory Hale there—or on antagonizing the once-peaceful natives, led by the formidable King Kiang.

Just as Budd started off the year with the non–Western *City Beneath the Sea*, so he ended it with this entertaining slice of nonsense, *East of Sumatra*, which could have been just as easily titled *Ambush on the Isle of Tunga*. But fans of Budd's Westerns shouldn't be turned off, because if *Red Ball Express* is a Western with trucks, then *East of Sumatra* is a Western in a jungle, replete with threatening natives, a nice native girl who falls for the white leading man and the usual treachery and action expected of an oater. The only real difference is that ominous-looking blowguns with poison darts replace the traditional bow and arrows.

Red Ball Express failed as a film, but it did try to say something meaningful about war and race; it just didn't know what it was saying or even how to articulate it. *East of Sumatra* has no such aspirations. It's patronizing and pointless, sporting a simple-minded Jungle Jim–like attitude. Universal knew how to grind out B Westerns and sword-and-sandal films (or tits-and-sand films, as they were sometimes called) on its assembly line every single day, and for this little stanza, the studio combined all those ideas into one. The film's lineage is closely tied to the Western in that the author of its source material is famed novelist Louis L'Amour. He shares co-story credit with Jack Natteford, but L'Amour wasn't happy with the final cut. "The idea was good, the cast was capable," he wrote in his memoir. "And instead of a meaningful picture, the producers or somebody turned it into a sex and jungle epic." L'Amour insists the film's downfall began with the expected scene of a beautiful native girl (here played by Suzan Ball) "swimming naked or nearly so in a pool" when the leading man (Chandler) finds her. From that point on, he wrote, the main theme of the story was pushed aside and the hopes of the protagonists, like the picture, "go down the drain."

He's right. The basic set-up pits commercialistic miners, including Chandler, against a peace-loving island community that's willing to let the Anglos denude their isolated paradise in return for modern medicine, doctors and a hospital. But what are the natives, led by a dour-looking Anthony Quinn as King Kiang, to think when the mining crew arrives replete with automatic firearms and pistols on their hips? The American interlopers have no idea what is in store when the resourceful islanders, angry at what they consider to be some double-dealing on the part of the whites, utilize their own brand of blowgun warfare, wisely staying hidden in the shadows of the jungle foliage to pick off the Americans.

If you are looking for a probing look at racial relations or the contrast between despoilers of the earth and peaceful conservationists, you will be disappointed. Budd called *East of Sumatra* "fun" and we all know what that means. He went in, did his work, picked up his paycheck and tried to incorporate some cool action bits here and there. And to that end, he succeeded, particularly in a tense sequence in which Chandler and his men feverishly work their way through the jungle trails to a forbidden temple to make a last stand while the poison darts from the blowguns knock them off one by one.

But it's tough to accept the presence of the mining magnate's girlfriend Lory Hale (played by Marilyn Maxwell) in the mix, particularly as she rather coincidentally once had an affair with Chandler's character. Even more ludicrously, she continually looks like she just emerged from the hair, costume and makeup department of New York City's swankiest salon. I swear she went out and got a haircut between one jungle scene and another, which makes no sense. Maxwell is not a great actress, but she was a good-looking woman and performed as adequately as any Universal contract player might have in the role. The press and public gave her a hard time, with many patrons telling Universal she "should have stuck to musicals." Interestingly, the Universal archives indicate that the studio scored big when it signed Gloria Grahame for the role of Lory on November 10, 1952, at $500 per week. By November 18, Maxwell was cast in the role with no explanation as to what happened to Grahame after her contract was signed. (Maybe she read the script and said, "You gotta be kidding me.")

It's equally challenging to swallow the notion that these somewhat primitive islanders all understand or speak some English for a variety of far-fetched reasons: One went to boarding school in nearby Sumatra, another worked for Chinese traders who spoke English, another encountered English-speaking missionaries, and so on. There's an awfully embarrassing sequence following Ball's really hot dance number in which the Americans teach the confused natives how to applaud.

Budd shot the picture from just before Thanksgiving to Christmas Eve, 1952. Typical of the Universal pace, he was expected to find five to ten minutes for rehearsal time here and there while knocking off 10 to 15 pages of dialogue and action per day. The studio and Hollywood press made a lot out of the fact that Chandler and Quinn worked late on Christmas Eve on their climactic hand-to-hand bout, but no one mentioned that a lot of extras had to give up family time that night too while they stood around in native garb watching the stars fake their punches. They were probably wishing they were home with their kids waiting for Santy Claus.

The Douglas C-47 plane is impressive, as well it should be: The studio contracted with the Johnson Flying Services of Missoula, Montana, to rent the plane and a small crew to operate it during filming. Universal received permission to remove the wings and then re-install them on the set, and took out an $80,000 insurance policy against any potential damage to the plane. Studio workmen had to tear down part of the studio's main gate and the watchman's building, remove some 3000 feet of power and telephone lines and clear all parked cars from the studio streets in order to help technicians tow the giant aircraft onto the lot, which inconvenienced everyone nearby for about half a day. This real-life touch gives authentic weight to the aerial footage, including the sight of the plane landing on the isle.

The original script called for Ball's character to swim nude in the idyllic tropical lagoon but the Breen Office told Universal to get some clothes on the girl. So she rather absurdly swims in her sarong, which then clings to her wet lithe body as she plays a dialogue scene with Chandler. The censors also told Universal to cut a Groucho Marx–like line intended for Chandler, when Ball's naïve native girl asks him a double entendre–loaded question and he responds, "There must be some way to answer that and not get slapped." I can't imagine Chandler pulling that off.

The usual minor problems slowed production every now and then. For some reason, Budd had trouble finishing the shots of Chandler and Ball meeting at the waterfall, causing delays on December 4. Ball got sick around that time and missed a few days of work, necessitating some re-arranging of sequences. Chandler hurt his ribs in an action scene on December 20 and was treated for his injuries on the set. Maxwell suffered a Charley horse and had to go to the studio doctor on a day when the cast was performing some run-bys in the jungle. A need for retakes brought Budd and some of the cast and crew back to the studio on December 30, but by the end of the calendar year, their work on the picture was complete.

The film was previewed in mid–April 1953, following a planned screening of the Alan Ladd film *Desert Legion*. In reviewing the preview card responses, I can't help but wonder if Universal rigged the audience: The vast majority seemed to love these B films, be they good, so-so or bad. "Were the story points clear to you?" patrons were asked. "Only the women's points," one wise guy remarked. But you can't blame him. The studio knew what it had, and it played that angle up in ads, sending out inter-office memos to "concentrate on key sex art of Jeff Chandler and Suzan Ball" and urging the producers of the trailer to get plenty of footage of Maxwell's bosom. (They did.)

And despite L'Amour kicking about the picture, he agreed to quickly write a 25-cent paperback version of the script to be released with the film. The deal fell apart when he couldn't get his publisher's commitment on such short notice. A Universal executive griped to the front office about the botched deal distracting everyone with "unnecessary paperwork." L'Amour also told the studio he would go on tour with the film for $175 per week plus expenses, so he couldn't have been that unhappy with the finished product.

And to Budd's credit, if old pros Chandler, Quinn and Maxwell gave by-now patented portrayals that seemed apt for their one-note characters, at least Graves, Earl Holliman and Scatman Crothers, as members of Chandler's crew, fleshed out their scripted characterizations and worked on developing relationships with one another. The bit where Holliman's easygoing character gets a poison dart to the back must have terrified children in the audience: He grasps at Crothers as he battles for breath and contorts his body in a manner to suggest paralysis. Crothers' reaction is smack-on-target. A second of grief, then anger as he fires wildly and without success at their unseen pursuers.

Universal asked United Artists for help in publicizing the film, requesting copies of UA's ad campaign for the Gary Cooper vehicle *Return to Paradise*—featuring a very different kind of American on a very different kind of tropical isle. "Man with a mysterious past… he came to this virgin paradise seeking escape…but remained to rule—and to love!" those ad campaigns proclaimed. So Universal shamelessly followed up with the similar tagline "The story of 'Duke' Mullane…the iron men he led, the jungle he plundered and the women he loved in the last forgotten corner of the earth!… East of Sumatra…where savage kisses feed the flame of men's desires."

It paid off. The patrons bought tickets everywhere it opened. What did the critics think? Just what you would expect. "The merry old tropical jungle is still good, even after the wear and tear of years, for another film story…" wrote the *Los Angeles Times* critic (September 12, 1953). "It has all the familiar plots, characters and gimmicks reshuffled for a new deal."

The same-day *Los Angeles Herald & Express* review recapped the plot in dull fashion without offering any critique other than, "Budd Boetticher's direction gets as much as possible out of the Frank Gill screenplay." *The Hollywood Reporter* (September 11, 1953) expectedly said all nice things, including "Chandler turns in an excellent portrayal of a rugged, two-fisted mining engineer with a yen for women and liquor."

Budd Boetticher, to Sean Axmaker:

> There were some damn good directors at Universal, and it was a fight every day of production to try to make better pictures. They wanted us to follow the script, and I think a director should approve the script. I would do things and they wouldn't like what I did… [I]t was a producer's studio, not a director's studio.

Wings of the Hawk (Universal, 80 minutes, released in September 1953) Director: Budd Boetticher. Producer: Aaron Rosenberg. Screenplay: James E. Moser. Adaptation by Kay Lenard. Cinematographer: Clifford Stine. With Van Heflin (Irish Gallagher), Julie Adams (Raquel Noriega), Abbe Lane (Elena Noriega), George Dolenz (Col. Ruiz), Noah Beery, Jr. (Orozco), Rodolfo Acosta (Arturo), Antonio Moreno (Father Perez) and Pedro Gonzales Gonzales (Tomas)

Synopsis: American miner Irish Gallagher gets caught up in one of the many south-of-the-border revolutions, falls for a female revolutionary and blows a lot of things up in the process.

If *Bronco Buster* is Budd Boetticher's best Universal picture, then it's fair to say that *Wings of the Hawk* is the most enjoyable. It's the closest Budd ever got to directing a Burt Kennedy movie in the sense that it builds and maintains an adventurous, often comic energy throughout its 80-minute running time. The picture was released in both 3-D and 2-D (flat) and the version I saw was like a 2.5-D, with some props (as well as Van Heflin's fist) flying at the camera.

The 3-D craze was still at its peak when Budd shot *Wings of the Hawk* on the Universal back lot in the spring of 1953, though by the time the picture hit cinemas four or five months later, 3-D had lost its novelty factor. By the end of the year, most studios had abandoned the process.

Budd would say that he shot the film flat—in 2-D—and that Universal went back in and shot the 3-D footage after he left the studio to go to Brazil to work on *The Americano*. This may be true, as the Universal archives do not suggest that the Budd was shooting in 3-D and the effects do seem added on to the plot. Budd told Sean Axmaker,

> I wasn't dumb over there. I knew [3-D] wasn't gonna last. Jack Warner had a meeting with all the well-known directors and producers in Hollywood at Warner Bros., held up a pair of 3-D glasses and said that every man, woman and child in the United States in one year from now will have a set of their own 3-D glasses. We looked at this idiot and said, "This guy is out of his mind." So ten days of filming with rocks going into the second row and arrows hitting people in the tenth row was released flat, and it didn't work.

Warner had in fact told the press that the studio was convinced "that the public will wear such viewers as effortlessly as they wear wristwatches or carry fountain pens." To be fair, Warner scored a big hit and used the 3-D process quite admirably in the horror film *House of Wax*. A few other big studio productions—*Kiss Me Kate* and *Hondo* for example—also benefited from the novelty. But most 3-D films emphasized horror or science fiction elements, including *Creature from the Black Lagoon*, *The Maze* and the infamous cult stinker *Robot Monster*. Robert Stack starred in the first big 3-D hit, 1952's *Bwana Devil*, featuring man-eating lions in Africa. Stack later said, "*Bwana Devil* was a freak picture that made money and the process zoomed to popularity overnight, then fell on its face."

The "in-your-face" special effects aside, *Wings of the Hawk* is a fun picture to watch. In a role intended for Glenn Ford, Heflin brings an impassioned dedication to his character Irish Gallagher. He exudes a confident swagger that you don't normally see in his work and helps carry the weight of the ensemble forward. The time is 1911, not long after the start of the Mexican Revolution, and Gallagher and his Mexican partner are quietly getting rich from a mine in Mexico when federal troops led by Gen. Ruiz (George Dolenz) show up to demand a piece of the pie in exchange for "protection." Within minutes, Heflin is punching out Mexican soldiers and hightailing it in a fast-paced horseback chase sequence as bullets fly past him.

Throwing plot caution to the wind, the scenario has him hook up with a small band of Mexican revolutionaries, led by a fiery but very inauthentic Julie Adams. (She tries to add a Mexican accent to her first few lines of dialogue, but gives up on it pretty quickly.) Heflin throws punches pretty well and adroitly tosses off comic one-liners, referring to Adams' character as "Little Joan of Arc in riding pants!" And he's also good at playing a Bud Abbott–like straight man, which gives supporting player Pedro Gonzales Gonzales an opening to fire off some funny lines. When Heflin comments on another character's penchant for casually shooting people down, Gonzales Gonzales deadpans, "He has his faults. Nobody's perfect." It's a hilarious line.

Budd recalled Heflin as one of his favorites, but added, "He wasn't comfortable in a Western-type thing like this." (I don't agree. I think Heflin wore the hat well and I wish he had the chance to wear it more often. He's terrific in *Shane*, *Gunman's Walk*, *Tomahawk* and the offbeat spaghetti western *The Ruthless Four*.) According to Boetticher, Heflin, who liked to knock one down every now and again, would say to the director, "Is this a ridin' day or an actin' day?" If Budd said it was an acting day, Heflin wouldn't drink. "If it was a riding day, he'd take a couple of belts before we started and feel no pain," Budd said. "But he was wonderful."

Adams, who sports a Frida Kahlo hairstyle, is a joy to watch too. In her autobiography she recalls that Bud Westmore oversaw her bandit girl makeup and hairdresser Joan St. Oegger "designed a hairdo of two black switches twisted high on my head" so they could apply black greasepaint to her hairline to make her light brown hair darker. She recalled that she got to ride James Stewart's horse Pie and that she took daily riding lessons with wrangler Jack Shannon.

For all of Pie's dedication to Stewart, he threw Adams for a loop during an action sequence in which she is riding him while following Heflin, who is driving a wagon, away from the bad guys. Pie was supposed to stop short in front of the camera so Adams could draw her pistol and fire twice at the pursuing bad guys. Instead, his actions flummoxed her and she shot once in the air and once into the ground—"Nowhere near the bad guys." Then her horse was hit from behind by one of the pursuing stuntmen, knocking her on the ground where she instinctively curled herself up as three other horses rode over her. "When the crew rushed up to check on me, I could see on their faces that they thought I was dead or seriously injured.... I was helped to my feet and was still feeling a little woozy when our stunt coordinator Davy Sharpe rushed up and said, 'You did good, kid. You tucked when you fell.'"

As she recovered, a stuntman murmured to her, "When you're riding in a chase, keep riding." She later learned that the five stuntmen playing bad guys had bet each other a dollar over which one would reach the camera first. "I didn't think it was as funny as they did,"

Adams recalled. "That was my first and last take of the day." Budd, she wrote, wanted his actors do to their own stunts but she left the film thinking, "If something seems too difficult, it probably is. Don't try to do it yourself; ask for a stunt person."

The Universal archives support Adams' story: The accident occurred on April 17 and the actress suffered "no serious injuries." As usual with a Budd Boetticher movie of this time period, actors and stuntmen did get injured. On April 7, stuntman Richard Farnsworth (later to gain recognition as a fine actor and net an Academy Award nomination) was injured in a horse fall. "No bones broken," the production log reported. A few days before, actor-stuntman Fred Carson got hurt in a horse fall.

Gonzales Gonzales gives a nicely tuned performance as one of Adams' underlings who develops respect for Heflin's macho Anglo. It is unfortunate that within a year or two he was cast almost entirely in stereotypical comedy roles, because he is given an effective moment of angry despair in *Wings of the Hawk* as his character watches federal troops kill his mother. Preview cards from audience members indicate that they loved Pedro. "I'm glad Groucho [Marx] found him," one theater patron wrote Universal, referring to Gonzales Gonzales' recent appearance on the popular TV quiz show *You Bet Your Life*. There he came off like two Mexican Chico Marxes to Groucho's sometimes bewildered host. When the latter asked Pedro how the two of them would be billed if they teamed up for a vaudeville act, Gonzales Gonzales got a huge laugh when he replied, "Gonzales Gonzales and Marx." Groucho topped that when he turned to the audience and quipped, "Two people in the act and I get third place." Incidentally, Pedro and his *You Bet Your Life* partner (a ski-shop employee) blew the big money when they couldn't name the two Biblical cities destroyed by God, Sodom and Gomorrah. Still, they won $313.82 on Groucho's show and Universal hired Pedro for *Wings of the Hawk*, initiating a long acting career.

The picture sports a feeling of exuberance that suggests Budd adopted an attitude of, "Let's make this one lively. I don't care how it turns out but I bet it's going to be a lot of fun." That attitude may be partially because Budd knew it would be his last film for Universal, a studio that served him somewhat well while limiting his capabilities at the same time. In his autobiography, Budd tells a story of deciding one morning to tell the studio heads that he wanted out of his contract, which was up for another yearly renewal in late April 1953. Budd's version goes like this: He met with studio executives James Pratt, William Goetz and Edward Muhl at two one afternoon and said, "Gentlemen, I don't want to work here any more." To which they said, "Whatever you say."

Budd expressed surprise, thinking they had not heard him, and reiterated, "I've had it here. I don't want to direct any more pictures for Universal. I don't want to drive or walk through your gate again. I want you to tear up my contract."

"We just want you to be happy, Budd," Goetz said. "It's whatever you want." Then they all shook hands and Budd left, running across the street to a bar to call his agent at MCA and pass on the news.

That's when Budd's agent told the astonished director that Universal had already decided not to pick up his option. In short, as Boetticher recalled, "I'd just been fired!"

The Universal studio archives do not paint such a clear-cut picture, but it is obvious that somewhere during the shooting of *Wings of the Hawk* the studio decided it could cut Budd loose. A March 27, 1953, memo suggests exercising a renewal of Budd's contract for another year at $1,250 per week. But an April 15 contractual memo notes that the studio was not obligated to exercise that option prior to completion of Budd's work on *Wings of the Hawk*. By that time, the studio had agreed to let Budd take a break to go shoot *The Americano* for Robert Stillman Productions as of mid–May 1953. The contractual dialogue makes it sound like the studio offered a limited extension to Budd's contract so he could finish *Wings of the Hawk* by early May and still make it to Brazil for *The Americano*, with the provision that

Budd could let the studio know if he wanted to extend his contract.

Budd also wrote in his autobiography—and repeated the claim to many interviewers, including me—that Universal would not let him loose to go film *The Americano* in Brazil. But late in life, he let slip that he had to get away from Universal because actress Julie Adams, who appeared in three of his films, was distracting him. Knowing he wanted out of his contract, Budd arranged to blow up the entire studio while filming the climactic action sequence to *Wings of the Hawk*. He claims this happened on the last day of filming, and based on production files, he's right: May 7, 1953, was the date that all the explosions went off, sending trees and rocks and stuntmen flying this way and that. The hilly studio back lot certainly took a pummeling, but it's an exaggeration to say he destroyed the whole studio. Budd recalls the sequence being set around a bridge between the *federales* and the rebels, but the blow-up business actually occurs around a mining set that Heflin's character is trying to wrest free from the *federales*. Budd says he actually set off the detonation charge, which knocked him backwards in his director's chair and split the seams of a lot of nearby swimming pools.

Interestingly, the film's daily production logs indicate that Budd repeatedly showed up on the set late and that he slowed down production by initiating some last-minute changes in camera set-ups. Perhaps this is an indication of his growing boredom on the lot. For the most part, the film was shot in sequence, which is something Budd really strived for in the Randolph Scott pictures he made later.

Wings of the Hawk's budget pushed toward the $900,000 mark—Budd's most expensive film on that lot, and more than he would be allotted to make any of the Randolph Scott movies. Van Heflin earned $7,500 a week. Universal paid Gonzales Gonzales $500 a week.

Universal spent money to make up 7,500 pressbooks in a 3-D format and 8,500 pressbooks in a 2-D format, indicating they were hedging their bets on the process but also playing to the fact that many smaller cinemas did not have the capacity to run 3-D movies. The plan was to release the picture with a 3-D musical and a 3-D Woody Woodpecker film, but somewhere along the way the studio got stuck with double bills that co-featured Johnny Weissmuller in *Valley of Head Hunters*. (One Los Angeles critic dismissed that film in a two-line review that said Weissmuller was "putting on weight.")

Wings of the Hawk did good business, even in theaters that did not offer 3-D, and preview audiences mostly wrote positive comments regarding the film, though several patrons asked how the title figured into the plot. It doesn't, a point also noted by *Los Angeles Times* critic Philip K. Scheuer who wrote, "No wings, no hawk." Amusingly, Scheuer also wrote that Heflin's acting came down to this: "When the good Mexican dies, Heflin folds one of his hands over his chest, but when the bad Mexican dies Heflin just lets him lie there." (It's true!) The *Los Angeles Examiner* liked the film and said when Heflin's character begins fighting back against the *federales*, "it is with a gusto that makes the screen crackle with satisfying violence."

The *Los Angeles Daily News* critic, Roy Ringer, had the sense to tell readers, "Boetticher, who has spent much time [in Mexico], knows Mexico and his characterizations emerge with more believability than bitter experience has taught us to expect from such a story." That's a nice sentiment but the Mexicans are all played in the stereotypical mold of the time: agreeable smiling peons or mustache-twirling, dishonest officials.

As much as I like Heflin in the film, I think *The Hollywood Reporter*'s August 27, 1953, review went too far when it said, "Heflin follows up his brilliant performance in *Shane* with another outstanding characterization."

By the time Universal was adding 3-D effects in the summer of 1953, Budd was gone from the lot. He would not return, though he came close when it looked like he might direct *Two Mules for Sister Sara* in 1970. In retrospect, Universal served him well, just as Columbia had in the mid–1940s. Unlike the actors in the films Budd made at Eagle-Lion and Monogram, the actors on the sets of his Universal pictures do look happy and enthused. As with his previous films, he was saddled with stars-in-the-making (Hudson, Murphy and Quinn), B+ stars who never quite made or held the A grade (Ryan and Chandler come to mind) and actors on the verge of stardom. But they all appear to be pushing themselves a little bit more under Boetticher's guidance.

Though the Universal 9 do not compare as a whole with the seven films Budd later made with Randolph Scott, several—*Bronco Buster, Horizons West* and *Wings of the Hawk*—are solid, if not better. With the exception of the somewhat embarrassing *City Beneath the Sea*, the rest are respectable time-fillers.

The Magnificent Matador (National Pictures, 93 minutes, released by 20th Century-Fox in May 1955) Director: Budd Boetticher. Producers: Carroll Case and Edward L. Alperson. Screenplay: Charles Lang. Story: Budd Boetticher. Cinematographer: Lucien Ballard. With Maureen O'Hara (Karen Harrison), Anthony Quinn (Luis Santos), Manuel Rojas (Rafael Reyes), Richard Denning (Mark Russell), Thomas Gomez (Don David), Lola Albright (Mona Wilton), William Ching (Jody Wilton). Eduardo Noriega (Miguel) and Anthony Caruso (Emiliano)

Synopsis: Aging matador Luis Santos tries to regain his wits and nerves as he returns to the bullfighting arena after a lengthy absence and contends with his illegitimate son, who wishes to follow in his father's footsteps.

Boetticher's involvement with the mediocre and talky melodrama *The Magnificent Matador* started in 1952, when he was working with Anthony Quinn at Universal. A June 1952 *Los Angeles Times* article notes that the two would reteam for a bullfighting picture to be scripted by Borden Chase, writer of 1948's *Red River* and several Universal–James Stewart Westerns. But the production got into gear only after Budd returned from Brazil and the ill-fated production of *The Americano*, which Budd was to direct with Glenn Ford starring.

The Americano is the only film Budd started and didn't finish. It stars Ford as an American rancher who takes some Brahma Bulls to Brazil to sell them and ends up in the middle of a typical range war—only one with pythons and other exotic creatures native to Brazil. Boetticher's contract with Universal indicates that by the spring of 1953 he requested an "out" to direct *The Americano* for Robert Stillman Productions. A May 12, 1953, document from the Universal studio files notes that Boetticher's contract included a suspension option and he wished to use 15 consecutive weeks to work for Stillman on the picture. "We have no objection," the studio memo reports, adding that Universal had no need of Boetticher's services once he finished *Wings of the Hawk* no later than May 20, 1953. But that letter indicates a sense of hope between Universal and Boetticher regarding future projects, being it includes a provision that reads, "Stillman agrees to notify us promptly upon completion of Mr. Boetticher's services if such completion occurs prior to the expiration of 15 consecutive weeks. They agree to notify us from time to time, upon our request, of the estimated date of completion of Mr. Boetticher's services for them." This doesn't sound like the attitude of a studio that just fired one of its best directors, as Budd liked to claim.

So Budd was out of Universal and off to Brazil for one of the most frustrating experiences of his career. Besides Ford, the cast included Arthur Kennedy, Cesar Romero and Spanish actress Sarita Montiel. In a very lengthy paragraph in his autobiography, Budd summed up the many problems that beleaguered the production, saying the Brazilian producers did not deliver anything they promised to Stillman and company; "There weren't even roofs on the stages in which we were to shoot." He said he spent 16 weeks there, mostly sitting around. "It got so bad that the top Brazilian producer, Bennie Dianissio, forced our cast and crew to stand in line, alphabetically, to receive our money for meals," Budd wrote. Money was slow coming in and co-star Arthur Kennedy had another movie commitment back in the States. Against Stillman's wishes, Budd filmed shots of "snakes, crocodiles, piranha—everything dangerous that you could only find in the jungles of Brazil. Glenn was wonderful. He worked closely with all

Anthony Quinn and Maureen O'Hara as former lovers now at odds in *The Magnificent Matador*.

these killers as long as the money held out." Then the money didn't hold out and everyone went back home by plane. Budd chalked up his work on the picture as "background footage" and says William Castle finished the film.

In Glenn Ford's son Peter's biography of his father, *Glenn Ford: A Life*, he wrote that most of the filming took place on the Mato Grosso plateau, with interiors shot at the Companhia Cinematografica Vera Cruz studio in Sao Paulo. "This would be the longest, most remote trip Dad had yet undertaken for a film," recalled Peter, who joined his father on location for the production.

Things went badly soon, Ford said, with key members of the crew not showing up as scheduled, bad weather shutting down the production, and problems occurring with Sarita Montiel's lack of English and horseback riding experience. One day Peter Ford found a worm in his string beans, and pretty soon everyone in the cast came down with some sort of stomach illness. "We were told that we might have swallowed parasites," Peter said. Ants, ticks and leeches added to the company's woes. Soon the production became "a virtual nightmare for all involved," Peter said. Lack of funding from local banks and RKO shut the production down in September 1953, according to the younger Ford. But he says his father shelled out the money for the cast and American crew members to get back to America by boat, whereas Budd says they returned by plane. Nearly a year later, production resumed after Stillman threatened a $175,000 lawsuit against Glenn Ford to force him to make the movie in Corona, a rural area southeast of Los Angeles. Actor Frank Lovejoy replaced Kennedy and German-born Ursula Thiess replaced Montiel. Romero returned and gave a delightful performance as a swaggering good-bad guy—making one wish Budd had hired him as the bad guy in one of the Randolph Scott Westerns. "The almost entirely new version of *The Americano* was completed by the end of August and released the following February to mixed notices and double bills. It was all aggravation and wasted effort," Peter Ford summarized.

Cut to: Budd Boetticher hastily writing a script about a bullfighter who loses his nerve, gets involved with a haughty American woman and tries to regain his bravery while worrying about his illegitimate son, who has decided to become a bullfighter and who, based on his father's visions, is doomed to die in the ring.

Here's Budd's reason for making *The Magnificent Matador*: "I intended to help Tony make himself a star." But this may make more sense: Budd gave up a Universal contract to make an independent movie with Glenn Ford in Brazil. Things did not go according to plan, his reputation was suddenly connected to an unfinished production, and—without the safety net of a studio contract—Budd found himself once again unemployed with the responsibility of an unfinished picture resting upon his shoulders. What better way to reestablish himself than to make yet another bullfighting movie to prove he still had what it takes? *Bullfighter and the Lady* pulled him out of the cinematic gutter and led to a contract at Universal; why couldn't he do it again with something similar—something like *Bullfighter and the Lady II*?

But signing with independent producer Edward L. Alperson to make the new film was a mistake. Alperson had started Grand National in 1936 and signed James Cagney to a couple of movies in an effort to launch that low-budget company into the big time. But instead of producing *Angels with Dirty Faces* (Alperson bought the rights with Cagney in mind), he made the mediocre musical *Something to Sing About*. By the 1940s, Alperson had a new company called National Pictures (instead of Grand National, just in case anybody remembered) and he either produced or presented such low-grade efforts as *Dakota Lil* and *Belle Starr's Daughter,* both with George Montgomery and Rod Cameron. If you wanted to

More excitement from *The Magnificent Matador*. Anthony Quinn and Maureen O'Hara are center-frame as Thomas Gomez (right) provides some energy. That's William Ching just above star Quinn's head.

(From left) Anthony Quinn, Maureen O'Hara and Thomas Gomez tried to inject some life into Budd Boetticher's 1955 misfire, *The Magnificent Matador*. This is nothing magnificent about the film, unfortunately.

restart your career in the mid–1950s, you wouldn't go to a guy making low-budget George Montgomery and Rod Cameron oaters. But Budd did, and he came to regret his decision. According to Budd, "[Alperson] promised me on a stack of Bibles (and I piled them up to be sure, there were a lot of Bibles there) that he would do nothing but put up the money. He interfered in everything." At one point during the shoot, he claimed, he had to throw a drunk and meddling Alperson out of the Shrine of Guadalupe.

Budd said he wrote the original script for the film, initially called *The Number One*. Alperson changed the title because it sounded like someone had to go to the bathroom. Alperson brought Barnaby Conrad's novel *Matador* to Budd with the hope he could convince him to retitle the picture by somehow stealing the novel's title without paying for the rights to do so. Boetticher, attempting to steer Alperson away from that idea, came up with the "most God-awful title" in *The Magnificent Matador* and Alperson said, "Christ, that's great!"

Charles Lang, not Boetticher, gets credit for the script. Was that an act of friendship on Boetticher's part to help out a down-on-his-luck pal? Lang had given up acting around 1950 but continued writing. His most recent credit, for the obscure Lincoln Productions, had been released by Hal Roach, Jr.—another Boetticher crony, making one wonder if Budd didn't hook the two up. Entitled *Captain Scarface* (1953), that cheapie featured the all-not-star cast of Barton MacLane, Virginia Grey and Leif Erickson in a soggy sea-faring saga of skullduggery. It has lots of talking and little action and characters you don't really care about—just like *The Magnificent Matador*.

But, if you ever wanted to see Maureen

O'Hara fake an orgasm, *The Magnificent Matador* is the picture for you. It happens just past the one hour mark, when her character—who has been knocked off her horse by an errant bull out on the Mexican prairie—sits, legs spread, watching as her bullfighter boyfriend Quinn tames the wild beast with his cape in long shot. O'Hara suddenly squeezes her legs together, tosses back her head and lets out a slight sigh of orgiastic glee. What other director could get the usually prim and proper O'Hara to do that?

Budd told me that O'Hara was one of his two favorite leading ladies, the other being Nancy Gates from *Comanche Station*. "Maureen is the most professional woman I've ever known," he said in a late 1980s interview. "She knew everybody's dialogue, she could set the cameras if you wanted her to and change the lights, she got there and she was ready to work right on the nose of the time she was supposed to." Despite the production's money problems, Budd insisted it was a enjoyable shoot all around.

Going by his autobiography, Quinn didn't see it that way, and O'Hara dismissed the film in her book *'Tis Herself*: "Critics disliked it and found it dull. I wasn't surprised. Even the people of Mexico seemed bored while we were filming. A bullfight sequence was shot and they booed it because the matadors didn't actually kill the bulls. Of course we didn't. We would have had to kill a bull for every take. It was a ludicrous criticism."

Quinn says they were booing because he, as an actor, refused to get into the ring to fight a real-life bull for the movie. The Mexican crowd members assumed he would be doing his own fighting as Boetticher's cameras rolled. "Even the appearance of a bullfight was

Anthony Quinn and Maureen O'Hara were once real-life lovers, according to Quinn's autobiography. But the fire had cooled off-screen and on-screen by the time they teamed up for 1955's *The Magnificent Matador*, which Budd Boetticher directed based on his original story.

Anthony Quinn (left) and Maureen O'Hara (right) don't seem too concerned that Richard Denning (being held back by William Ching) wants to belt Quinn in *The Magnificent Matador* while Lola Albright watches.

enough to get these people going; they poured in through the stadium tunnels as if we were giving something away," Quinn recalled in his autobiography *One Man Tango*.

Quinn appeared in the set-up scenes leading up to the bullfight and then disappeared into one of the tunnels where his double—a local ranchero—took his place, clad in identical costuming. The crowd didn't buy it, Quinn said. "They knew the ranchero was not me and they would not accept a substitute.... [T]o these people I was a coward." To add to Quinn's discomfort, his real-life girlfriend, a society girl who was sitting in the stands, turned against him, calling him a "fucking coward."

Bullfighter Antonio Ordonez told Quinn he had no choice but to face the bull: "Look, all you need is to make one or two passes. That's all these people want, to know that you have balls." He assured Quinn that he (Ordonez) and Carlos Arruza would be nearby to protect him in a worst-case scenario.

Budd didn't help matters by giving Quinn grief from the director's booth via an earpiece Quinn wore. "Goddamn it, Tony, where are you? We're losing the scene. We're losing the picture. This fucking crowd is out of control!"

And so Quinn—in a scene more exciting than anything you will find in the film—entered the arena. "I was a bullfighter and I would live or die by my instincts," he wrote. When the bull charged him, Quinn said, "He buzzed me so close I almost ejaculated. It was, without exaggeration, one of the most thrilling passes in the history of the ring, and I was not through. I was hard with excitement... My God, I was hooked!"

The bull gave Quinn a second pass—"even more thrilling than the first. The crowd erupted in applause," he said. "There followed, I believe, the greatest ovation in the annals of bullfighting and it was meant for me, alone…. It was better than winning ten Academy Awards."

Afterward Quinn chose to forsake his lover and take one of her friends to bed instead. "I was Antonio Quinn, conqueror of the bulls, and I would not take shit from anybody!"

That's a lively tale and maybe it's true, but little if any of that energy and excitement is seen in *Magnificent Matador*'s final cut. A double wearing Quinn's outfit is clearly gouged by a bull in the film—Boetticher later said they got lucky when that happened—but mostly our hero stands around talking with a lot of other people. They talk in hotel rooms and living rooms and dining rooms and barrooms and then, when they get out on the prairie, they talk some more. The first bit of action—a brief bit of fisticuffs between Quinn and Richard Denning—doesn't occur until we are headed toward the middle of the movie. A racquetball game nabs our attention around the 50-minute mark and finally, as the film slowly moves toward the hour-mark, we get that outdoor horse-and-bull play with O'Hara coming with pleasure as she watches her lover protect her from the raging bull.

Lang's script borrows heavily from the 1947 prizefight drama *Body and Soul*, with Quinn's matador visiting a church the night before a big fight and flashbacking to his roots, when he had integrity and courage and a belief he could conquer the world. Unless you know something about bullfighting or really like Quinn and O'Hara, the film is a slog. It's unfortunate that Budd struck out with a project so dear to his heart.

The picture was shot in Mexico late in 1954, and the color is nice. The pomp and circumstance of the arena is well captured by Boetticher, and Lucien Ballard deserves praise for his cinematography. If nothing else, the film served to introduce Budd and Ballard, who would work together again several times. Budd enjoyed telling the story of how, upon meeting Ballard, he blew up, telling Alperson off in front of Ballard. "I read the riot act. I was the director, it was my script and I was the associate producer. No one, no one else was to be hired unless I was consulted," he wrote in his autobiography. Then he turned to Ballard and said, "I must tell you that, when we film in the bullrings, I have very definite ideas as to where I would like to put my cameras."

To which Ballard responded, "Mr. Boetticher, as far as I'm concerned you can take your cameras and stick them up your ass."

The two became fast friends.

New York Times correspondent Paul P. Kennedy visited the set shortly before Thanksgiving 1954 and wrote a very engaging *You Are There*-type piece capturing the turmoil that went on behind the scenes. He said that matador Antonio Valezquez was "very nearly gored on his very first time at a charging bull" because the bull in question did not follow "the script or the cape… [H]e was knocked down and about to be gored when the bull was drawn off and the matador was borne from the ring." Some 20,000 spectators watched this spectacle and then got to witness another bull knocking a *bandillero* partially unconscious. A third bull, no doubt inspired by the rebellious nature of his companions, jumped over the arena barriers and started chasing crew members who scrambled hither and yon. Some spectators in the amped-up crowd, itching for blood, displayed their displeasure at the antics by engaging in a "comic seat-cushion fight." According to Kennedy Boetticher was delighted by the impromptu hijinks. "You can't write a bullfight for bulls," he told the correspondent.

Boetticher on *The Magnificent Matador*: "It wasn't a success. There was too much money at stake, and I let myself be influenced. I shot it too fast. I promised myself that it would be the last time I didn't do exactly what I wanted."

In 1960, co-producer Carroll Case sued Alperson and National Pictures for back distribution pay, winning about $180,000 several years later. By that time, 1963, Boetticher was in Mexico, probably wishing he could sue for some back pay himself given the financial grave he was digging for himself with yet another film about bullfighting, *Arruza*.

The critics didn't buy *The Magnificent Matador*. The *Los Angeles Mirror News* (June 17,

1955) said it had a "limping story.... Quinn is impressive as the troubled toreador.... [T]he rest of the acting and the dialogue are not likely to impress anybody." The *Los Angeles Times* review (same date) called the picture "dull" and "pallid." *Cue* (May 28, 1955), summed it up as a "slim story."

The *New York Times'* Bosley Crowther, never an easy man to please, wrote,

> The weaknesses are simply in the story and the direction of Budd Boetticher, in the acting of Miss O'Hara, in the illogic of the character of Mr. Quinn and in the fact that a picture about bullfighting never conveys any real sense of peril. As near as you can make out from this picture, they kill the bulls by running them to death. And, for that matter, Miss O'Hara nigh kills Mr. Quinn the same way.

Some of the Hollywood trade reviewers found nice things to say. *Variety* (May 18, 1955): "It was lensed south of the border with an authentic flavor that bolsters a regulation story.... Boetticher's direction and story move along conventional, but acceptable, lines." *The Hollywood Reporter* went much further in its May 18, 1955, review, saying producer Alperson "hits the jackpot" with the film and that Richard Denning, of all people, gave "a standout performance." Budd's direction, the reviewer said, was "understanding and judicious."

A Cogerson Movie Scores.com blog that ranks Maureen O'Hara's 53 films puts *The Magnificent Matador* at 49, above *Lady Godiva* and below *The Battle of Villa Floritas*.

The Killer Is Loose (Crown Productions, 73 minutes, released by United Artists in March 1956, 73 minutes) Director: Budd Boetticher. Producers: Robert L. Jacks and Robert Goldstein. Screenplay: Harold Medford. Story: John and Ward Hawkins. Cinematographer: Lucien Ballard. With Joseph Cotten (Sam Wagner), Rhonda Fleming (Lila Wagner), Wendell Corey (Leon Poole), Alan Hale, Jr. (Sgt. "Denny" Denning), Michael Pate (Chris Gillespie), Virginia Christine (Mary Gillepsie), John Larch (Otto Flanders) and Dee J. Thompson (Grace Flanders).

Synopsis: After police officer Sam Wagner inadvertently kills the wife of a wanted man in a stake-out gone wrong, the widower criminal vows revenge. His target: Wagner's wife Lila.

Originally intended as a 20th Century–Fox production to co-star Orson Welles as the killer and Victor Mature as the cop, *The Killer Is Loose* remains one of Boetticher's best non–Western films. The ensemble cast members all give natural, credible performances and the script and pacing build and maintain tension for the heroes and empathy for the villain. One of the screenplay's many graces is how it gets the audience to develop sympathy for the killer. When the cops stupidly kick in the door to bank robber Leon Poole's apartment, they don't seem to think he may return fire or that someone else—like his wife—may be in the room. When the fast-paced firefight in the dark comes to an end, Poole glances lovingly at his now-dead wife and quietly tells police officer Sam Wagner (Cotten), "Don't you see how wrong it was to do that? To kill her?" Up until that point, Poole was the myopic mastermind behind an inside bank robbery. Now, with his beloved wife dead, he is a killer with one goal in mind: to make Wagner feel the same pain he feels by killing the lawman's wife.

As with so many of Budd's films, the picture is full of people who almost became stars, briefly became stars or would never become stars. The scenes between Joseph Cotten, who rarely projected sensuality on the screen, and Rhonda Fleming have real sexual spark and they engage in some nice back-and-forth dialogue about the cost of sacrificing their marriage because of his love of his profession. "I've got a job to do," Sam Wagner tells his wife, sounding not unlike Gary Cooper's Will Kane in 1952's *High Noon*. What he has to do is set himself, and then his wife, up as targets to bring Poole out in the open after the latter escapes from a prison work farm.

Poole's murder of an honor farm guard is handled with creepy restraint. The myopic Poole can only escape an extensive police hunt and roadblocks because of his failing eyesight: He takes off his glasses and blindly drives a stolen truck through a slow-moving police roadblock and outwits the law at every turn because he doesn't have a plan. He's making it up as he goes along, right down to disguising himself as a woman to get close to the heavily guarded Wagner house in a suburban neighborhood.

Budd plays more with camera angles in this film than he had in recent endeavors. Perhaps working once again for an independent company and left somewhat unsupervised, his inherent creative side came out. He and cinematographer Lucien Ballard sharply captured Los Angeles' bustling downtown, creepy side streets and seemingly safe suburbs to present a portrait of an ever-changing environment where there is too much sprawl to prevent anarchy or murder.

The picture includes the now well-regarded sequence of Poole calmly shooting one of his former tormentors, Otto Flanders (well played by John Larch), in the stomach by way of a milk bottle that Flanders is holding. It's a scene that would set the stage for the sudden violence that would erupt without warning in the upcoming Randolph Scott Westerns.

Still, the picture is marred by an overreliance on the sort of hokey scripting that hurt the Boetticher Columbia Bs of the 1940s. Alan Hale, Jr.'s agreeable cop is a dunce, bungling a bugged-phone surveillance assignment and getting easily distracted by the offer of sandwiches and coffee when he's supposed to be protecting Fleming. When Cotten tells Fleming that he's having police officers Hale and Michael Pate stay at their house as extra protection, calming her with the news that

The Killer Is Loose is one of Boetticher's best non–Western films.

only one in 1000 prisoners who escape remain free, Hale stupidly blurts out, "We just want to be all set in case he's the 1000th." These are words that would hardly calm the somewhat hysterical Fleming.

Fleming is good. Budd said he stripped her of her glamour and worked with her to get a realistic performance out of her, given she was accustomed to appearing in second-rate Technicolor Westerns or swashbucklers or providing window decoration for Bob Hope or Bing Crosby at Paramount. "Rhonda Fleming had never been wet, never not looked gorgeous," Boetticher told *Filmfax* magazine's Sean Axmaker. He said the studio sent her to Magnum's for her costumes, but he made her go to the smaller-scale Lerner's so she would look like an ordinary housewife. (Budd: "She didn't like that either, but she can wear a rag and look better than most anyone else in movies.") Budd told her, "Rhonda, no one's ever let you act. She didn't speak to me for weeks, until the premiere of the picture when she said, 'Thank you.' Because she'd never been a human being before.... She was wonderful in that picture."

When I interviewed Fleming for my book *The Films of Randolph Scott*, she confirmed much of what Budd said, saying Budd was one of her favorite directors because he allowed her to play a real character. In later years, Fleming would show up at film noir festivals to accompany *Killer Is Loose* screenings and she always spoke well of it.

In various interviews, Budd told the same story about how he came to make *The Killer Is Loose*. He and cinematographer Ballard had just finished *The Magnificent Matador* in Mexico where they had free rein. Back in Hollywood and free of his Universal contract, Budd said he wanted to "prove that I could still make an 18-day picture and not go over schedule and budget." That comment makes one think he knew he had to convince Hollywood he was reliant and professional. He said Cotten, Corey and Fleming had already been signed to the production and he had nothing to do with the main casting. He then set out to make the picture in 15 days. "I know some people would be shocked to read that, would wonder how I could put some personal vision into a 15-day project. But I don't have a personal version to get in the way of making pictures. If you're a boxer, when the bell rings, you come out fighting" (From *Film Noir Reader 3*, First Limelight Edition, 2002).

In his autobiography, Budd says he made the film to get to know Cotten better, and in an interview with Wheeler Winston Dixon, he called Cotten "a complete professional, always knew his lines... [H]e was great to work with." Cotten does not mention the film or Boetticher at all in his 1987 autobiography *Vanity Will Get You Somewhere*.

Corey dominates the picture. Watching him create such a pitiful and sympathetic creature out of a murderer, it's sad to think that some seven or eight years before, he was considered one of those "stars of tomorrow." Producer Hal B. Wallis discovered Corey on stage in *Dream Girl* and brought him to Paramount, where he starred or co-starred in *Desert Fury* and *Sorry, Wrong Number*. Later he moved nicely into character roles in bigger pictures, including 1954's *Rear Window*, but no director seemed to get more out of the quiet, bland and alcoholic actor than Boetticher. Within a decade, Corey would be appearing in terrible horror movies and A.C. Lyles Westerns, looking and acting like a man reading his lines from an off-stage cue card held enticingly above a bottle of rye. He died in 1968, at age 54, of liver ailment.

The picture was shot in the early summer of 1955 on location in Hollywood and at RKO, which was slowly dying. On the last day of the production, John Wayne approached Budd on that lot with Burt Kennedy's script of *Seven Men from Now* and said, "Read this." Had Budd not been working on *The Killer Is Loose*, it is doubtful he would have landed that job.

Blake Lucas, in the original edition of *Film Noir: An Encyclopedia Reference to the American Style* (edited by Alain Silver and Elizabeth Ward), convincingly wrote that Corey's Leon Poole character is "a thematic forerunner of the Randolph Scott hero, who typically seeks revenge for his wife's death."

In the sort of snarky movie review that subscribers to the *New York Times* may have enjoyed reading back then, Bosley Crowther dismissed the film, writing in his March 3, 1956, review, "A couple of first-rate actors, Joseph Cotten and Wendell Corey, are caught in *The Killer Is Loose*, a third-rate crime film, which came to the Palace yesterday." After giving away the plot and climax to the film, he added, "Don't look for anything original or exciting in this round of hide-and-seek. Harold Medford, who wrote the screenplay, must have done it with a set of rubber stamps. And Budd Boetticher...must have been thinking of nothing but quitting time when he did."

Variety didn't think much of the picture either (February 1, 1956): "So poorly done that the plot is seldom convincing.... While Medford's script is no great shakes, neither is the direction of Budd Boetticher as attested by the listless performances of Cotton as the Sherlock and Miss Fleming as his hunted helpmate."

Modern-day bloggers seem to appreciate the film more now than their in-print counterparts did some 60 years ago. On "Laura's Miscellaneous Musings" (a terrific movie-lover's blog that I cannot recommend enough), she calls *The Killer Is Loose* "creepy... flawed yet worthwhile." The blog "50 Westerns from the 50s" (also recommended) recently chose a non-Western Boetticher film to highlight and called *Killer Is Loose* "tight, tense and terrific."

Seven Men from Now (A Batjac Production, 78 minutes, released by Warner Bros. in July 1956). Director: Budd Boetticher. Producers: Andrew V. McLaglen, Robert Fellows and Robert E. Morrison. Story and Screenplay: Burt Kennedy. Cinematographer: William Clothier. With Randolph Scott (Ben Stride), Gail Russell (Annie Greer), Lee Marvin (Masters), Walter Reed (John Greer), Don "Red" Barry (Clete), John Larch (Bodeen), Stuart Whitman (Lt. Collins), John Bernadino (Clint), Chuck Roberson (Mason), Steve Mitchell (Fowler) and Pamela Duncan (Nellie)

Synopsis: Seven bandits rob a Wells Fargo payroll, killing the female clerk on duty. Soon her husband, ex-lawman Ben Stride, is on their trail, bent on burying them.

The first of Budd Boetticher's seven pictures with Randolph Scott—and the first of six that writer Burt Kennedy worked on in some capacity—*Seven Men from Now* features a protagonist who has no interest in bringing back his quarry alive. He wants them dead and he knows how to do the job. The film rescued Scott from a slowly sagging career in routine oaters made at both Columbia and Warner Bros., and almost overnight it re-established Boetticher's reputation—much like *Bullfighter and the Lady* had done five years before.

As created by Kennedy, Scott's Ben Stride is a man who makes others uneasy with his silence. His character seems to have no backstory and no plans for a future beyond killing, and that defines him as a man of the moment and unpredictable. It takes the viewer and the other characters who are dealing with Stride 25 minutes of screen time to find out who he is and what he's all about when Masters (Lee Marvin) simply says, "Yeah, they killed her—the sheriff's wife." And then everyone figures out why he is riding hell-bent for vengeance, almost indifferent to the plight of those around him.

But not entirely indifferent. Kennedy's script presents us with a hero who feels responsible for his wife's death. He wasn't man enough to accept a secondary post as deputy after an election brought in a new sheriff, and so his wife had to take a job in the Wells Fargo office to make ends meet. When Stride sees the well-meaning and easygoing misfit John Greer put his wife Annie in danger by taking her through dangerous territory, he tags along to escort them, unaware that they will inadvertently draw him closer to his human prey—and that he will slowly fall in love with Annie.

Much has been written about the Boetticher-Kennedy-Scott films—easily referred to as the Ranown cycle after the production company that Scott set up with partner Harry Joe Brown. (Brown had nothing to do with *Seven Men from Now* but was smart enough to see that it sparkled with cinematic gold.) It is clear now, some 60 years after the film's release, that it served as the logical successor to the string of Anthony Mann-James Stewart Westerns featuring similar heroes out for revenge or redemption. Budd—and Harry Joe Brown, for that matter—hated the term "psychological western," and Budd once rather famously said, "The Western has no meaning."

"The films are not as bleak as some may have made them out to be," said Western film historian Jim Kitses, a Boetticher fan, because of Budd's natural exuberance for the material. *Seven Men*'s script, written by Kennedy, is chock full of humor as it is, right down to an empathetic and cynically amusing main villain in the persona of Masters. He goes around practicing his fast draw at every moment, sometimes letting loose a little boy's "Pow!" as he does so. Budd often said that you could imagine the character doing the same thing as he stopped to urinate on the side of the road.

Budd and Burt's films with Scott feature colorful, animated bad guys who you wish would ride away from the final showdown. The likes of Dan Duryea and Arthur Kennedy—playing good-bad guys in Mann-Stewart films—certainly provide initial danger to the protagonist, but long before the end credits come up, the Stewart character has already proven his superiority to them, setting them off-balance. The Boetticher-Kennedy villains do not lose their way so easily. They are sure they can take the Scott hero and display no vulnerability when it comes down to it. "We struck something that was good," Boetticher told me. "Because somebody was born on the other side of the track, it doesn't mean that he was basically a bad person. He was a gunslinger and he was fighting for his life."

Kennedy's script sports a devilish sense of humor. Annie Greer takes a pratfall in the mud, Masters has fun kicking a chair out from under a sleeping saloon bouncer and a garrulous old drunk cackles with delight as he recounts how a small patrol of Army soldiers took off once they heard that some hostile Chiricahua were in the territory. "Guess they figured jobs are easier to come by than hair," the old coot chortles before ambling off with a mule loaded down with liquor bottles.

There's even a touch of dark humor in the opening moments when Stride encounters the first two of his seven human targets. Seemingly settling down in a small cave to enjoy a cup of coffee with them—but well aware that they won't survive the cup of coffee, let alone the night—Stride explains that he has lost his horse and is on foot because "Chiricahua jumped me 'bout ten miles back."

"They stole him?" one of the two bandits stupidly asks.

"They ate him," Stride says, finishing a sip of coffee.

Kennedy—with some help with Boetticher—filled the story with memorable dialogue. "I'd hate to have to kill you," Stride tells Masters shortly after they meet. "I'd have to have you try," Masters quickly replies, without emotion. It's unfortunate that Burt liked to recycle his own material and overused this line of dialogue, as he did another one from this

A fading Gail Russell and an aging Randolph Scott brought a subtle sexual chemistry to 1956's *Seven Men from Now*, which, like *Bullfighter and the Lady*, helped right Budd Boetticher's directing career after a misfire or two.

film: "Man don't ride south in this territory without a reason. You got a reason?" Kennedy himself admitted as much in an interview in the late 1960s:

> I sometimes have a tendency to fall back on things I've done before. For example I wrote a character for Lee Marvin in *Seven Men from Now*. I later put that character in different situations, the same fun-loving gunfighter, and I think just about every character actor in town played it: Jimmy Coburn, Brian Keith, Richard Boone, Jim Arness...just about all of them played it. Most of the good ones have now become leading men but they were all hangdog heavies in the old days. They were great, the reason being that they had something to do. The poor leading man would just walk through the picture.

Randolph Scott just doesn't walk through *Seven Men*. He anchors the picture. Probably few in the audience expected the easygoing Southerner, who had become accustomed to making mostly by-the-numbers Westerns for Warner Bros., to suddenly use his minimalistic acting style to convey such deadly power. The Scott character accepts the risk of likely death as the price to pay to get the job done. And the job is killing.

Years later, Budd said that Burt was on the set reworking the script with him day by day. And in this case that appears to be true. "I usually just sat down and wrote them [the Scott Westerns] and then we'd get together and this was wrong or that was wrong," Kennedy said of his on-the-set collaboration with Budd. He went on to say that *Seven Men*, *The Tall T*, *Ride Lonesome* and *Comanche Station* are almost entirely his, word for word. "It is the script," he said of the finished film *Seven Men from Now*, to Thomas McNulty (in a 1998 *Classic Images* article).

Not exactly. Burt's script, dated August 10, 1955—about two months before filming began in Lone Pine—originally included a pair of children for the Greers and a dog. Some of the byplay involving Masters in the deserted saloon was altered on the set, and the demise of Masters' sidekick Clete is quite different in the script than in the finished film. Budd said he came up with the idea of having one character, riddled with bullets, die standing up in the tight crevice of rocky caves, and he also insisted that it was his idea to make Masters a big kid playing fast draw all the time because nobody in Hollywood could outdraw Lee Marvin. (Actors John Ericson and Claude Jarman, Jr., both told me Marvin was always playing "quick draw" on the sets of the films *Bad Day at Black Rock* and *Hangman's Knot*.) So Budd did add stuff and filtered out some unnecessary material to create a minor classic of the genre.

Burt said he was on board to "protect the words." He was on the set when he heard Marvin's character say, directly to the camera, "Seven men from now...," which was a little too obvious. But that doesn't make sense when you see the film, since Masters has already come across the graves of the first two of the seven that Stride has killed and would thus know there were only five men left. "Luckily Budd and I had a good rapport," Kennedy said. "He listened."

Kennedy said it was also his idea to have the Scott character, after the final gun battle, collapse on a rock and keep his pistol in his hand rather than drop it. "I told Budd, Randy wouldn't even pay attention about putting his gun away, he'd just sit down on this rock with the gun in his hand. Little things, but they make a lot of difference. The director has an awful lot on his mind—he can't always see the little things." Years later, Kennedy told *Daily Variety* (October 30, 1984), "There was a four-minute comedy scene with Lee Marvin. They scored it as a dramatic scene and the preview audience couldn't laugh. I said, 'Take it out,' and they looked at me like I was crazy. They took it out and it played. Then when he said something funny, they laughed."

Of his relationship with Kennedy, Budd told Sean Axmaker, "We just agreed on what was good and what was bad... [H]e would write a script and maybe I would have three suggestions, because he knew that no matter what kind of script he wrote, no matter how good it was, I would make it better and he wouldn't worry." Kennedy did not disagree, telling Axmaker, "Budd always made a good film from my scenarios. He managed to make them much better than they were on paper."

Scott loved the script, telling Budd it was probably the best Western script he had ever made up to that point. Kennedy recalled Scott as an easygoing, professional actor who came in, did his work and went home, usually to peruse *The Wall Street Journal* to see how his investments were faring. Budd spoke of Scott in glowing terms more often than not, usually saying, "If the Confederacy had just 100 soldiers like Randolph Scott they would have won the Civil War." He said Scott didn't need Boetticher or Kennedy because he was ready for retirement (probably true) and that he was more concerned with the value of his oil wells than his adopted children. "He was the greatest gentleman in the world and a wonderful, wonderful guy," Budd told me. "The only trouble with Randy was…he was perfect. He never did anything wrong." But, Budd added, "When he did disagree with me, he never showed it. And I had very definite ideas about what I wanted to do and it probably rubbed him the wrong way."

Budd would admit that he had to accept Scott's limitations as an actor. "Not a lot comes from Randolph Scott," he said during a Pinewood Dialogue with curator David Schwartz in 2000. "And when I said that Randy didn't have too much to do with it, I meant that with great love and affection. He just played Randolph Scott and allowed us to use all these new fellows you'd never seen before" (Coburn, Marvin, Claude Akins, etc.). Budd told Schwartz, "He was more classic than we could put him on film. He was so beautiful. Such a great guy. And he didn't need me. He didn't need Burt. He just needed to buy some oil wells. He was really for real."

In yet another interview, Budd described what Scott might have brought to his roles:

> If he thought I was wrong about something, he would just be very quiet and walk away and I would wonder what was the matter. I was so fond of him that I'd say, "Wait a minute Randy, do you have an idea on this?"
>
> "Well, I thought maybe if we did this and this…" And he was usually right. Usually it only pertained to what he thought about his charac-

Randolph Scott primed for action in *Seven Men from Now*, the first of seven collaborations between Scott and Boetticher.

ter. He never said, "I think Richard Boone should say this and do that." He'd say, "I think that maybe if I stop here as if I was gonna take a drink and then I'd change my mind, there might be a little beat in there that…" I'd say, "That's great. Let's do it."

Film historian and author Jim Kitses accurately notes that Budd learned to deal with both the qualities and limitations of Scott and credits the actor with carrying the movies all through the Ranown cycle. Scott's performances, he said, give us "more a sign of an icon than a man." Actors who worked on the Boetticher-Scott films told me that Budd would wander over to Scott on the set, out of earshot of everyone else, and talk with him for a few minutes. Were they exchanging stock exchange tips or talking character? It's tough to guess today. But Scott, who had been acting in films for about 25 years, suddenly exposed both a sentimental soft side and a cold exterior that spoke volumes about a man trying to find a reason to live by killing.

And *Seven Men from Now* certainly set Scott off on a small, gradual comeback and prepared the actor to work with Sam Peckinpah in 1962's *Ride the High Country*. Scott and his partner Harry Joe Brown were smart enough to see what Boetticher and Kennedy brought to the mix: fresh energy, unpredictable characters and a sense of story quality that had been lacking in Scott's recent oaters. Scott and Brown immediately began scheming (if such a verb can be attached to Scott) to hire both Boetticher and Kennedy to start making movies. And two more Boetticher-Kennedy Westerns featuring Scott—*Ride Lonesome* and *Comanche Station*—faithfully follow the *Seven Men* storyline in introducing a character with a mysterious past who is out to settle a score or find a way to redeem himself in the face of human jackals, warring Indians and unrequited love. Burt Kennedy put it this way: "Randolph Scott was wonderful for Budd to work with because Randy liked the way he came off the screen in Budd's pictures—as a tough guy, which he wasn't."

The combo worked well for both Scott and Boetticher. Actor Rand Brooks, who knew them both, said,

> Randy was such a gentleman and Budd was raised correctly. Budd had good schooling and good manners and Randy appreciated that. I think Randy had respect for Budd because he realized he'd line up good action and line up some good scenes and hire the best people. I think they were a good team, frankly. If there was any irritation at all, I didn't see it, nor would I believe it would happen, because it wouldn't be sensible for either one of them.

As for the relationship between Budd and Burt, Brooks said, "Burt loved Budd. But we'd get together and talk and [Burt's] favorite words about Budd were, 'That son of a bitch.' I think we both felt the same way about Budd." Brooks said Budd would rewrite Burt's scripts when he needed to. "Budd had a way of getting things out of people, even if he had to sneak them out... [H]e had a great ear for dialogue."

Budd and Burt agreed about the genesis of *Seven Men from Now*. John Wayne had placed Kennedy, who up to that point had worked as a bit player, stuntman and writer, under contract but didn't give him anything to work on. With a pencil and an old-fashioned pad of paper or two, Burt concocted *Seven Men from Now*. He pitched it to Wayne, who put it on a shelf. Somehow Robert Mitchum, who was looking to produce a film, got wind of it and asked to see the script. He wanted it and offered Kennedy $15,000. That got Wayne's attention and he decided to look at the script himself. (I'm guessing Wayne, unhappy that Mitchum bowed out of the Wayne production of *Blood Alley* about the same time, was reluctant to throw the actor any bones.) Kennedy says Wayne then sent the script to Robert Preston and Joel McCrea, both of whom turned it down. Wayne biographer Scott Eyman reports that Wayne did not want to act in "another western about revenge" and then sent the script to Gary Cooper, who also passed.

Wayne's next choice was daring but sort of odd. "Wayne developed a strange enthusiasm for Richard Egan, telling Jack Warner, 'This is the most manly guy I've seen on the screen since Gable,'" Eyman wrote, and so Wayne made a bid to borrow Egan from 20th Century–Fox. Fox wanted $50,000 to loan him out, Eyman reports, and Wayne was ready to pay it. But Jack Warner, of all people, may have suggested Randolph Scott, who was under contract to the studio and making not-so-good oaters like *Tall Man Riding* and *Riding Shotgun*.

Boetticher was shooting *The Killer Is Loose* on the RKO lot, where Wayne was shooting interiors for John Ford's *The Searchers* and perhaps still involved in Dick Powell's ill-fated RKO production of *The Conqueror*. Wayne gave Boetticher the script and asked him to look it over. Budd read 35 pages or so and then told Wayne at lunchtime that it was the greatest script he'd ever seen. Wayne set up a meeting with Boetticher and Kennedy to discuss casting the picture. At that point, both Budd and Burt agreed, it was Wayne who said, "Let's use Randolph Scott. He's through."

And so, as Budd liked to put it, "We took Randolph Scott and shoved him up Wayne's ass."

It's a good story and rings with some truth. But I wonder if Wayne, who made two pictures with Scott in the early 1940s for Universal, wasn't smart enough to see that the leathery-looking cowpoke from Virginia still had some box office pull. In the early 1950s, Wayne was comfortably near the top in most Top Ten box office polls. But if he looked around, he would find Randolph Scott down near the bottom of that Top Ten list—maybe at seven or eight or nine or even dead last, but still galloping strongly in the Top Ten. Scott's Westerns made money for Warner Bros. and Columbia. And Wayne generally chose well when it came to casting non–John Wayne movies for Batjac, putting solid stalwarts like Glenn Ford and Robert Mitchum into his pictures, or taking a gamble on up-and-coming talent like James Arness (which paid off) and William Campbell (which didn't). Randolph Scott meant money, and Wayne probably wouldn't cast someone in a film just to make him look bad or because Jack Warner told him to.

Scott warmed up to Boetticher fast. "Randy was a craftsman," said actor Steve Mitchell, who plays one of the bad guys trying to ambush the Scott character in a canyon late in the film.

> He knew Budd made him look good, and he knew Budd was a good director. So when you have a guy who looks good to you and you're a star, you ride with a winner.
>
> Budd was a good director but a madman. He let Randy alone, I didn't see him jumping on Randy. He didn't make any loud calls. Randy was extremely nice and pleasant, but Randy had a reserve about him. I don't think he was distant—that was just him by nature.... I think he was probably underrated as an actor. He didn't just do a "yep" or a "no." He was always very believable.

Wayne and Boetticher worked together to assemble the rest of the cast. Duke chose Gail Russell as the sensitive Annie Greer. She had not made a film since 1950, shortly after her contract with Paramount ended. "I think [Wayne] was more fond of Gail Russell than any of them," Boetticher said. "And I think Duke had a crush on her. I think she was the one leading lady that he really cared about in anything but a professional way." Wayne had co-starred with Russell in two films at Republic in the late 1940s: *Angel and the Badman* (she was the angel) and *Wake of the Red Witch*. Years later, he defended his choice to cast her in *Seven Men from Now*:

> Gail was such a beautiful young girl that some of those fucking sons of bitches at the studios had taken advantage of her. You know about the old casting coach? She'd been there a number of times. Well, it didn't happen with me. I gave her the part on her own merits. She was the only person I never shouted at because I knew she was insecure. She had an anxiety problem, which I understood because I'd had that when I was just a kid. I felt all she needed was someone to show her kindness.

Some friends and professional colleagues of Wayne's feel there was some sort of personal relationship there; others do not. Burt Kennedy said, "Duke hired her as they were lovers years ago. She was gorgeous and a dear girl."

But, Kennedy added, "Gail Russell was an alcoholic, that was her big problem. If it had been a bigger picture, it could have been a bigger comeback for her. It was kind of sad because she was a lost soul. She was quite good as an actress." Walter Reed, cast as Russell's husband in the film, told me, "Wayne was really infatuated with her. She was absolutely gorgeous, even when she was drinking."

And she was drinking. By the time filming began in the autumn of 1955, Russell had already racked up a couple of drunk-driving incidents and well-publicized court cases. Once an "overnight star" at Paramount, which used her to great success in the 1944 ghost chiller *The Uninvited*, Russell was tormented by doubt, low self-esteem and, over time, the bottle.

Director Lewis Allen, who directed her in two Paramount films, said she could only pull off six or seven lines of dialogue at one time before breaking down in tears on the set because "she was scared to death." Allen told Tom Weaver that Russell's hairdresser and makeup person began taking her out for after-hours drinks to loosen her up: "They wanted to give her confidence. And after she started going with them and having a drink at night, she had a little more courage during the day." She also had a little more alcohol during the day too—and then at night again.

By 1950, the studio washed its hands of her. She did one picture for Universal, *Air Cadet* (director Joseph Pevney told me he didn't have any problems with her, but she still seemed insecure) and then she disappeared for a while, marrying actor Guy Madison and occasionally making the headlines for some drunken shenanigans.

As she began working on *Seven Men from Now*, Russell, who turned 31 in September 1955, a month before filming began, told the press not to consider the production a comeback for her because she wasn't sure she would act again. She said Randolph Scott treated her with kid gloves on the first day and guided her through their first scene together with a gentle hand, which helped.

Budd, Burt and Walter Reed all recalled that soon after shooting began, Russell lost her nerve. "She wouldn't do a scene," Reed recalled. "Budd took her behind a wagon, talked to her and she came back and did it. She was a girl you had to handle with kid gloves because she was so sensitive. She was an alcoholic. We had to have someone on the set watch her. She had the most beautiful eyes and was a terribly sensitive girl but you could hurt her by saying 'boo.' She had no confidence in her own abilities."

What did Budd say to her behind the wagon? He told her he'd put her across his lap and spank her in front of the cast and crew, and she believed him. At night, at the lodge in Lone Pine, she could drink, but not during the day, he told her. (One wonders how the sometimes insensitive Lee Marvin treated her. They seem to have developed a strong on-screen respect for one another.)

Wayne cast Don "Red" Barry, a fellow B-series cowboy star from his Republic days, as Marvin's outlaw pal. Budd said little about Barry in later interviews, although he told me with a tone of scorn in his voice that he thought Barry was lucky to get the job. Years later, Barry told the press, "It was very tough to start playing character roles after the Westerns had faded away. It was like starting over again. I dropped the 'Red' from my name and went back to Donald Barry, hoping to divorce myself from the stereotyped Western image producers had of me. Then I did every kind of bit part that presented itself, just to prove myself as an actor. I loved playing heavies… heavies were the acting parts." He worked as a character actor until taking his own life in 1981 at the age of 68.

Budd had worked with Lee Marvin in *Seminole* a few years back. Dwayne Epstein's biography of Marvin, *Point Blank*, does not explain how he landed the role of Masters but does quote Boetticher as saying Marvin came up with his own wardrobe ideas: "When he came on set for me to approve this costume…he had a hooker's bright red garter on his left arm. It was just magnificent. He wore it through the whole picture, keeping the audience guessing when he was going to explain and he never did. That's the kind of thing Lee Marvin would bring to a part." Years later, Epstein wrote, Marvin claimed that his *Seven Men* death scene was his favorite. And the author tells a great story of Marvin meeting John Wayne for the first time on the set of *Seven Men*. According to Burt Kennedy, Marvin had a coat on and he walked up to Duke and introduced himself and said, "This coat had your name in it at wardrobe but it's a little tight for me." Duke loved the compliment and he would work with Marvin three times in the early 1960s, including on two John Ford films.

Burt Kennedy and Walter Reed recalled Marvin as an intense, sometimes unpleasant person who liked to intimidate them. When Reed made a $5 bet with Marvin and won, Marvin contemptuously took a five dollar bill out of his pocket and threw it on the mud-strewn set of the wagon sequence in *Seven Men*, forcing Reed to bend down and pick it up. (The action is not unlike the on-screen verbal sexual assault that Marvin's character seems to perpetrate on Reed's character in the wagon sequence. I'd rather not tell you more about it—see it for yourself.)

Budd shot the picture in October 1955 in Lone Pine. He liked to tell a story of how he found an isolated location high up in the rocks that no man had ever set foot in before, a place where he knew he could get a terrific shot of Scott's character riding through the twisting rocks and hills. But then he hit his foot on a camera spike that had been put there by director Raoul Walsh decades before, and he immediately realized how many filmmakers had already taken advantage of Lone Pine's natural beauty. Budd turned the area into his own version of Monument Valley, creating an ever-changing environment that spoke to the winding and unpredictable plots of the Ranown films.

Batjac budgeted about $700,000 for the film, and it went slightly over-budget. Worldwide it made somewhere between $1.5 and $1.6 million, so it was a small but surprise hit for everyone involved. In publicity materials for the film, Scott said he performed the stunt in which his character is dragged behind a wild horse, and that sure looks like Scott in close-up in the first half of that sequence. Warners and Batjac agreed to pay Scott his usual $100,000 salary but he did not get to profit-share on this one. He *would* on the successive pictures Boetticher directed for Scott's company at Columbia.

The reviews were positive almost all around. "[W]ell played and well directed, with an excellent storyline," wrote *The Hollywood Reporter* (July 11, 1956). Scott, the reviewer wrote, "is a master at the deadpan approach but he always manages, as he does here, to suggest humor and warmth so that his characterization never seems flat.... Boetticher's direction is good, pulling the picture together and achieving all the values possible in the production." The review noted that while *Seven Men* follows the usual chase formula, "it has enough psychological overtones so that it escapes the routine classification."

The Independent Film Journal (July 21, 1956) called it "a first-grade western drama... boosted by a really fine script. Scott is quietly appealing as the sheriff." The *Los Angeles Times* (August 9, 1956) cited it as one of Scott's "better entries in the giddy-up" field while *Showmen's Trade Review* (July 14, 1956) said it was "an outstanding action picture."

I love the *Cincinnati Time Star* review of August 3, 1956, which must have burned producer Wayne up: "Randolph Scott is the greatest living phenomenon in motion pictures. The man must be at least 200 years old and he still looks young enough to be John Wayne's son." Scott was 57 when filming took place and Wayne was about 48.

Many media outlets praised Russell's work, hoping perhaps to encourage her to pursue a comeback. The *Los Angeles Times* (August 9, 1956), said she "does a nice job" while *Variety* (July 11, 1956) wrote, "Gail Russell, off screen for some time, has not lost her appeal and is good as the woman who becomes interested in Scott."

Russell gives a poignant, honest portrayal of a woman who loves her husband but yearns for another man (Scott's character). Russell's eyes speak to a fire slowly going out but still holding enough warm embers to spark a man's interest. But she looks well past her 31 years of age, and she would continue to age fast.

A comeback was not to be. Russell did appear in three more films, fourth-billed in Universal's *The Tattered Dress* (1957), third-billed in Republic's *No Place to Land* (an appropriate title for her career at the time) and top-billed in a forgotten grade-C kiddie picture called *The Silent Call*. There were even a few television spots. About a year after *Seven Men* was released, she made headlines again after drunkenly ramming her vehicle into Jan's Restaurant on Beverly Boulevard, hitting a porter who was cleaning the place. She failed a sobriety test, annoyingly telling the police, "I had a few drinks. I had two. No, four. Oh I don't know how many I had. It's nobody's business anyway." She and Madison divorced in 1954. Budd said Andrew McLaglen fell for Russell during *Seven Men* and tried to help her. At the wrap party, she got bombed and disappeared and he couldn't find her for three days.

Hollywood columnist Erskine Johnson wrote a September 1957 profile of Russell that said she was busy painting in her small apartment. One of her paintings, Wilson noticed, was of a matador thrusting his sword into a bull—a nod to Budd, perhaps, for his taking a chance on her. While Wilson put a little too much emphasis into her being on the "comeback trail," the piece also accurately confronts her problems with the bottle and failed efforts to stay sober. "I guess Hollywood was bad to me but how can I give up acting in movies when it's my life?" she asked him. That year there would be another car accident involving alcohol, for which she was fined $420, put on three years' probation and lost her license.

In a moving tribute to the actress that ran in the Summer 2014 *Films of the Golden Age* issue, producer Andrew J. Fenady recalled casting Russell in a 1961 episode of his TV series *The Rebel*. He called her "a fragile beauty who did the best imitation of John Wayne's walk I've ever seen." He recalls the difficulty the cast and crew had with Russell's inability to recall and recite the simplest of dialogue, and how he was preparing to cast someone else in the role when she came up to him, sober, and begged for another chance. "She sailed through on the first take," he said. "Never kicked another line. We finished the picture on time and Gail Russell was absolutely radiant."

It would be her last work as an actress. She died alone, on the floor of her small West Los Angeles apartment—for which she paid $130 a month in rent, the newspapers reported—in August 1961, surrounded by empty liquor bottles. Neighbors said they had not seen her in days.

Even before *Seven Men* hit theaters in the summer of 1956, Batjac announced it planned to film Elmore Leonard's short story *The Captives* as a film for Wayne, with either Andrew McLaglen or Boetticher directing. But by the summer of 1956, when filming began, Scott played the hero in that adaptation, retitled *The Tall T*, with Boetticher directing for producer Harry Joe Brown and Burt Kennedy scripting.

For decades a washed-out print of *Seven Men* popped up on TV stations every now and then. Budd liked to tell the story of how he ran into John Wayne's son Michael at a poolside party and cajoled him into agreeing to pay to restore the film. But Wayne didn't do that right away, despite repeated calls from Budd. Boetticher said that taught him a lesson: "The next time I run into Michael Wayne by a pool, I'm gonna push him in." It's a good laugh line, but give Michael and Batjac credit. They did eventually restore the film, which remains a popular choice for any Budd Boetticher retrospective.

In August 1956, to coincide with the release of the film, Berkley Publishing released a 125-

In the summer of 1956, Berkeley Publishing quickly put out a 25-cent paperback adaptation of Burt Kennedy's taut script *Seven Men from Now*, calling it *7 Men from Now* and crediting Kennedy with authorship. However, he said he had nothing to do with it. The book was released to cash in on the success of the film, the first to pair Budd Boetticher with actor Randolph Scott.

page paperback version, entitled *7 Men from Now*, for 25 cents. The stark and intriguing cover features an illustration of the Scott character, pistol in right hand, standing atop a cemetery bearing seven crosses. Though the text is credited to Burt Kennedy, he said he had nothing to do with it and knew nothing about it until decades later when interviewers asked him about it. It bears a surface resemblance to the film, but includes a lot of extraneous "western pulp" dialogue and nonsense, including an Indian attack in which both John and Annie Greer prove to be deadly shots.

And, finally, Budd Boetticher would later bristle a bit in telling people that Wayne or one of the producers cut about a minute of footage out of *Seven Men from Now*. He never specified what was cut, but there is an abrupt dissolve after Marvin's character rides up to the wagon carrying Walter Reed and Gail Russell's characters and it looks as if he is about to speak to her.

The Tall T (A Scott-Brown Production, 78 minutes, released by Columbia in April 1957) Director: Budd Boetticher. Producer: Harry Joe Brown. Screenplay: Burt Kennedy. Based on Elmore Leonard's short story "The Captives." Cinematographer: Charles Lawton, Jr. With Randolph Scott (Pat Brennan), Richard Boone (Frank Usher), Maureen O'Sullivan (Doretta Mims), Arthur Hunnicutt (Ed Rintoon), Skip Homeier (Billy Jack), Henry Silva (Chink), John Hubbard (Willard Mims), Robert Burton (Tenvoorde), Fred E. Sherman (Hank Parker) and Chris Olsen (Jeff)

Synopsis: Three brutal outlaws take mining heiress Doretta Mims and cowhand Pat Brennan hostage while they await a ransom bounty for her life. But the captives learn how to use a shotgun and the allure of sex to turn the tables.

It hasn't been my day.—Pat Brennan (Randolph Scott)

Imagine eight-year-old boys excitedly buying their popcorn and soda as they anticipate seeing a brand-new Randolph Scott Western on a Saturday afternoon in the spring of 1957—and being horrified at the wholesale killing of man and boy within the first 20-some minutes of *The Tall T*, a taut, darkly violent suspense Western rather faithfully based on an Elmore Leonard short story.

The Tall T's characters have simple wants: Scott's Pat Brennan wants a ranch. Richard Boone's outlaw Frank Usher wants friendship. The spinsterish Doretta Mims (Maureen O'Sullivan) wants love. And Usher's young sidekicks, Chink and Billy Jack, want to kill. It's a recipe for bonding and bloodletting.

Perhaps more than any other Boetticher-directed Randolph Scott picture, *The Tall T*—the title was vaguely tied to the Tenvoorde ranch that Scott's character visits in the beginning of the film—plays up the doomed relationship of love and respect between the protagonist and antagonist. Unlike characters in most of the other Boetticher-Scott films, Brennan and Usher do not know one another before they meet at a stage relay station. Within the span of a day or two, it's clear Usher wishes he could be more like Brennan—owning a spread, honoring the land and other men, and not running from the law. "A man should have something of his own, something to belong to," Usher says to Brennan at one point, clearly hoping that he can find a way to avoid killing this captive. Later, Usher surprises Brennan with, "I like you, Brennan. Ain't many men I can say that about."

But Usher's words are not enough to win over a man who won't compromise his morals, even at the point of a gun. We have little sense of Brennan's worth with a gun, unlike the ex-sheriffs, bounty hunters and mercenaries that Scott played in the other Boetticher films. But something about his ethical resolve makes us believe he's capable of killing if push comes to shove. "Some things a man can't ride around," Brennan tells the near-hysterical Doretta Mims when they do get a chance to break away but he won't take it. He's got to finish the job, and the job in this case is killing. Brennan wants to live, and suddenly that frames him as a man who is more desperate than his captors.

What is it about Randolph Scott that makes you realize that while he just was not as good an actor as John Wayne, he was the better choice for all those parts in the Boetticher Westerns? His economic acting style works wonders here, as he uses a minimum of emotional expression to display shock, fear and sadness in a matter of seconds, before his character comes to the realization that above all else he wants to live. Early in the picture, the only goal his character has is to earn enough money for a seed bull. Once captive, even if he's left without a ranch, he just wants to wake up one more day. Scott projects a quiet dignity in his characterization that gives you just enough doubt as to whether he's going to get out of this alive, but it's these very qualities that attracts the good-humored Usher—who claims to have never pulled a gun on a man because he's content to let his murderous underlings do that kind of dirty work—to Brennan.

More than any other Boetticher film, *The Tall T* hints at a homoerotic attraction from Usher to Scott—a point Boetticher liked to play up in later interviews when he said the villains of the Burt Kennedy movies were in love with the hero. I don't think that's the case in any of these films except *The Tall T*. The bad guys in those other films clearly respect the Scott character, and they have enough sense to ride around him until they have no choice, but it's a long stretch to suggest there's anything more to those connections. But in *The Tall T*, Usher is smitten enough with Brennan's adherence to the laws of the west that he starts dreaming of turning that way himself. But like Brennan, he can't ride away from who he is. In the end, given the chance to escape himself, Usher foolishly levers his rifle and comes riding headlong at Brennan, receiving a shotgun blast in the face for his efforts. Usher's last word, uttered in pain, dismay and desperation, is "Brennan." It's almost as if he is apologizing for forcing his new friend to kill him.

"I felt Boone really loved Randy in the picture, to the point of being terribly attracted to him physically," Boetticher told Eric Sherman and Martin Rubin in *The Director's Event* (Atheneum, 1970). "He would have liked to have been Randy. There's no reason that a man can't love another man. It doesn't have to be a homosexual thing. I think only weak people are afraid of that." More than a decade after making the picture, Boetticher himself said of his star and producer, "I fell in love with Randolph Scott and Harry Joe Brown." Brown, he said, kept him anchored as a director. "When you decide to make an 18-day picture, you can't fool around."

Most of the pictures were broken down to the basic needs of mankind: success, money, sex, living and dying. Set against the isolated, arid backdrop of the Alabama Hills in Lone Pine, *The Tall T* accentuates those wants by setting its characters so far away from humanity—in the form of a town—that they are forced to take action or die in the middle of nowhere.

But that's heady analysis, and both Budd and Burt hated that sort of criticism. When

Randolph Scott waves down a passing stagecoach in this energetic still from *The Tall T*, the second of the Boetticher-Scott Westerns.

some critics suggested the Scott character, when surrounded by a semi-circle of hostiles early in *Comanche Station*, was representative of Boetticher as a matador and the Comanche warriors serving as the arena, Budd said simply, "Wrong. I wasn't thinking of bullfighting. Randolph Scott is surrounded by Indians because he is in a hell of a lot of trouble."

Novelist Elmore Leonard deserves a lot of credit for the film's success. His 1955 *Argosy* short story "The Captives" provides the basics for the film, starting off about where the picture arrives around the 20-minute mark, with the taking of the hostages and the discovery of the murder of the station man and his young son. Leonard, who was getting about two cents per word for his literary efforts in the dying pulp trade of the 1950s, told writer Courtney Joyner that he was aiming for the Hollywood market from the start. "I liked the idea of using as much dialogue as possible with imparting any kind of information you need," he said. He liked what Brown, Scott, Boetticher and Kennedy did with his story: "I thought it was wonderful. I really liked it because he stayed right with the story. There weren't any asides that I noticed.... The type of villain in these stories was often more charismatic than the hero."

Budd liked to say he had a hard time convincing the studio heads to hire Boone, then finishing up two years of playing a doctor in the television series *Medic*, as the bad guy. Budd said Columbia executives said Boone didn't have a sense of humor. When Budd called Boone to tell him of their concern, Boone said, "Well, Budd, you've got to admit those heart attacks are pretty fucking hilarious." That, Budd, said, was enough for him to hire Boone.

Still, that story doesn't make sense. Why would Columbia executives, who pretty much let Harry Joe Brown and Randolph Scott alone, weigh in on who played the bad guy? And anyway, Scott and Brown had already used Boone in 1955's *Ten Wanted Men* – in which Boone was not allowed to display his sense of humor. Budd said Columbia gave the

Randolph Scott readies for trouble in the form of Richard Boone in *The Tall T*.

Scott-Brown unit autonomy because "we weren't anybody." The powers-that-be at Columbia knew and trusted the team of Scott and Brown, who had been operating under the Scott-Brown production company aegis for about a decade by the time *The Tall T* went into production in the summer of 1956.

As with *Seven Men* and the later *Buchanan Rides Alone*, Scott, Brown, Boetticher and Kennedy benefited, albeit indirectly, from John Wayne. Wayne's company had bought the rights to Leonard's short story, perhaps with the notion of starring Wayne as Pat Brennan. When Wayne and partner Robert Fellows split up, Fellows got to keep the rights to "The Captives." According to Kennedy, Fellows set up the deal to have Columbia do it with Scott and Brown if Boetticher directed. The studio responded by saying, "Sure—if Burt Kennedy rewrites the script." Kennedy's recollection is that Columbia offered Fellows $17,000, and he in turn offered Kennedy a measly $1000. Kennedy said that he countered with an offer to rewrite it for $1000 a page. "You've got me over a barrel," Fellows told Kennedy.

Kennedy, who said Fellows once did him a wrong, replied, "I don't want you anywhere but I'm not doing a thing on the script unless I'm paid a thousand bucks a page."

By Kennedy's estimate, he only rewrote five pages for a total of $5000. This suggests to me that Kennedy had less to do with the finished project than we all think, but the truth is, most of the story was there to start with, plucked directly from the pages of Leonard's short story. By both Burt and Budd's accounts, Burt was on the set during most of the three-week shoot of *The Tall T,* perhaps adding a line or two and tweaking some dialogue. The normally taciturn Randolph Scott was happy to be working with Maureen O'Sullivan, best known for her portrayal of Jane in the 1930s MGM Tarzan pictures. Boetticher said he cast her because he needed a plain-looking woman, and in fact the years had dulled O'Sullivan's hidden sensuality. (Take a look at some of the revealing photos of her clad in the Jane loincloth in those pre–Code Tarzan movies.) O'Sullivan later said of the film, "It was fun making it and I had my own way for once. I did it without makeup and I had long red hair. It was shot at the foot of the High Sierras and we [she and Scott] used to ride a lot and take long walks…. I thought Budd Boetticher was a great director and I liked the story." Burt and Budd said Scott was happy to be around an old social pal from the 1930s and he often had dinner with O'Sullivan after a long day's shoot. "She was the kind that nobody's going to marry," Budd said of O'Sullivan's portrayal of Doretta.

The rest of the casting—with the exception of the dull clod playing the ranch foreman early in the picture—is near perfect. Boetticher said he remembered Skip Homeier's turn as a Nazi brat in 1944's *Tomorrow the World!,* so he cast him as one of the two young hellions. "And he was so good I used him again in *Comanche Station,*" Budd said. Henry Silva, Budd recalled, had never straddled a horse before and put the wrong foot in the stirrup the first time he climbed aboard. Budd pulled John Hubbard in because "I wanted a weak actor to play that guy because he was a bum."

Drunks. They always cause hijinks on the set. Budd said Arthur Hunnicutt was inebriated to the point that "we did that dolly shot across the street with Randy 28 times. Next time you see it, look at Randy's face. He's trying not to laugh because Hunnicutt is ad-libbing." This may be accurate. Hunnicutt does tend to repeat a few words, as if trying to remember his lines, and he seems thrown when Scott's horse suddenly bumps into him, but he's game and has a nice, natural gait to both his physicality and his delivery of dialogue. Boetticher and Scott couldn't figure out where Hunnicutt was getting his alcohol from until assistant director Joe Kenny noticed that Hunnicutt sucked oranges all day long. "We discovered he would take a hypodermic needle and fill the oranges full of vodka," Boetticher said. "You have things like that and you go absolutely crazy because drunks are brilliant."

Budd pulled some matador-like touches off, having fun with a scene in which a Brahma bull goes wild and pursues the Scott character around a pen. Bulls, Boetticher said, don't like water, so he convinced the stuntman filling in for Scott to dive for cover in a water trough. "Are you kidding?" the man said. "No," Budd replied. "He's not going to get you." The stuntman did what he was told, and darned if that big bull didn't briefly jump into the trough, making me wonder if he hit the poor guy submerged in the water below. Boetticher convinced Scott to mount the bull as it is being let loose, but that's clearly the stuntman taking the ride and the fall afterward.

There's a fun bit of physical comedy when Scott's Pat Brennan comes out of the small cave-side shack where he and O'Sullivan's Doretta are being held and bangs his head on the roof of the hut, leading Boone's Usher to break out in delightful and derisive laughter. Budd said it was an accident and Scott was really groggy as a result. Burt Kennedy confirmed the story and said Boone just rolled with the punches (or head bang) and let out the laugh, and the two actors just went on playing the scene as written.

Kennedy said these Boetticher-Scott movies were made for about $500,000—less than the cost of a Universal Audie Murphy Western. "I designed them so there were no interiors," he said. "They were done cheaply. We had a magic number and it had to be cheap, so there's a lot of scenes where people sit around and talk. We just didn't have a lot of money. *Seven Men* cost $750,000 because it was Wayne's." Budd confirmed this when he told me, "We were making second features as far as the price was concerned…that became A pictures." Years later, someone told Boetticher that three of the Scott Columbia movies utilize portions of the same Mischa Bakaleinkoff film score. "How cheap can you get?" Budd laughed.

Maureen O'Sullivan and Randolph Scott seem to have the drop on bad guy Richard Boone in *The Tall T*. But the shooting ain't over yet.

Scott, Kennedy said, "was very real. He didn't really act, though. He was very much a Southern gentleman. He didn't have the stature that Duke had, but he had great dignity. That's what it was. Duke didn't particularly have dignity." Scott, he said, was well aware that the villains had all the good lines and fancy death scenes. "He knew the bad guy roles were the best."

Kennedy saw Harry Joe Brown as a nice fellow who was "not exactly really talented. He knew how to put people together for a film. He was a good partner for Randy because he did the nuts and bolts. He worried about making the movie." Harry Joe Brown, Jr., among others (including the late Western film historian, author and literary agent Jon Tuska), believes the elder Brown's input is overlooked. Brown, Jr., told me:

> My father knew a lot about Westerns, having made them from about 1920 up until his death. He knew stuff like where the right cliffs and the pretty deserts were. My father was the one who made choices about the directors. He liked Budd Boetticher quite a lot... [M]y father's job was to find a great team and getting Kennedy and Boetticher together on those late pictures was his doing. The formula of the movies was all my father's conception and the basic finding of the stories and setting them up and getting good actors was all his job.

According to Brown, Jr., Scott fit the elder Brown's moral sense of a hero:

> Randolph Scott stood for a certain kind of person...this screen image was important to my father. He believed in the image of integrity, strong character and making moral choices. I think that was what Randy was able to project. It was kind of a slant from him being a Virginia gentleman—a certain code of behavior, which was the Code of the West and really, in Scott's case, a Code of the South, a certain kind of behavior that needs to be observed in a place that could be very lawless. Randy stood for something.

And, Brown, Jr., said, it was his father's idea to return to Lone Pine, a shooting locale he had used long before Boetticher ever did. He said that his father "saw the frontier as a kind of ecological wonder. The scenery is very important. That whole idea of location—the natural beauty of the land, the red cliffs, the streams, the wild horses—that view of the earth is very important to a Western. Later on, those wide open spaces just weren't there any more."

The working titles of the movie were *The Captives* and *The Tall Rider*. Budd said Columbia was so cheap it didn't want to pay $200 to purchase the copyrighted title *The Captives*, and that's why *The Tall T* was chosen instead. Kennedy said he earned about $15,000 per screenplay. Scott-Brown and Columbia paid Budd about $30,000 per film, a big jump from his salary at Universal—and he was having a lot more fun. "We just worked ourselves to death," he said of those years.

By October 1, 1956, Columbia had put together press materials for the film, though it delayed releasing *The Tall T* until the spring of 1957. It's unfortunate that by the late 1950s, the big newspaper outlets, including the *New York Times*, were cutting back on reviewing second features and B+ Westerns like *The Tall T*. *Variety* (April 3, 1957): "There's a wealth of suspense in the Burt Kennedy screenplay. Scott impresses as the strong, silent type."

Though Scott could see the decline in box office receipts for his own productions from the mid–1950s on as television cut into the movie business's profits, pictures like *The Tall T* could still make a profit for him and his partner. Their deal, struck a decade before with Harry Cohn, was a 50–50 cut with the studio. Both sides invested half the production money and both sides split the proceeds. In a May 1955 interview with Hollywood columnist Bob Thomas, Scott said, "There's no doubt television has cut into our business. We used to count on two to three million domestically and four million worldwide. But you can't expect that nowadays. The little monster [TV] has brought a lot of changes in the picture business." But a half-million dollar project like *The Tall T* could still bring in a million in profits, giving both Scott and Brown and Harry Cohn a half-million for less than a month's work.

Scott and Brown continued to work with Budd and Burt on a picture-by-picture basis—

though both Budd and Burt said the last two films in the series were set up on a two-picture deal following Cohn's death in February 1958. While Burt went to work on other projects, including some Warner Bros. films, Scott and Brown hired Boetticher to direct another Western, *Decision at Sundown*.

Shortly after Columbia released *The Tall T*, Budd's wife Emily sued for divorce, citing cruelty and asking for about $1500 a month in alimony and the Van Nuys house they shared, which was reported as being worth $50,000. The couple had two daughters, Georgia and Helene. Budd gave her what she wanted, and staggered into a romantic relationship with one of the leading ladies of his next Randolph Scott film, *Decision at Sundown*.

Decision at Sundown (A Scott-Brown production, 77 minutes, released by Columbia in November 1957) Director: Budd Boetticher. Producer: Harry Joe Brown. Associate Producer: Randolph Scott. Screenplay: Charles Lang. Story: Vernon L. Fluharty. Cinematographer: Burnett Guffey. With Randolph Scott (Bart Allison), John Carroll (Tate Kimbrough), Karen Steele (Lucy Summerton), Valerie French (Ruby James), Noah Beery, Jr. (Sam), John Archer (Dr. John Storrow), Andrew Duggan (Sheriff Swede Hanson), John Litel (Charles Summerton), Ray Teal (Morley Chase), James Westerfield (Otis), H.M. Wynant (Spanish) and Richard Deacon (Zaron)

Synopsis: Civil War veteran Bart Allison rides into Sundown to kill town boss Tate Kimbrough. But no one, including Kimbrough, seems to know why.

Decision at Sundown is a misfire, but not a mediocrity. The truth is, despite my criticism of it in my 2004 book *The Films of Randolph Scott*, I'm growing to like the movie a bit more each time I see it. It's a mess, but an interesting mess, and I think it fails because the actions of the protagonist, Bart Allison, change the town—but not him. He is out to avenge himself on the man who he thinks caused the death of his wife Lucy. Allison leaves Sundown as he entered it: bitter, angry, and having accomplished nothing other than the inadvertent death of his best friend Sam.

In fact, this may be the only Boetticher-directed Scott in which our hero could be mistaken for the villain. Though John Carroll's Tate Kimbrough is a womanizer and town tyrant, he has his own set of morals that includes owning up to his past mistakes and strapping on a six-gun to meet Allison head on. As such, Kimbrough displays more moral fortitude than the Scott character, and accepts his dethroning as town kingpin with grace and dignity.

Budd repeatedly dismissed the film, calling it an "old Randolph Scott story" that had been lying around the Columbia lot for a while, waiting for some hack director to take it on. That doesn't make a lot of sense to me. First of all, it's based on a 1955 short story by Vernon L. Fluharty so it couldn't have collected dust for more than a year and a half. Second, Budd's pal Charles Lang scripted it, and I can see no reason why Scott and Brown would have hired Lang—who had no other connection to them before they started working with Boetticher—unless Budd recommended Lang for the job. Burt Kennedy recalls Budd calling him around this time and asking if was okay if Charles Lang get credit for one of the Scott Westerns because he (Lang) was trying to get his screenwriting career going. "I wasn't asked to do the film," Kennedy told me. "In fact, I wasn't even asked to *see* the film!"

Budd shot *Decision* almost entirely on the Columbia back lot in April 1957. He cast actors he had worked with before, including Noah Beery and Frank Chase, while Brown and Scott likely chose some of the lesser players like Bob Steele, Ray Teal and James Westerfield, who had appeared in previous Scott films. How or why Boetticher cast Karen Steele remains a bit of a mystery. By some accounts, Boetticher met her while his marriage to Emily Cook was unraveling and before he began work on this picture, and then decided to cast her in it. But Budd said he met Steele during the picture and broke one of his own laws of directing: never sleep with your leading lady unless it's the last night of the shoot.

"It's funny how those of us who are natural romantics keep looking for 'Lady Guinevere' when we've got her right at home," Boetticher reflected in his autobiography. He continued:

Emily Boetticher was a saint—still is. She was beautiful and she loved me—for a long while. But damn if I didn't keep looking. Well, I thought I'd discovered all the "Guineveres" in the world rolled into one. She was elegantly beautiful, extremely talented and she just worshiped the ground I walked on. Now isn't that a pile of crap!"

My "Guinevere" turned out to be "Morgan le Fay" and I ended up getting exactly what was coming to me—a belly-ful of misery, absolutely ill about my family and thoroughly disgusted and angry at my own stupidity. A motion picture director should only become involved with an actress in spite of her profession, not because of it.

Budd does not mention his Morgan le Fay by name, but it is Karen Steele. She cost him his friends over the length of their romantic relationship—which started around April 1957 and ended in the autumn of 1959, when Budd wrapped *The Rise and Fall of Legs Diamond*, his fourth and last film with Steele as his leading lady.

Steele is stunning to look at, that's for sure. And though I think she grew into a decent actress in *Ride Lonesome* and better than decent in *Legs Diamond*, she is one-note pouty in *Decision at Sundown*, which doesn't help an already problematic production.

Perhaps Budd's personal discord dissipated some of his focus on *Decision at Sundown*, but boy, does it start out promisingly. With a few days' stubble on his face, Scott first appears to be holding up a stagecoach. It turns out he is waiting on his friend Sam (Noah Beery, Jr.), who has been scouting out the town of Sundown, where the cad Tate Kimbrough lives. The duo arrives in Sundown just before Kimbrough's morning marriage to Lucy Summerton (Steele), and within a minute or so we get the picture: Kimbrough likes women, has a mistress on the side (sensitively played by Valerie French) and he rules the town. But Kimbrough seems to be a fairly benevolent Napoleon, and that's one of the film's many problems. Whereas a lack of backstory helps both *Seven Men from Now* and *The Tall T*, here it really mucks up the potential. We don't know how or why Kimbrough came to rule Sundown, other than to win it over with money and by buying the sheriff (Andrew Duggan).

"It was the story of a town," Budd would say in explaining *Decision at Sundown*'s failure, and he's right. As with *Red Ball Express*, the focus is pulled away from the individual and redirected to a colorful but stereotypical array of characters, none of whom have any depth. They sit in the bar and drink and pontificate after Allison, having shown up at Kimbrough's wedding to let the man know he intends to kill him, hides out in the livery stable, pulling his hapless pal Sam into the battle with him. Kimbrough's men lay siege to the place, but nothing much happens except for some ineffective flying lead and lots of talk. And the talk

Randolph Scott in the least interesting of Columbia's Boetticher-Scott films, *Decision at Sundown*. But that doesn't mean there's not plenty for the viewer to chew on in this offbeat misfire. Note the shadow of technical crew equipment on the building just above the overturned wagon.

isn't nearly as interesting as the type we find in a Burt Kennedy script of the period.

Little that Allison does makes sense, and Scott's portrayal doesn't hint at a psychological disorder that could perhaps serve as an explanation for the illogical actions he takes. Time and again, other characters in the film—including Sam—comment on Allison's strange behavior in confronting Kimbrough and then holing up in the livery stable, where our hero can do little but dodge incoming bullets. And when John Archer's Doc Storrow (sometimes pronounced as "Sorrow" by other characters, making me wonder if there was a change in the script that some actors caught on to and others didn't) starts offering a litany of well-meaning bits of advice to the townspeople to get them to act on Allison's behalf, it's clear that he has become the moral conscience of the story, and not Allison. Archer is earnest and determined, but he—like most of the actors in the film—displays little nuance, making an interesting line like "What man knows how a life should really be lived?" come off as flat and forgettable.

On the plus side again, there's fine work by both John Carroll and Valerie French. Carroll was a star-in-the-making at MGM in the 1940s, when matinee idol Clark Gable was off serving in the military. "He was duly hired by MGM as a threat to the cinema king but was never given the proper showcasing to live up to his promise," James Robert Parish and Ronald L. Bowers accurately report in *The Golden Era: The MGM Stock Company* (Bonanza Books, 1972). "Hollywood decided that, after all, he was only a poor man's Rhett Butler." By the late 1940s, Carroll was shoring up Republic's cowboy star William "Bill" Elliott in a trio of films, one of which—*The Fabulous Texan* (1947)—showcases Carroll at his best. One senses an introspective actor beneath the showy Errol Flynn-ish exterior, but only in a few cases—including *Decision at Sundown*—did Carroll get to show what he was made of. His Tate Kimbrough has humor, softness and a self-critical eye, and you believe him when his eyes fill with confusion and fear as he plans to face Allison in the street.

Carroll's career stopped abruptly following the release of Republic's final movie, a terrible offering called *Plunderers of Painted Flats* in which the actor rather too convincingly portrays an aging, alcoholic gunman and womanizer who is aware that he has galloped into his last box canyon. Sordid headlines—including a *Confidential* magazine piece on an all-nude swim party Carroll threw and allegations by an elderly widow that he stole a quarter of a million dollars from her—likely hurt his career at a time when he could have segued into some regular character work. Boetticher said he cast Carroll after watching the actor lose $40,000 at a crap table in a Las Vegas casino and not bat an eye. (No wonder he allegedly stole money from aging widows!) "He was just such a great character," Boetticher said. "He could sing 'Around the World in 80 Days' better than any singer in the world. And he was intrigued with my career and who I was, that I had been a bullfighter. We spent a lot of time together, and that's how he got in the film… [H]e was good."

Valerie French worked in a few more films but really concentrated on stage work, winning acclaim as a theater actress. She died of leukemia in 1990, two years after Karen Steele passed away in Arizona. Jon Tuska, in a series of letters he sent me from the late 1990s until his passing in early 2016, often referred to Steele as being a bit unbalanced. He wrote,

> Neither [Harry Joe] Brown nor Scott thought much of Karen Steele as an actress, but they accommodated Budd who was obsessed with making her a glamorous sex symbol. Randy did not particularly like her and confided that the only pleasure he had found working with her was when he got to slap her buttocks—and he didn't hold back because Budd said he wanted it to be "realistic" and, after all, as Randy noted, Budd was the director.

Scott *does* let Steele's backside have it when he spanks her in *Decision at Sundown*.

Budd didn't like to see Scott playing drunk, but Scott does it very well. The actor gives an admirable, unfiltered performance, projecting a sense of sorrow, despair and futility that had not been seen since his fine work in 1937's *High, Wide and Handsome*. Scott is also intimidating in the early scenes, anticipating his character in Sam Peckinpah's *Ride the High Country* by a few years. Scott is also intimidating in the early scenes, anticipating his character in Sam Peckinpah's *Ride the High Country* by a few years. But there's little room in the script for Scott to display warmth or humor, two personal assets sorely missing here.

Boetticher on *Decision at Sundown* (to the author):

> You know why it was the least one? Because it was already written. It was my second picture after *The Tall T*.... It was already written and it was an old Randolph Scott picture and I didn't like the idea that he had to be drunk in a lot of the scenes. That didn't befit him at all. And it was a disastrous picture for me because that's when I met Karen Steele... [S]o I didn't like that one.

To Sean Axmaker, Budd said of this picture and *Buchanan Rides Alone*,

> They were very different and they weren't as good; they were too complicated. In *Decision at Sundown*, [the Scott character] had mental problems that he really didn't have in Burt's pictures. It wasn't a Randolph Scott character. It was the story of a town, the story of a lot of people. It was like *Westbound*, it was the old-fashioned Randolph Scott picture, it wasn't one man who had to do a job, the kind of pictures that Burt and I made together. The scripts weren't as good.

The comparisons to *Westbound* are apt, and Boetticher would end up shooting *Westbound* next, though that film would not be released until 1959.

Yet there is something within *Decision at Sundown* that continues to call to me as a viewer. I don't think anyone involved with it dug deeply enough to figure out what that something is, and I don't know that at this point I can pull out a big enough shovel to do it myself. If it is the least interesting of the Boetticher-Scott Columbia pictures (and it is), it's heads and shoulders above so many other Westerns made around the same time—and still more intriguing than most of the Westerns Scott made at Warner Bros. in the 1950s.

Actor H.M. Wynant told me,

> I remember Andy Duggan and I were cast around the same time, and I overheard Boetticher saying that he hired Andy because he liked the sound of his voice and the way he talked. And then he told me that he hired me because of my physicality. I remember that upset me because I wasn't being referred to as an actor with a voice like Andy, but as someone who could move well, which I did. Randolph Scott was very much known at the time for making B Westerns, but *Decision at Sundown* was not that way at all. It had a substance that went well beyond the standard "shoot 'em up" stuff and everybody involved knew that. This movie had literary power.
>
> Budd did a tremendous job of casting it. By that I mean actors who were not normally very good gave good performances under his direction. I didn't have much to do with Karen Steele, but the rumor on the set was that she got the part because she was Budd Boetticher's "lady." I loved John Carroll. He was like the evil side of Clark Gable. He gave a wonderful performance and I credit that to Budd Boetticher. Budd liked to talk to actors, but not to me because it was all about the way I moved [laughs]. Budd and Randy acted really like one. They got along beautifully, that was obvious.

Decision at Sundown netted not-so-good reviews, though *Variety* (November 1, 1957) cited the "generally high staging quality by director Budd Boetticher.... Scott plays his role very well."

The Hollywood Reporter review of the same day called the film "a passable western, although, considering the ingredients, it is a disappointment. The chief fault seems to be that Scott is made a man of mystery and that when the mystery is dispelled, it turns out not to have been a good enough reason for the obscurity." *Film Daily* (November 26, 1957) found the film "on the slightly slow and heavy side" with characters who "inspire little sympathy or express much conviction." On November 21, 1957, The *Los Angeles Mirror-News'* Fred W. Fox wrote that Boetticher "gets away fast and is doing handily with *Decision at Sundown* but at the halfway mark he pulls up awkwardly and flounders." Of Randolph Scott, Fox wrote, "He'll probably have his spurs and saddles long after reviewers like me are hobbling around the Home for Aged News Stiffs."

Composer Heinz Roemheld's melancholy score works to the film's advantage, though it is over-used.

In October 1956, *Variety* announced that George Montgomery was going to produce a picture written by actor Leo Gordon called *Decision at Sundown*. This turned out to be the Warner Bros. production *Black Patch* (1957), one of Montgomery's most offbeat and ambitious efforts.

Buchanan Rides Alone (A Scott-Brown Production, 78 minutes, released by Columbia in August 1958) Director: Budd Boetticher. Producers: Harry Joe Brown and Randolph Scott. Screenplay: Charles Lang, based on the novel *The Name's Buchanan* by Jones Ward. Cinematographer: Lucien Ballard. With Randolph Scott (Tom Buchanan), Craig Stevens (Abe Carbo), Barry Kelley (Lew Agry), Tol Avery (Judge Simon Agry), Peter Whitney (Amos Agry), L.Q. Jones (Pecos Hill), Manuel Rojos (Juan de la Vega), Jennifer Holden (K.T.), Robert Anderson (Waldo Peck) and William Leslie (Roy Agry)

Synopsis: Happy-go-lucky Irish-American mercenary Buchanan inadvertently gets caught up in a familial struggle for a small California border town.

Buchanan Rides Alone is the *Casablanca* of B Westerns, both in terms of the number of double-crosses and last-minute plot twists that take place onscreen and in terms of the behind-the-scenes, make-it-up-as-we-go-along writing of the script. And like *Casablanca*, there remains a lot of debate and contention about who is responsible for the screenplay.

First, let's give credit to "Jonas Ward," a pseudonym for a number of different writers who wrote the long-running *Buchanan* literary series. About an hour of the film's running time is filled with characters, dialogue and plot points pulled directly from the novel, making me wonder what all the fuss was about when it came to the argument of who wrote the script. Only in the last 15 or 20 minutes does what happens onscreen deviate considerably from the novel, and frankly, in this case, the movie's better than the book.

Now that we got that out of the way, let's look at who said what about the writing of the script.

Budd Boetticher, in *When in Disgrace*: "Burt's *The Tall T* was the second of seven straight films I made with Randolph Scott. Burt wrote four of the seven; my long-time pal, Charles Lang Jr. (who also did the script for the *Magnificent Matador*), wrote the other two that I really liked."

Bill Krohn, in his forward to *When in Disgrace*: "[Boetticher] had the help of the great cameraman, Lucien Ballard, and his favorite writer, Burt Kennedy, on many of them (including *Buchanan Rides Alone*, a frontier *Revenge's Tragedy* that Boetticher and Kennedy improvised during shooting when the credited writer's script proved unsatisfactory)."

Budd Boetticher to the author:

Charlie Lang was the screenwriter, he was one of my best friends. He was known as Froggy Lang. He was getting a divorce and he was drinking. And Burt and I were working out the treatment for *Buchanan* and it was called *The Name's Buchanan*. It was a damn good script from the book and we worked out what we wanted to do. And I went with Karen [Steele] to Mexico City for Christmas vacation and sent the script to Charlie. And Charlie made $25,000 polishing the script up. So on the way back—Karen had left me in a huff—I drove to Tucson because I wanted to pick locations with Lucien [Ballard]. I was sitting having breakfast all alone, and Lucien walked in and threw the script down at me. He said, "Did you read this?" I said, "What do you mean, did I read it? I wrote it!" He said, "Well, read this piece of shit." It was just awful. We couldn't shoot a goddamned thing. I called Burt. I said, "Burt, come to Tucson. We're gonna make a piece of shit if you don't get over here." We ad-libbed the whole goddamned picture. There wasn't a script...and when you see the poster from Columbia, there are no credits because they couldn't say what we did. They couldn't say, "Written, directed, produced and everything by Budd Boetticher and Burt Kennedy, ad-libbed."

Burt Kennedy to the author: "I worked on *Buchanan Rides Alone* just a little on the beginning, not much."

Burt Kennedy to Sean Axmaker, replying to the question of whether he worked on the script:

KENNEDY: "Yes. I forget exactly whether it was... the opening was more of a problem than any-

thing else, as I remember, and I worked mostly on the opening of it. I really can't remember. I know I worked on it and there was a writer who was a friend of Budd's..."
AXMAKER: "Charles Lang."
KENNEDY: "Yeah, that's who it was."

Burt Kennedy to C. Courtney Joyner: "[Scott and Brown] hired me to write two screenplays, and I didn't have the foggiest idea what I was going to do. And so I wrote, I think, *Ride Lonesome* first, yeah, and they made that. And then right on top of that I was working on *Comanche Station* and they made that. And then all the other pictures that Budd did, like *Buchanan Rides Alone*, and those things, I didn't have anything to do with those."

Lucien Ballard told Leonard Maltin that John Wayne originally optioned the rights to the *Buchanan* book and sold it to Scott and Brown. "And everyone thought it was great.

Wayne said it was the best story he'd had in years and he was angry at having let it go." Ballard then echoes Boetticher's words about their breakfast-time meeting in Tucson, claiming he said to Budd, "You better read it, it's the worst piece of crap I've seen in years. So [Boetticher] started rewriting it at night, during lunch breaks, all over shooting. He was still working on it during lunch hour on the last day we were shooting."

Actor Craig Stevens to the author: "The character [Carbo] was really created on the spot. It was originally a very small role, but Budd built it up on the set. We did a lot of improvising."

L.Q. Jones to the author: "Burt wrote the script and kept writing while shooting. I imagine they were adapting as they went along... Burt recommended they look at me to do the part. But he wrote so many of the films for

The easygoing soldier of fortune Buchanan (Randolph Scott, left) bids goodbye to rival Carbo (Craig Stevens) in *Buchanan Rides Alone*.

Randy that Harry Joe did—at least four—so it gets hard to say, "Who wrote this one?" If you pinned me in a corner and asked me, I'd say, 'Burt wrote this one [*Buchanan*].'"

Finally, screenwriter Charles Lang, Jr., told me in a brief phone conversation in 2000 that he wrote the screenplay and Budd may have changed a few things on the set while he (Lang) was away. He said Budd was taking credit for the film because that's the way Budd was, but he (Lang) didn't want to go on the record because he was afraid Budd would beat him up.

So where does that leave us?

Well, given the absence of a final shooting script (God knows it's probably full of penciled-in changes and crossed out words), I suggest we forgot all about the script's origins, since just about everyone involved with the production is dead as of the writing of this book.

Buchanan Rides Alone is just a hell of a lot of fun. It is the most darkly comic of the series, and the one that really displays enough twists to the usual tropes of the genre to suggest it influenced the later spaghetti westerns. Scott is clearly enjoying himself as the easygoing Buchanan, a man confident enough to enjoy his last steak and beer, knowing the armed man at the next table is going to kill him. Caught up in a killing he had no hand in, Buchanan survives an attempted lynching and assassination, breaks jail a couple of times, and regains the $2000 he earned fighting below the border so he can ride off into the sunset to start a ranch of his own. At 60, Scott's age is finally beginning to show in a few scenes (he is wearing a lot of eye makeup, for one thing), but he still conveys a youthful, animated energy as he uses his six-guns to blast away at anything that moves. *Buchanan Rides Alone*, like *Decision at Sundown*, doesn't always focus on the Scott character, letting the story unfold through the eyes of a lot of different people, including the trio of underhanded Agry brothers who quarrel among themselves.

Still, it's not a film with a lot of memorable dialogue, and some of the best stuff—"This sure is a ten dollar town"—comes right out of the Ward novel. And once the picture veers away from the novel, it really goes off-track like an out-of-control rollercoaster car, indifferent to the potential for a crash. Characters turn on one another at the last minute, blasting each other to pieces. The familial battle over control of a border town will be seen in Sergio Leone's *A Fistful of Dollars,* which is based on the 1961 Kurosawa film *Yojimbo.* If Budd and/or Burt did construct the final escape-chase-shoot-out scenes on the spot, it shows: There's a loose complacency to it all that erases the potential for real danger. *Buchanan* has a comfortable ease to it that belies all of its violence. Buchanan never really seems to be in that tight of a fix, even with a rope around his neck, but he's easy to root for because nearly everyone around him, except for the friendly Juan de la Vega and the gunman Carbo, are greedy killers or amoral idiots.

As with *Decision at Sundown*, what's missing here is a real sense of connection and conflict between hero and main villain. Buchanan and Carbo—who is the paid bodyguard of one of the Agry brothers—have few scenes together and exchange little dialogue, making their last-minute truce rather unbelievable. (In the novel, the two engage in a knife duel and Buchanan kills Carbo.) Here, we are at least left with another memorable ending to a Boetticher-Scott film, when Buchanan cedes control of the town to Carbo while just about everyone else lies dead around them.

CARBO: I advise you not to stay here. Like you said, this is my town now.
BUCHANAN: Mr. Carbo, you can have it.

After Buchanan rides away, Carbo eyes the corpses around them and then turns to the last surviving Argy brother, the unfortunate halfwit Amos, and says, "Don't just stand there, Amos, get a shovel."

Boetticher claimed to have injected that line into the script on the last day of shooting because in so many Westerns, "there's been a big battle and there's a lot of dead Indians out there and they smell the next day... [S]o I thought, 'What a great thing, if only we could make it funny.'" The preview audience for the film "just went nuts" at the line, he said. (Note: Look closely at actor Craig Stevens' mouth when he says the word "shovel." It actually looks like he uttered a one-syllable word, like "spade," and that it was re-dubbed as "shovel" in the post-production phase.)

Boetticher and Stevens both say that the film was shot in 12 days, whereas most of the Brown-Scott films were shot in 18 days. The American Film Institute reports that the film was shot in three weeks in February 1958, wrapping on February 27—the same day that studio head Harry Cohn died in Phoenix, making this the last of the Scott-Boetticher films to be completed under his watch.

The Breen Office examined the script and urged the producers to cut down on a scene where the bad guys beat up Buchanan and Juan and to eliminate a bit where Amos gets whipped (that last part was removed from the final production). On January 24, 1958, the Breen Office noted in a memo that the *Buchanan Rides Alone* producers had submitted "an incomplete script" to which they still had objections, but by January 31, the final script was approved by the censors. This somewhat backs up Budd's claim that the film was thrown together at the last moment. An April 21, 1958, Production Code Administration document gives Charles Lang, Jr., credit for the screenplay; the PCA gave its final blessing to the picture just a few days before.

The Protestant Motion Picture Council wasn't too happy with the finished film: "The parts are assembled in a brutal pattern with underhanded scheming, gunplay, liquor and unwarranted killing," a council memo stated, adding that the picture was "for adults only." In England, the censors removed shots of Buchanan and Juan getting beat up and all the shots of one character's dead body hanging in

Columbia emphasized the violent aspects of 1958's *Buchanan Rides Alone* which is nonetheless the most playful of the films that star Randolph Scott made with Budd Boetticher.

(From left to center) L.Q. Jones, Randolph Scott and Manuel Rojos hold some baddies (actors unidentified) at bay in *Buchanan Rides Alone*. Most of the people in this still end up dead by the climax—but not Scott's Buchanan!

a tree. Germany's censors suggested cutting a very amusing eulogy delivered by L.Q. Jones' Pecos, saying it was only suitable for those age 16 or older!

Critics liked *Buchanan Rides Alone*. "Turned out on a relatively modest budget (as these things go these days), released with no special fanfare, still it is an honest picture, made with skill and craftsmanship," said *Variety* (August 1, 1958). They also called the screenplay "well paced." The *Motion Picture Herald* (August 2, 1958) said that Boetticher's direction "sparkles with action, character study and offbeat situations. [Randolph Scott gives a] becoming, carefree portrayal of a soldier of fortune."

The Hollywood Reporter (July 31, 1958): "It is a much better than average western. The scripter, Charles Lang, and the director, Budd Boetticher, succeed in making human values supercede plot mechanics so that you're always pulling for the good guys." The *Los Angeles Examiner's* S.A. Desick (August 14, 1958): "The proceedings get somewhat involved, but they're carried off with flair, good characterization and branding-iron humor."

Film Daily (August 7, 1958) was somewhat critical: "The film is in the standard outdoor action groove, story-wise, and has a fine pictorial quality and production know-how." But, the reviewer added, the script was in "constant movement...often sacrificing credibility for action."

L.Q. Jones to the author:

Budd worked from the seat of his pants which is one of the things that made him so good. Look at the stuff he did with Randy and Harry Joe Brown. They were making them for spit. I think our budget on *Buchanan* was somewhere between $300,000 and $325,000. When you have that sort of budget and limitation, can you be a John Ford?

Craig Stevens to the author:

That was the only Western I ever made.... Budd was an "on-his-feet" type of director. He had ideas and I listened. And he was open to his actors having ideas.... The film had a lot of quality and I'm proud of it. It was really fascinating to play: There were good guys and bad guys and some in between and Budd was fascinated with that.... Randolph Scott was a wonderful man. He was really a Southern gentleman, professional and polite. He was greatly underrated.

Some have said that *Buchanan Rides Alone* influenced Sergio Leone's *A Fistful of Dollars*, which in turn inspired the decade-plus run of spaghetti westerns. Budd often told the story of visiting Milan, Italy, for a film festival some time in the late 1980s and discovering that Leone was in attendance. One day Budd was walking up the stairs of the hotel lobby and Leone was walking down. Before Budd could say anything, Leone said, "Buddy, darling, I stole everything from you!" and the two hugged.

While Budd often spoke fondly of the film in later years, he told me he considered it one of the "lesser" entrees in the Randolph Scott canon. In 1965 he told a *Cahiers du Cinéma* journalist that it was "the weakest film in the series."

Scott's mother died during the production of the film, which may speak to the aged and pained look he displays throughout. Harry Cohn's death may have thrown Scott too, for the two maintained a friendly and professional relationship that dated back to at least the early 1940s.

Following Cohn's death, Columbia fell into the hands of lesser-known (and less talented) professionals who, for a few years, maintained the steady flow of B pictures before the studio system came to an end. "Columbia went into the red," author Clive Hirschorn wrote in *The Columbia Story* (Octopus Publishing Group, 1999). "An era was over."

A final thought: Audie Murphy would have been perfect casting for Buchanan, a war veteran who is in his mid–30s, likes women, has a wry sense of humor and doesn't mind killing people. Producer Harry Joe Brown put together a two-picture deal with Murphy in 1956 that resulted in the misfire *The Guns of Fort Petticoat* before the two had a falling-out. (The second film on that contract was never made.) Harry Joe. Brown Jr., told me that that while Murphy possessed many of the same personal qualities that Randolph Scott had, the World War II hero and actor was more unpredictable and sometimes clashed with his father.

Ride Lonesome (A Ranown Production, 74 minutes, released by Columbia in February 1959) Producer-Director: Budd Boetticher. Associate Producer: Harry Joe Brown. Screenplay: Burt Kennedy. Cinematographer: Charles Lawton, Jr. With Randolph Scott (Ben Brigade), Karen Steele (Carrie Lane), Pernell Roberts (Sam Boone), James Best (Billy John), James Coburn (Wid), Lee Van Cleef (Frank) and Dyke Johnson (Charlie)

Synopsis: Bounty hunter Ben Brigade takes outlaw Billy John into custody. But as the two near civilization and pick up a few companions, it becomes clear that Brigade has bigger prey in mind.

After the clutter of people and the confusion of plot points in both *Decision at Sundown* and *Buchanan Rides Along* (as well as *Westbound*, which was already shot but not yet released), *Ride Lonesome* is a welcome return to the austere essentials of the Kennedy-Boetticher-Brown-Scott partnership. The creative team stripped away almost all externals as they created a stark, still composition of a man who prefers to speak only with his six-gun. Scott's Ben Brigade must kill one more time to be free of killing. And he does his job in a West almost entirely devoid of civilization. Peter Coonradt, writing in *Cinema* magazine (December 1968), laid it out perfectly when he said of the Scott character in *Ride Lonesome* and *Comanche Station*, "He is so sure of what he has to do that he never stops to wonder why he is doing it and he never tries to justify himself to others."

But one can see subtle growth and differences in Scott's Ben Brigade, especially when compared to his characterization of Stride in *Seven Men from Now*. In that film, the Scott hero couldn't turn his back on a pioneer couple who need him to survive, and he was continually on guard against Lee Marvin's gunman Masters. In *Ride Lonesome*, Brigade accepts—with just a hint of suspicion—the company of former outlaws Sam Boone (Pernell Roberts) and Wid (James Coburn), helping them to achieve their own freedom by allowing them to share in the bounty of the immature man-boy Billy John (a wonderful James Best). As with Stride, Brigade looks down upon a man who puts his wife in danger but he is less protective of the oversexed widow Carrie Lane (Karen Steele, achieving a passable sense of decent acting in the role) than he was of Annie Greer in *Seven Men*. In this case, carting Mrs. Lane along doesn't cause delays or distractions (and at least she can handle a rifle). Brigade knows where he is going and rides at his own pace, aware that his prey—Billy John's older brother Frank—is coming after him to save Billy John from the hangman's noose. Brigade is riding the trial of patience, waiting for his fate to catch up with him.

It's to Burt and Budd's credit that, as with most of their pictures with Scott, they set up a good mystery angle regarding their protagonist's wants. Billy John has no idea why Brigade is really after him—nor do Sam Boone or Wid figure it out for a long time.

Kennedy's script features more sex than any of the other Scott films. Nothing explicit, of course, but the feeling of sexual desire for a woman as attractive as Carrie Lane is played up repeatedly in scenes between Sam Boone and Brigade and Boone and Wid. "Can you imagine having her around all the time?" Boone asks the more naïve Wid as they eye the full-figured Carrie Lane combing her hair. "All those days. All those nights." Later, Boone tells Wid it is unlikely that Mrs. Lane will remain a widow for long. "Some get along without," he says. "She's the type that has a need—a deep lonely need only a man can get at." It is the most openly sexual commentary Kennedy makes regarding the marriage of love and lust. And Burt softens his development of the so-called bad guys, molding Sam Boone as a tough customer who is nonetheless capable of a gentleness we do not see in the likes of the Lee Marvins, Richard Boones and Claude Akinses who populate the series.

Boone asks Mrs. Lane if he can take care of her, but he does not demand it. There is only the slightest hint that maybe they will try that set-up some time down the line, after Brigade has finished his job.

Gone too is the sloppiness of continuity errors and dumb gaffes (Scott's leg wound moving from the right to left leg in *Seven Men from Now*; Henry Silva moving his feet together after his character is already dead in *The Tall T*). *Ride Lonesome* looks perfect. Boetticher frames some scenes so that the men look bigger than the desert environment they are traveling. He pays homage to John Ford with an Indian chase and attack, and he convinces Scott to jump his horse over a wall and take a fall with the animal within the relative safety of an abandoned relay station. (That sure looks like the 60-year-old actor doing the stunt.) And he and Kennedy even allow Lee Van Cleef, reduced to a dim and distant reflection of the Lee Marvin-Richard Boone characters of old, to soften his character's approach to his own mission. When Van Cleef's Frank realizes why Brigade is drawing him in, there's almost a touch of remorse when he tells his men, "I did him a hurt once." Later, finally facing Brigade in the last showdown, Van Cleef's Frank is aware that the odds are against him, but with that fear comes a sense of regret as he begs Brigade to not force the hand. When all is said and done, Brigade is left standing alone in the middle of a clearing (one that resembles an arena, so perhaps Budd was throwing in a bullfighting reference here), watching the so-called Hanging Tree—where Frank once strung up Brigade's wife—slowly burn. Whether the fire will serve as a cleansing of Brigade's guilt and pain is unclear. *Ride Lonesome* sees three of its five main characters riding to a place called Hope. Only Billy John is likely to meet a bad end. As for Brigade, who knows?

Kennedy gave his two supporting villains time to develop a relationship with one another. We discover that Boone and Wid have ridden together for some time without talking much. They've done some robbing though it is unclear if killing was ever part of their criminal past.

When Boone lays out his plan for a renewed life, a life bought with amnesty if he and Wid can bring in Billy John, he tells Wid he wants him as his partner. Wid, confused, asks why. "Because I like you, Wid," Boone replies, to which Wid deadpans, "Why, I never knew that." It's a great laugh line, perfectly delivered by Coburn.

Budd said that Randolph Scott suggested giving Coburn more lines on the set, so Budd fixed that scene up on the spot. He also said the original script called for Scott's character to kill Boone and Wid. According to Budd, he called Columbia and spoke to either executive Sam Briskin or associate producer Harry Joe Brown—the latter having been demoted by the Columbia brass who no longer saw his contribution as being necessary to the success of the films—and said he wanted to change the ending to let the two bad guys live. Briskin or Brown (depending on which version of the story Budd told) said Budd didn't have a choice: "Well, you have to—they're the bad guys." Budd claims he told Columbia he'd shoot the ending both ways. In one, Brigade lets the two go with Billy John, buying them a shot at freedom. In the other, Brigade shoots them down.

Then, Budd said with great glee, he just never got around to the second version. Either the light of the day faded too fast or the transportation trucks showed up and got in the way or something else happened to interrupt the plan, he claimed. When he brought the finished film back to Hollywood and the studio, he claimed he showed the studio execs the ending as it is now—with Brigade letting the two bad guys become good guys—before turning to the studio bosses and asking, "Do you want to see the other version?"

"No, no, this is great, leave it as it is," the studio boys told Budd.

That's another good Budd Boetticher story, one not challenged by any journalist, including me, when Budd told it. But it's not true.

Randolph Scott (left) perfected the strong silent Westerner who sets out to do a job and gets it done. Here he plays a bounty hunter out to rope in some prey in the form of James Best in *Ride Lonesome*, another top Budd Boetticher Western.

Kennedy's final shooting scripted, dated August 1958—which is when filming commenced in Lone Pine—ends the same way the picture ends. Why Burt or Pernell Roberts or James Coburn or anyone else involved with the picture didn't question Budd on this fact is unclear. They were probably all being polite. Burt once told me that Budd told the same stories the same way so many times that he could no longer tell truth from fiction. Budd once told me that if Burt said something that contradicted Budd's version, I should believe Burt. Either way, it's not that important because *Ride Lonesome* is a damn fine picture, probably the purest Burt Kennedy script of all the Boetticher-Scotts.

Budd and Burt both said that once Harry Cohn died, Columbia had little use for Harry Joe Brown. The studio heads felt Boetticher could produce and direct the next two films to save them some money and maybe some headaches, though by all accounts Harry Joe was a sweet man who didn't meddle too much. But when he did meddle, well... "While good directors like George Marshall would be having lunch, Harry Joe would go out and put everybody in the wrong costumes and shoot second units," Budd told Sean Axmaker.

> So Randy would come riding over the hill in a red shirt, we'd cut back to the close-up, and he's in black. I didn't want anybody screwing around with those two pictures, so Harry Joe was the producer and he had two things that he could do: He could come on the set and tell me the rushes were great, or he could have a cup of coffee. That wasn't being tough, because I really loved him. Columbia wanted to cut him out completely.... No, I never produced the pictures. Harry Joe did the job but I still made the pictures with Burt and Randy and Harry Joe gave us what we wanted. A producer should help you get the cast, should make suggestions about the script, he should handle the financing so that you get enough of what you need. But we didn't have any official bothering or second unit work during lunch.

Ride Lonesome and *Comanche Station* were made on a two-picture deal under the newly organized Ranown Production Company banner as the new Columbia regime tried to figure out what to do with the Brown-Boetticher-Kennedy-Scott contingent, well aware that Scott's long-term contract with the studio was coming to an end. Budd and Burt recalled the budgets of the last two films as being somewhere around $500,000, and maybe even a bit lower, suggesting a belt-tightening policy instituted as the last vestiges of the old Hollywood studio system began to wash away.

Change was in the air. In the summer of 1958, when *Ride Lonesome* was in production, Republic Pictures shut down for good, and RKO followed suit shortly thereafter. Dore Schary, who succeeded Louis B. Mayer at MGM in 1951, was ousted from that studio in 1957. The studio head of 20th Century–Fox, Darryl Zanuck, disappeared in Europe for a couple of years to chase women and pretend to be happy. With Harry Cohn dead, only Jack Warner survived as the last of the studio moguls, and he would hold on until the middle of 1967, when old age and boredom led him to sell out to Seven Arts. The fact is, the days of the B Western were coming to an end, and the days of the really good B Westerns were therefore in jeopardy.

Ride Lonesome features the film debut of James Coburn. He would next appear in Columbia's *Face of a Fugitive*, a neat little noir Western starring Fred MacMurray, in October 1958. *Ride Lonesome* was released in February 1959 and *Face of a Fugitive* in May of that year. Years later, Coburn had little to say about his work with Boetticher, though the two remained friendly and Coburn vowed to act in one of Budd's films in the 1980s and 1990s *if* he ever got it made. Coburn was one of several Boetticher actors to go on to work for Sam Peckinpah (L.Q. Jones, Lee Marvin, Chill Wills and Don "Red" Barry are some of the others) and the actor always seemed more comfortable talking about Sam rather than Budd. Budd said that director John Sturges, who also cut his directing teeth at Columbia in the 1940s, asked Budd to send him some footage of Coburn from *Ride Lonesome* as the director was considering him for a part in *The Magnificent Seven*. Robert Vaughn said he recommended Coburn to Sturges, but it's still possible Sturges wanted to see the footage.

Lee Van Cleef, Budd said, was either drunk or suffering from hangovers during the shooting of his few sequences, which necessitated cutting some of them short. While driving back home from the shoot following its completion, Van Cleef got involved in a bad car accident that sidetracked his career for some time. All the same, within a decade he became a star, albeit in European Westerns.

James Best, who had already made two films with Budd, signed on for another although he must have known that Budd was expecting him to do his own stunts. And he did. Budd told Best he wanted to hang him, and not a stuntman, in the final sequence. "I want to see pain as you hang," Budd said. Best, in his autobiography, said the rope in question had a steel cable running through it that was attached to a harness that he wore. Best's wife Jobee was on the set, so Best gave her a camera and said, "Take a picture of this. They're going to hang me here. I won't really hang unless the steel cable breaks. If it does break, then you'll have my picture and a good lawsuit."

Budd called, "Action!" and Best acted in desperate pain as his horse rode out from under him. "I kicked and acted as though I was really being hanged," he recalled. "All of a sudden, some of the crew members rushed in, grabbed me and lifted me up. They thought I was really dying. Budd had a fit."

Budd cussed out the crew members and told Best they had to do the scene again. Best said no. Budd said he had to: "I've got to shoot it close enough so that I can recognize your face."

"Well, then," Best replied, "It's $500 if I do it again."

He got the money.

Budd, on how he worked with Burt on reshaping the scripts (to David Schwartz): "Burt would write beautiful scripts. And I would read them and just marvel at what he had done. Then we would be on the set together. We would say, 'Why don't we do this? Why don't we do that?' And I would guess maybe 30 percent of each finished picture was never on paper."

Author, to Budd Boetticher: "There's always an abandoned way station somewhere."

Budd: "Yeah, you have to have some place out there where they can stop and have a cup of coffee."

Film Daily (February 10, 1959): "Competent acting all around, some good humor, fine direction by Budd Boetticher... [F]act is the ending is quite moving."

Variety (February 4, 1959): "Another good western from the Ranown Productions team of Randolph Scott and Harry Joe Brown.... [Boetticher] had a tough, honest screenplay by Burt Kennedy, and he has given it perception and tension.... Boetticher and his cast handle it well, only occasionally over-reaching in brief scenes where Miss Steele's sex seems stressed beyond reason."

One reviewer took time out to complain that it would have made for better clarity had the film not involved a gang of five chasing another gang of five on horseback, "as occasionally in the long shots it is difficult to tell which group is which." In re-watching the film after reading this review, I must admit he has a point.

The American Film Institute Catalog reports that both *Ride Lonesome* and *Comanche Station* were shot in 12 days, a reflection of Columbia's cost-cutting measures in the waning days of the studio system and Hollywood's lack of faith in the Western.

Westbound (Warner Bros., 72 minutes, released in March 1959) Director: Budd Boetticher. Producer: Henry Blanke. Screenplay: Berne Giler. Story: Giler and Albert Shelby. Cinematographer: J. Peverell Marley. With Randolph Scott (John Hayes), Virginia Mayo (Norma Putnam), Karen Steele (Jeannie Miller), Michael Dante (Rod Miller), Andrew Duggan (Clay Putnam), Michael Pate (Mace), Wally Brown (Stubby), John Day (Russ) and Walter Barnes (Willis)

Synopsis: Union officer John Hayes goes undercover to stop the South from preventing the North from delivering gold to the east to fight the Civil War. No one goes west.

It's a challenge to get enthused about *Westbound*, a convoluted oater that plays out like a mid–1930s Republic B. In fact, the plot owes something to Warner Bros.' epic *Virginia City*, which starred Scott as a Southerner trying to move a gold shipment from the west to the east in an effort to finance the Confederacy's struggle.

Westbound demonstrates how lost at sea Boetticher could become when left with a drifting script and a not particularly exciting support staff. Boetticher once said of the Warner Bros. Scott Westerns, "Black horse, black hat, black chin strap. Crap!" And yet here he was making the same sort of nonsense to help Scott out of a jam.

An introvert by nature, Scott came west on a whim in the late 1920s. By 1932, he had secured a contract with Paramount to appear in a slate of Zane Grey–like B Westerns. He soon established himself as a Western star, but the next decade was a frustrating mix of good Westerns, bad Westerns, good non–Westerns, bad non–Westerns, a few almost-great pictures and a few embarrassments. If Scott never gained the heft of a John Wayne or Clark Gable or James Cagney, he nonetheless held his own in the box office race, never coming in first or even second at the finish line but still making a show and maintaining popularity around the world. By the late 1940s, he had teamed with both producer Harry Joe Brown (for a series of Westerns co-produced with Columbia) and producer Nat Holt (for a series of Westerns Holt produced for RKO and 20th Century–Fox) and began making solid B+ oaters on budgets averaging about $750,000. "I have always been a fatalist about my career," Scott once said. "What was to be, was to be."

He used the money he made from his films to invest in uranium, oil wells and real estate, and by the time Budd Boetticher and Burt Kennedy started working with him, the only thing keeping Scott in pictures was his enjoyment at doing so little work. (Think about it: even at three pictures a year with each movie averaging about 18 days to make, Scott probably didn't put in three months of work each year.) Between 1949 and 1955, Scott appeared in ten Westerns for Warner Bros., films that were generally budgeted in the $600,000–$950,000 range.

But Scott was tired of appearing in the lesser Warner Bros. offerings. There wasn't much he could do about it. He had signed two amendments to his original contract—one in 1952 and one in 1954—that earned him more money ($12,500 per week with a guarantee of ten weeks salary per picture) and increased the number of projects he owed the studio.

By Budd's recollection, which is validated by documents in the Warner Bros. archives, Scott called him one night in the summer of 1957 to say that he still owed Warner Bros. another movie and the studio would not release him to make Columbia's *Buchanan Rides Alone* until he fulfilled the contract.

"Oh, shit," was Boetticher's response.

The director drove over to Warner Bros. to talk to producer Henry Blanke. Budd said he wanted to direct the picture. Blanke told him they could not afford his salary, which at that time was in the $30,000 to $35,000 range.

"Do you have two and a half dollars?" Budd asked Blanke. The studio signed Budd—probably to keep Scott happy and increase the quality of the production—for $25,000.

The studio gave *Westbound* a $700,000 budget and a four-week shooting schedule in September 1957. The studio heads probably figured that Boetticher and Scott were working magic with that kind of schedule and budget over at Columbia, so why not let them mirror those efforts on Scott's home lot? What the studio didn't calculate into the equation was the input of writer Burt Kennedy and producer Harry Joe Brown. Without their creative juices flowing around the production, *Westbound* was left to move along at a trot. "As far as my films with Randolph Scott are concerned," Budd wrote in his autobiography, "I have never included *Westbound*, which in my opinion could have continued right into the Pacific Ocean.... I did have the opportunity to make the film a little better."

Well, maybe a little. Some critics may say that the picture is not as bad as many people (like myself) claim it is. One expects more from both Boetticher and Scott, and again the script plays up how limited both men were when it came to reaching full potential when they didn't have a strong storyline to carry forward. Scott looks tired and doesn't seem nearly as committed to the material as he was to the work he did for his own company. Film historian Jon Tuska said that Harry Joe Brown told him that Brown's advice to Scott was, "Do a nice job for Warners, but save your best for us."

Scott pulls off the very rare line of charm and humor here and there, but he's also rather embarrassingly reduced to standing still and holding his coattails up in the air, sort of like a little girl conducting a bow following a recital of some sorts, while bad guy Michael Pate cleanly blows Scott's holster and gun off his hip. Pate is the sort of one-note miscreant who needs a good beating or shooting to set things right, but all we get in the end is Scott taking careful aim and blowing Pate out of the saddle as the latter tries to scram out of a street gun battle. It's a very unsatisfying conclusion to a mostly unsatisfying film. In fact, the most hero-like thing Scott pulls off in the first ten minutes of *Westbound* is to force a surly station manager to eat a piece of heavily salted pie!

Here and there, Budd and company manage a few nice moments, as when Karen Steele joyously hugs her long-departed soldier husband and, midway through the embrace, realizes he has lost an arm in the fighting. And Scott and Michael Dante partake in a rain-swept raid on a line cabin to steal back horses that were stolen from them in a well-orchestrated sequence in which Scott is clearly doing his own stunts. But these moments are akin to finding two good apples in a barrel of rotten ones. You're just kind of relieved that the lot wasn't all bad.

Budd tried to inject some excitement into the script, actor Michael Dante said. A scene where Scott's character teaches the one-armed Dante character to handle a Winchester was an unexpected challenge, Dante recalled. He said once he read the script, he asked Budd to arrange with the studio prop department to let Dante take a prop Winchester home for the weekend to practice the one-armed lever-action draw and firing of the gun. Dante, a former baseball player, had the grace and athleticism needed for such a stunt.

But when he arrived on the set the following Monday, he discovered that Scott, for all his dignity in the saddle, couldn't do the same trick easily. "I had to flip-flop—I had to teach Randy how to do it," Dante recalled with a laugh. He continued:

> Randy didn't have the weekend to work on it and if you don't have the time and coordination of it down perfectly, it will cut you up. We did one take, two takes, three takes—I think 32 takes in all. Randy was bleeding. They had to put heavy makeup on his hands so you couldn't see the blood. It was awful. He was a coordinated man but not as athletic as I was. They came down from central office to ask what was going on. "You're shooting all day and you haven't even gotten one shot in the can," they told Budd. Budd was impressed with my work because it added to

Rare behind-the-scenes shot of stars Virginia Mayo, Michael Dante and Randolph Scott relaxing between scenes of *Westbound* (courtesy Michael Dante).

the scene as written, so he told them, "We either get this shot or you get another director." And they backed off. We finally got the scene around four in the afternoon. I think it gave my character more self-esteem and confidence and added to the scene.

Dante recalled Steele as cooperative, pleasant to work with and a good actress. Steele is a little more relaxed here and develops a nice rapport with Dante, an actor who projects an honest sincerity to his role as a vet trying to regain his manhood by helping Scott run a stage line. Virginia Mayo, fulfilling one last contractual obligation to Warners, has about ten minutes of screen footage as the mopey wife of bad guy Andrew Duggan. She looks in pain, and by her own account, Budd's account and studio records, she was in pain, suffering from an abscessed tooth that caused her to miss some workdays. "It wasn't a good part," Mayo told me. "I did the picture, but the fact is, I wasn't in the picture at all. Karen Steele was the director's girlfriend and it was not my picture. Scott was very courteous and mannered, but I didn't get to know him at all…. I think this was his last picture for [Warner Bros.] too." Mayo dismissed the film with similar comments in less than a paragraph in her autobiography *The Best Years of My Life*.

Budd said when Mayo called in sick one Monday morning, he decided to get creative with a shot that involved Dante's one-armed war vet trying to tame a wild horse. First he told Steele to put on a period nightdress but discard her underclothes. "No brassiere, no panties, no nothing," Boetticher said. Then he shot a scene of her rising from her bed and heading outdoors to investigate the commotion with the horse.

Then Budd said, "I put the camera on a dolly and I went all the way down the porch and her knockers are going like this [*Budd demonstrated breasts bobbing up and down*] and it's not censorable, you can't see a thing, but it's really sexy." He's right, it's sexy, and you can start convincing yourself that you can see underneath the white cotton nightie and it sure looks like Steele's got nothing else on under it. But the scene does not take place on a porch—Steele just gets out of bed, goes to the door and walks out into the yard where Dante is grappling with the horse.

The next day, Mayo came to work and apologized. Budd told her not to worry; that he got some great stuff in the can, and wouldn't she like to see it? She said yes. So he showed her the scene and Mayo—a pretty sexy dame and much better actress than Steele—"was never late again." (Note: I for one would have liked to see Mayo play the Steele part in *Ride Lonesome*.)

Dante said he felt none of this animosity and that the atmosphere on the set was warm. "There was no temperament among the cast or the crew that I recall. It was a happy family. That was Budd's doing." Pate, in a letter he wrote to me in the mid–1990s, echoed that sentiment, saying it was all fun and games on the set.

Dante called Budd "the young John Ford of the Western genre" and said he was his favorite director because of his passionate approach to the material and ability to make action scenes come alive. And Boetticher, Dante said, "was by far the greatest storyteller I ever met. He had more interesting stories to tell in between shots than anyone I've ever encountered."

Dante said Budd's direction took Scott

> to another level of his work. It gave him a rugged, two-fisted kind of image against the heavies who played opposite him in all those films. He and Budd worked well together. You hardly saw the process. There was no interference, no difficulty, it was just smooth as silk. Randy looked great in the saddle. He had the right voice and the right quality of the Western hero—and that Southern twang. He didn't have to act it. The Western was his baby.

Burt Kennedy also tried to help *Westbound*—again, like Budd, "just a bit." In an interview, he told me,

> After Budd finished *Westbound*, Steve Trilling, hatchet man at Warners, called me up at Warners and said, "Come on down to projection room number two."
>
> I went down and he shows me a rough cut of *Westbound*. When it was over, he sat there silently. Then he said, "Why did you call the town Julesburg?"
>
> I said, "I didn't call it anything. I didn't write this."

He said, "You didn't?"

"You see, the end of the original film has a gunfight in town with all the people standing behind Randy, backing him up. But there's no reason for them to be there because earlier on, they had said to him, "If you cause any trouble, we won't back you." And then at the end, they back Randy up even though they told him they wouldn't.

So Trilling said to me, "What am I going to do?" So I worked on it for a bit and wrote an extra scene where the town doctor says they will help Scott after the Michael Dante character is killed. They took my scene and shot it in about an hour. Now when Randy turns around and all those guys are behind him, it makes sense."

It does make sense, but two extra scripted bits and an hour of extra filming still can't help *Westbound* rise above its barely passable rating. The two extra scenes, involving an unbilled Walter Reed as the doctor, do appear to have been shot separately as an afterthought. Trilling probably asked Budd about the name Julesburg because some actors in the cast unfortunately pronounce it Jewsburg.

Budd did provide a nice death scene for a 30-year-old stagecoach that had been on the Warner lot since the days of silent movies. Infested with termites, it was sent rolling over a big cliff for one of the better action scenes in the film. During shooting, one of its wheels came off and nearly ran into Steele, who escaped harm.

Columbia managed to get *Ride Lonesome* into theaters by February 1959, about six months after that film wrapped. But for some reason, Warner Bros. kept *Westbound* on the shelf for some 18 months, releasing it in March 1959, right after *Ride Lonesome*. Perhaps the studio had no faith in the finished project and figured if it had any chance, it would be by riding the coattails of the much superior *Ride Lonesome*.

Boxoffice (March 3, 1959) said of Scott, "Like Tennyson's poetic brook, square-jawed Randolph Scott will apparently go on forever—making Westerns, that is.... [*Westbound*] should prove satisfactory to his fans."

Variety (March 25, 1959) noted, "*Westbound* is bound for the bevy of action houses corralled these many years by its star, Randolph Scott." *The Hollywood Reporter* (March 20, 1959) inaccurately called the film an "actionful shoot-em-up Western" but accurately reported that the screenplay was "not up to the standards one expects from a Henry Blanke Production. Fortunately the acting is better than the writing."

Westbound didn't end Scott's contractual obligations to Warner Bros. He still owed the studio another film, but on December 31, 1959, the studio paid him $110,000 *not* to make that final film on his contract. The actor happily agreed to the deal.

Financially, *Westbound* made a little money for the studio. Its final cost was about $722,000 and it earned some $700,000 in foreign sales, nearly breaking even just in that market. In America, however, it brought in a light $544,000, suggesting that audiences were losing interest in run-of-the-mill B Westerns.

Thankfully, the Boetticher-Kennedy-Brown-Scott team was about to make a stop at the beautiful *Comanche Station*.

Comanche Station (A Ranown Production, 74 minutes, released by Columbia in January 1960) Producer-Director: Budd Boetticher. Executive Producer: Harry Joe Brown. Screenplay: Burt Kennedy. Cinematographer: Charles Lawton. With Randolph Scott (Jeff Cody), Claude Akins (Ben Lane), Nancy Gates (Mrs. Lowe), Skip Homeier (Frank), Richard Rust (Dobie), Rand Brooks (Station Man) and Dyke Johnson (Mr. Lowe).

Synopsis: Ex–Army officer Jefferson Cody (Scott) searches the southwest desert for his wife, who was abducted by Comanches ten years back. A trio of human jackals and a woman complicate matters.

> Full Shot: Jeff Cody and his animals ride lonesome through a sea of empty heading for Comanche country as we:
> FADE OUT
> THE END

So ends Burt Kennedy's compact script for the last Boetticher-Scott-Kennedy-Brown production, shot in the late summer of 1959 and released early the following year. In its way, it is the most hopeful of the series, and in some ways, it is the saddest. It is the story of a man who is searching for something he will likely never find. The man has no other purpose, no visible means of financial support, and not much of a backstory other than he was an officer at Fort McKavett (Texas) and his wife was taken by the Comanches. He is hard and tired and not prone to much emotion or exposition, and when he finds he has traded goods for the wrong woman (Mrs. Lowe, played by the fine actress Nancy Gates in her last film), he realizes he has no choice but to put aside his own mission to save her.

Naturally the hostile desert terrain throws a monkey wrench into the works—or in this case three monkey wrenches when a trio of no-goodniks led by Ben Lane (Claude Akins) show up. They want the woman for themselves because of the $5000 bounty her husband has offered to get her back dead or alive.

Kennedy borrows a lot from his *Seven Men from Now* script, but it doesn't seem to hurt *Comanche Station* one bit. He also makes one of his bad men, Dobie (Richard Rust), a sensitive kid who wants to do the right thing but doesn't know how to go about it. And he injects Mrs. Lowe with a dignity and vulnerability.

Her character is even more dignified in the script. The film diminishes her stature somewhat by having Scott's Cody character toss her into a water trough at the start of an Indian raid; the ensuing slapstick reaction—offset somewhat by the joy of seeing the well-built Gates in what amounts to a wet T-shirt—brings her down a notch or two from the more sober-sided and anxious woman Kennedy created on the page. The trough bit was added during production. In the script, the Scott character simply shoves her behind the trough when the shooting starts.

A comparison of the script to the finished product once again calls attention to how much influence Budd had once he got the film on its feet in the remote mountains of Lone Pine, far from the prying eyes of studio executives. The script calls for Mrs. Lowe to take a nude swim and let the audience see as "much as convention will allow." Budd wisely altered that so that we catch her after the swim, buttoning up her clothes. An exciting sequence in which Cody and Lane team to fend off attacking Comanche on horseback is laid out in relatively straightforward and frankly boring detail in the script: The two men just hide behind rocks and fire away, scaring off their attackers. But Budd added some marvelous little touches, with Cody picking up a saddle and throwing it at one Comanche, knocking him off his horse, and then using that fallen Comanche's body to shield himself from incoming arrows. None of that business is in the script and it highlights Boetticher's inventive on-the-set contribution.

Other changes are minor but notable. The script does not include a sequence we see in the film in which Cody, astride his horse, faces off against Lane and Doby and pretty much lets them know he's on to their planned ambush; it's a beauty of a scene that was dreamed up on the spot. A dog hanging around the station in Kennedy's script (and which disappears without any explanation as the humans ride away from the station without it) was dropped. On the other hand, in the script Mrs. Lowe does not have a child, and in the movie she does, and in my view the little kid is annoying and unnecessary.

In his excellent 1976 book *They Went Thataway,* James Horwitz says of Scott as an actor and the movies he made with Boetticher:

> Randolph Scott…always serious and straight-faced, drawling that Virginia drawl, a kind of remoteness in his manner, an icy-coldness in his tone. In many ways the Lonesome Cowboy, but alone with himself, you cannot help feeling, because he prefers the company…but the most outstanding series of Westerns he ever made was the Ranown Cycle that he starred in and produced with Harry Joe Brown… [T]hey were tight, serious and remarkable. All directed by Budd Boetticher. All dealing essentially with the Lone Cowboy, whose strength is in his aloneness, but who usually carries with him dark memories of disastrous involvements. There is usually regret and bitterness that he feels he must revenge or answer to himself for, or he is confronted, as he goes about his own business, with new involvements he cannot avoid.

That description really fits *Comanche Station* and in no other Boetticher film does Scott so fully embody the Lonesome Cowboy who doesn't mind being so alone. The final shot, of Scott's Cody once again taking to the rocky hills to chase an elusive dream, provides a fitting ending to a wonderful series of pictures that none of the participants could top—though Scott did when he returned to the movies one more time for Sam Peckinpah in *Ride the High Country* (1962).

Burt Kennedy created a memorable and sympathetic character in the part of Dobie, played by Richard Rust. He can read (which surprises his illiterate friends), he questions decisions and he yearns to amount to something. "Man does one thing in his life—one thing he can look back on, go proud," he tells his saddle pal Frank at one point. Arguing that the Code of the West dictates that a man—even a bad one—shouldn't shoot a woman, he tells Frank, "My folks, they brought me up to treat a woman kind. You know, 'yes ma'am,' 'no, ma'am,' open doors, get up'n give 'em my chair...not go killin' 'em." His ambivalent nature costs him his life late in the film, when Lane turns on him and puts a neat bullet hole in his back. "That's probably a tremendous comment on my own attitude toward life," Boetticher told Eric Sherman and Martin Rubin for *The Director's Event: Interviews with Five American Film-Makers*. "I haven't time for wavering. I haven't time for wishy-washy producers and writers…. I hate insecurity. Although I never thought of it before, I probably don't like those middle-of-the-road characters in my films, so I get rid of them."

Comanche Station does have a few problems. Somebody gussied Gates up with a nice hairdo and lots of lipstick, which glamorizes her character and takes away from the reality of the situation. The Comanches are inexplicably sporting Mohawk-style haircuts. As Richard Rust's Dobie rides away, seconds before he is to be shot in the back, we see the bullet hole already laid out in the back of his shirt.

Randolph Scott (center) leads the ensemble of the last Budd Boetticher-Burt Kennedy-Randolph Scott film, *Comanche Station*, out of danger. That is, until the final gun duel.

Now why do the bad guys always try to outgun Randolph Scott? Here Scott puts villain Claude Akins in his place in *Comanche Station*.

And though I like Skip Homeier, at 30 years of age he already seemed too old for the role of Frank, who may be a bit more brutal than Dobie but who is, nonetheless, still a young innocent. Homeier was an underused actor who never attained stardom and who was too-often cast in surly "punk gunman" roles. He's a joy to watch in a James Garner–type comic role in 1956's *Thunder Over Arizona* (a so-so film) and in many B or C movie projects he projected a deep introspection that went far beyond their requirements. He even displayed flashes of comic potential in something as silly as *The Ghost and Mr. Chicken* (1966); *Chicken* co-star Joan Staley told me he was in good humor and often clowning around on the set behind the scenes. It's too bad no director—including Boetticher—captured these inner talents. He worked mostly in television in the 1960s and 1970s and pretty much disappeared from the business by the early 1980s, when he was still in his early 50s. He eschewed all interviews in the ensuing years and by some accounts developed a bitter attitude about his career. He died in the summer of 2017, pushing 90.

Kennedy said he was on the set of *Comanche Station* "very little" and Gates said that in Lone Pine, she never once saw Harry Joe Brown—once again reduced to playing the role of executive producer and staying out of Budd's way. So this may have been Budd's purest Randolph Scott film in that, with the screenwriter and producer out of his hair, he wielded more control than he did on the previous entries. Still, many Western film historians believe Burt—and Harry Joe Brown for that matter—deserve more credit than Budd gave them in terms of the quality of these pictures. "What the Scott Westerns directed by

Budd had that they didn't have with [Andre] de Toth or [Bruce] Humberstone directing comes to this—Burt Kennedy," the late Jon Tuska said. "To an amazing degree, in retrospect, the Scott character was reinvented in the Kennedy scripts and Scott was inspired because he could see how the added depth had a powerful effect on him and on his screen work." Comparing the films Scott made with Boetticher to the six Westerns he made with Andre de Toth earlier in the 1950s, Tuska said, "Neither de Toth nor Boetticher was particularly concerned with directing Randolph Scott. They pretty much left him alone to do it himself."

Nonetheless, Tuska said that Scott "thought very highly of Budd Boetticher as a director, and he very much liked the characters that Burt would create for him to play.... Scott was as concerned about the character he played in these films as John Wayne was about the image of John Wayne in his films."

Budd Boetticher, on the Randolph Scott character, to Eric Sherman and Martin Rubin:

> Yeah, I think that Randy exemplifies a figure that we have always known as the straight-line hero. You see, he never makes mistakes. However, in the pictures we made together, for example *Comanche Station*, I let you see in his eyes that maybe he thinks Nancy Gates is pretty cute, even though he never takes her to bed. I didn't want him to be so inhuman that it looks like he never thinks about it. Then he's not a man at all.... I think Randy might have ended up with most of the leading ladies if they were available. Because if you don't have that going for you, you're a pretty stuffy guy. I thought the Scott character, before the pictures we made with him, was a pretty stuffy guy.

Nancy Gates to the author:

> Budd was the best. He had the greatest sense of humor and he would let me do anything. I had my first home-movie camera with me and he let me get on the crane of the camera truck and ride all over the place and film behind-the-scenes shots. He said I was the only one on schedule, as a matter of fact. For the most part he was very easygoing. Of course if you did something one way he'd sometimes say, "Give me a little more" or "Try this instead."
>
> Randy Scott—we both belonged to the same country club at the time—I had met him before. He was a great guy. Everybody liked Randy. He loved his horses. He was great to work with.... As an actor, he knew what he was doing—always. He'd been around a long time.... You meet some people in the business who aren't nice but Randy wasn't one of them. He was, I think, more interested in stocks and bonds. He was always reading *The Wall Street Journal* on the set. He was just a great guy. Always very quiet—he never made you die laughing. He was just himself. He was great. I loved him.

Rand Brooks to the author:

> I respected Randy tremendously. He was an "old school" gentleman. He did some straight parts very well. The little scene I had in *Comanche Station* was nothing, but I was very comfortable working with him. I felt if I were living that part, he was living his.... Randy is one of those people who it is very hard to say anything bad about him. No one could. He was a perfect gentleman. His voice was wonderful. The most perfect English in the world is spoken in Dublin, Ireland, and the second most perfect is spoken in Virginia.
>
> Budd had the ability to keep everybody alive and happy. He was his own worst enemy. He damaged his career through some of his actions and his desire to do something different than anyone else—like the story of Carlos Arruza. Budd was not a phony but he was a little bit bigger than life. He had many detractors, some of whom were jealous. I think some of them are right. He did a few things, possibly, that are over the line but he was a gutsy and imaginative man who didn't end up too well, but he was fighting right up to the end.

Harry Joe Brown, Jr. to the author: "I remember my father thinking that the violence that was in those films was an important thing. He felt people should see it.... He thought the audience would like the excitement."

Budd Boetticher (to the author, about Nancy Gates and Richard Rust):

> I liked Nancy Gates as much as anybody I worked with. Of course I was in love at one time with Julie Adams, but not counting that, my two favorite ladies were Nancy Gates and Maureen O'Hara. Great ladies.
>
> Richard Rust] never went anywhere.... I was in the Pantages Theater sitting alone, watching a movie, and a kid came in with a cowboy hat on and sat right in front of me and didn't take his hat off and I was trying to see the picture. I

thought, "Jesus, here's a kid who has no class." And I tapped him on the shoulder and it was Richard Rust. So obviously that's what happened to him. He was a horse's ass. But he was good. Very good.

No one involved with the film seemed to know that it would be the last one. Conversely, no one seemed to expect that there would be another one. Scott's deal with Columbia had come to an end, particularly with Harry Cohn dead, and Budd was set on heading to Mexico to start work on his Carlos Aruzza film. Kennedy wrote another script that fits right into the Ranown cycle, *Six Black Horses*, and set up a deal to direct Richard Widmark and Anthony Quinn in it for Universal. But the studio paid him an extra $5000 *not* to direct it. Audie Murphy and Dan Duryea played the leads, and it turned out to be a respectable B picture for director Harry Keller.

Still, Budd claimed he didn't know *Comanche Station* would be the last one with Scott. "I think it had a lot more to do with the price," he said, noting that $500,000 Westerns were finding it difficult to break even in a culture dominated by television, gimmicks and an ever-changing Hollywood.

According to Burt Kennedy, "Every year a hundred [medium-budget Westerns] would be made, and you can count on your hand the number of great ones. So if you were under contract, you got stuck in one. They were all George Montgomerys.... There were so many of them. You couldn't turn on your TV set without seeing one."

Kennedy has a point. In 1955—a year after the last of the B-series Western films featuring the likes of Rex Allen and Wild Bill Elliott—some 63 Westerns were in release. In 1956, there were 75 and in 1957, there were close to 70. In 1958, there were over 55 and in 1959, close to 40. In 1960, the year *Comanche Station* was released, there were a mere 24, and in 1961, 21. By 1962 and 1963, just a dozen American Westerns were finding their way out to cinemas. The glory years were over. Plus, Kennedy said, Randolph Scott "was tired of the business. He'd been around all those years and never got any recognition."

Adding to the problem, according to Jon Tuska, was the fact that the new Columbia executives thought the productions all looked the same. And they were not happy with the 50–50 deal that Scott and Brown had made with the studio in which they shared both costs and profits, thus cutting into potential box office riches for the studio.

And the times were a-changing. The 1960s would usher in civil unrest, an unpopular war, racial strife, X-rated movies and heroes who didn't act like heroes and usually didn't dress like cowboys. Add the sudden popularity of the violent, often nonsensical spaghetti Western, and you have a recipe for a funeral for the good ol' American Western.

In his *Comanche Station* review, the critic for the *Motion Picture Herald* (March 12, 1960) wrote that Brown and Boetticher "know the

Director Budd Boetticher and actress Nancy Gates—one of his favorites—on the last Budd Boetticher-Randolph Scott outing, *Comanche Station* (1960). It had been a good run (Photofest).

business of Western film backwards, frontward and down the line." *The Monthly Film Bulletin*: "The situation does not develop with the tension it promises, and a lot of reflective explaining is only broken by the bouts of conventional action, in themselves efficiently staged."

Variety (February 24, 1960): "The characters are vivid and Boetticher's direction of his cast keeps interest high." The picture, the reviewer aptly noted, was "likely to slip out unheralded."

Harry Joe Brown's days as a producer were nearing an end. He produced two more pictures in the 1960s, neither of which was very good, before retiring. He died in 1972 at the age of 81.

Burt Kennedy got the opportunity to direct a not-very-good Western called *The Canadians* (1961) for 20th Century–Fox. Budd said Burt called him one night and asked for some advice, and Budd said, "Just don't change a word of your screenplay." Burt probably shouldn't have listened, since *The Canadians* is a dry affair with traces of familiar dialogue from his previous Western films. He moved into television to gain more directing experience, and returned to write and/or direct a few better-than-average films for a dying MGM in the mid–1960s: *The Rounders*, *Mail Order Bride* and *The Money Trap*. Burt hit his peak as a director in the late 1960s, making, in fairly quick succession, the fun John Wayne-Kirk Douglas film *The War Wagon*, the hard-hitting Western drama *Welcome to Hard Times* and the comedy hit *Support Your Local Sheriff*.

But just as a turn into the 1960s set Budd Boetticher's career off-track, the 1970s derailed Burt Kennedy. He worked, to be sure, mostly as a director, sometimes as a producer or writer, for another 20 years, but for the most part the output is disappointing. *Dirty Dingus McGee*, *Hannie Caulder*, *The Train Robbers* and *Support Your Local Gunfighter* are not good films, and most of his television films are watchable and forgettable. (Burt jokingly called them "mortgages of the week," admitting he did them for the money.) But he remained a friendly and upbeat character, rarely displaying bitterness over his life or career, and to the end he was working on various projects, including a stage play.

In 1997, Boulevard Books published Burt's autobiography *Hollywood Trail Boss: Behind the Scenes of the Wild, Wild Western*, which is, like his career, uneven. It does include very amusing anecdotes about some of the people he worked with. He closed the book with, "There was an old saying in Vaudeville: 'When your act is over, be sure you don't get hit on the head when the curtain is coming down.' My act is over, so I'll get off before I get hit in the head or somebody ties me to a horse-truck. That's a wrap."

So it was. Burt Kennedy died less than five years later, in February 2001, about nine months before Budd Boetticher passed away.

And as for Budd, he was at the top of his creative game in 1960 and he just didn't give a damn. John Wayne wanted him to direct *The Comancheros* for 20th Century–Fox, and several sources, including Budd and Burt Kennedy, say that because of Randolph Scott, Budd was in the running to direct *Ride the High Country* for MGM in 1961. But he didn't pursue either option, instead disappearing into Mexico for most of the 1960s, chasing a crazy dream and earning the label of "nutcase" by the time he re-emerged in the late 1960s.

By that time, his Hollywood was long gone. And so was his career.

The Rise and Fall of Legs Diamond (A United States Production, 100 minutes, released through Warner Bros. in February 1960) Director: Budd Boetticher. Producer: Milton Sperling. Screenplay: Joseph Landon. Cinematographer: Lucien Ballard. With Ray Danton (Legs Diamond), Karen Steele (Alice Diamond), Elaine Stewart (Monica), Jesse White (Leon Bremer), Simon Oakland (Lt. Moody), Robert Lowery (Arnold Rothstein), Judson Pratt (Fats Walsh), Warren Oates (Eddie Diamond), Gordon Jones (Sgt. Cassidy), Frank deKova (Chairman) and Dyan Cannon (Dixie)

Synopsis: As the title implies, this is the so-called "real-life" up-and-down tale of the notorious Depression-era gangster Legs Diamond.

"This is the way it happened," the opening title card of *The Rise and Fall of Legs Diamond* reads. Not exactly.

Irish-American Jack "Legs" Diamond was born in Philadelphia in 1897 and, following the death of his father in 1913, drifted into crime. He rose in the ranks of New York City's criminal underworld, rubbing shoulder holsters with the likes of Lucky Luciano and Dutch Schultz. Married to the somewhat dowdy and slightly overweight Alice Schiffer, he maintained a string of mistresses, including then-famed showgirl Kiki Roberts. (Google her for a visceral kick.) Diamond survived about five shootings in which his body served as a handy receptacle for bullets, and he quickly developed a reputation for being the bad guy no one could kill. His downfall, by all accounts, began when he started stealing other gangs' liquor shipments, including some of rival gangster Owen "The Killer" Madden's. (Madden was a crony of George Raft's. In 1961, Danton played Raft in a cheap Allied Artists movie biopic.)

After surviving various legal attempts to put him behind bars, Diamond went celebrating in a town in upstate New York in December 1931. Two men entered his room and shot his head to pieces. Someone shot and killed his widow a couple of years later. No one knows who did the dirty deeds, though some fingers point to rival gangsters and others point to the local political machine, which may have hired police officers to do their dirty work.

Photos depicting Diamond show a dapperly dressed sourpuss who looks like an out-of-work character actor. Boetticher cast handsome Danton, a Jewish-American New Yorker who was, at least, about the same age as the real-life Diamond. Boetticher always intimated that he cast Danton as a favor to Julie Adams—who Budd often said he was in love with—as their marriage was hurting and Danton was getting frustrated with a stagnating career.

According to Budd, he ran into Danton at the MCA agency and the two went to the Hamburger Heaven restaurant to discuss the role. He said Ray asked Budd if had slept with Julie. Boetticher's response would not have satisfied any man: "You go home and you ask Julie if that's true and if she says no, believe her, and if she says yes, believe her."

Danton told a different story to a *Los Angeles Examiner* reporter (March 27, 1960): He said neither Budd or producer Milton Sperling paid him any attention. "My friends in casting finally got a test for me," he said.

Meanwhile, Karen Steele, who was still involved in a love affair with Boetticher, approached him to say that if he didn't cast her as Diamond's mistress-turned-wife Alice, she would never sleep with him again. Budd claims he shot some audition footage of her and showed it to Jack Warner, who, enamored of Steele's breasts ("Are those things real?") approved. Budd later said, "So we made the picture and [Danton and Steele] were great and they hated each other. They'd be screaming at each other. The best performances of their lives."

Budd filled in the rest of the cast with an interesting array of up-and-comers including Dyan Cannon as Southern moll Dixie and Warren Oates as Diamond's tubercular brother Eddie, plus some veterans including Gordon Jones and Robert Lowery. Jesse White, later to gain television commercial fame as the Maytag repairman, turns in a sensitive portrayal of a rival gangster who gives in to Diamond's violent demands. Elaine Stewart, who always offered up a pinch of pulchritude, does so again here as the mistress of Arnold Rothstein (Lowery).

In terms of entertainment, *The Rise and Fall of Legs Diamond* mostly succeeds. The picture does not waste time in introducing us to Legs and his brother as they plot an intricately timed heist of a jewelry store with the unwitting help of Alice. Soon Legs is behind bars, and he only returns to a life of crime—in the movie—because his sickly brother pushes him into it.

No one quite knows how Diamond got the nickname "Legs" though the two big theories are (1) he was a great dancer, and (2) he moved fast in escaping both the police and the graveyard. In the film, Rothstein impulsively nicknames him "Legs" though no reason is given.

Nor is much reason given to Legs' turning on the people who supported and loved him, including Eddie and Alice. It's even hard to figure out just what Legs does for a criminal living aside from steal from other bad people and shoot a lot of folks. In the film, Legs survives two shootings and kills seven or eight people. "The bullet hasn't been made that can kill me," he tells one doctor operating on his wounds.

What's catchy about Boetticher's version of the Legs Diamond story is that it is the first and only time he made one of his villains the leading man. Imagine Lee Marvin or Richard Boone carrying a Boetticher picture not as the hero, but as the bad guy, and you get the idea.

There are scripting challenges, and Budd knew it. He later said he knew he had problems when the initial script, set to be written by Philip Yordan, didn't arrive until way past the deadline. When Budd read it, he recalled, "I couldn't believe it. It was as if three different people had written it, and none of them was Phil Yordan. Yordan had had a kind of script factory going for a while, fronting for guys during the blacklist, and I guess old habits die hard."

But Budd wished to make his own *Triumph of the Will*, as he told many an interviewer. For Wheeler Winston Dixon ("Budd Boetticher: The Last Interview"), he said,

> The greatest motion picture I ever saw was made by a woman, Leni Riefenstahl, *Triumph of the Will*, about one of the most despicable men of all time, Adolf Hitler. So I wanted to make a picture about a miserable, no good son of a bitch that when you walk out of the theater you say, "God, wasn't he great!" And then you take two steps and you say, 'Wait a minute, he was a miserable son of a bitch."

But neither Boetticher's direction nor a screenplay credited to Joseph Landon can make Legs Diamond an empathetic character for long. And though Danton gets a couple of great moments in which he conveys the lonely desperation of a man who has no one to turn

Ray Danton never made it as a star, but he was perfect as the title character in Boetticher's *The Rise and Fall of Legs Diamond*.

to, it's mostly a matter of style over substance. The character nuance is missing from the script, and that's not Danton's fault: Legs' sudden abandonment of his weak-willed and sickly brother makes no sense, and his hard-headed response to a syndicate of criminal Italians seems self-destructive and even suicidal.

Not surprisingly, Boetticher said he played a hand in shaping the story and helped write the script. In preparation for filming, he recalled, he visited bars and restaurants frequented by hoodlums in Detroit, Chicago and New York City. There, men who claimed to have been associates of Diamond's came out of the woodwork to talk to him, but only after first inquiring what sort of film he planned to make about their old pal (or enemy). Boetticher told them, "I don't think that anyone who reached the top, even in gangdom, had to be all bad. He must have had something, even if it was a sadistic sense of humor, but something I can pin a motion picture on." He claims that approach won over the pistol-carrying Doubting Thomases and they came forth with stories "to make Legs a very charming character."

"I made *Legs Diamond* because I had a feeling I could make a gangster picture that was completely different from any other: It had a sense of humor," Boetticher said in another interview. But in the finished film, very little humor comes through. Steele does get a nice bit of comic schtick in an otherwise poignant drunk scene, and Danton conveys a touch of coy charm when trying to seduce the innocent Alice early in the proceedings. But very little else in the film could be construed as amusing. Even a neat sequence wherein a machine-gun–wielding Legs pops out of a restaurant's dumbwaiter is played seriously.

And, in reading various interviews in which Boetticher discusses the film, I have to wonder if he had seen it since 1960. "When he stuck the gun in Dutch Schultz's mouth, that's a horrible thing to do, but we played it for humor. You thought, 'Now isn't that cute?'" Boetticher told Sean Axmaker. But Legs doesn't stick a gun in Dutch Schultz's mouth; he presses the machine-gun against gangster Leon Bremer's forehead. To Boetticher's credit, it's a tense moment.

Even as far back as 1964, just a few years after finishing the film, Boetticher seemed to have trouble remembering his approach to the material, telling Bertrand Tavernier that he decided to make a comedy out of it: "I adopted a comic style and a comic tone, treating tragic scenes in quite a light manner, with gags." That's just not true.

Where the film does work is in the trademark Boetticher style of action scenes, as when Diamond uses a pair of revolvers to shoot down two men who tried to kill him outside of a movie theater, or when a hit man pumps some lead into a wheelchair-bound Eddie. Boetticher and/or Landon also added a wonderfully flashy bit of nonsense at the end, when an unarmed Diamond, aware that two gunmen are about to shoot him down, attempts to bluff them by telling them he is invincible—the first hit man's bullet having missed Legs' head by an inch. It's a great moment with Danton having the time of his life as he plays Diamond as a man with nothing to lose. The two bit players playing the hit men seem genuinely doubtful and scared. Boetticher later said of the ending,

> The nice thing about my deaths in movies was that somebody cared, even the guy who did it. Karen Steele really cared, and when you left the theater with *The Rise and Fall of Legs Diamond*, who was a despicable character, when the lights came on and you pull back in the rain and the thing was over, 90 percent of the audience were crying, "Aw, that poor bastard." Poor bastard, hell! If I made a picture and Eva Braun was the leading lady, I'd make you cry when they kill Hitler, until the lights come on. That's good direction.

Hiring Lucien Ballard as his cinematographer once again was smart. Ballard and Boetticher worked to make the film stock look dated and grainy, so much so, as Boetticher told Eric Sherman and Martin Rubin for *The Director's Event*, "At certain points in the film, it's impossible to tell which is the footage we shot and which is stock from that period. That's exactly what we wanted."

The effect backfired when producer Milton Sperling, watching the rushes, accosted Boetticher on the set. "I thought you said that Lucien Ballard was a great cameraman."

"He's a genius," Budd replied.

"But, good God, this stuff looks like it was shot in 1920," Sperling said. Budd then knew he had struck gold with Ballard.

"We had to go a little Hollywood, which is why I'm not crazy about that film. But we did hit in the newsroom montage that his world had left him," Boetticher said of Diamond. He's right: The cycle of sequences in which Legs, vacationing in Paris with his wife, sees American newsreels (with French narration) depicting the end of New York City Mayor Jimmy Walker, Chicago Mafia head Al Capone and the cycle of Prohibition, is a highlight and neatly encapsulates the beginning of the end for Legs.

Howard Thompson, the *New York Times*' second-string film critic, liked the film. His February 1960 review suggests the audience liked it too:

> A crammed Forty-second Street theatre audibly expressed appreciation yesterday morning, and small wonder. Take the script, rather loosely based on the crime czar's climb from the gutter to power, written by Joseph Landon. Against producer Milton Sperling's handsome background of period décor, Mr. Landon has pinpointed just enough underworld names and actual violence to give the film a ring of authenticity.
>
> However, there is nothing loose about the writing. Nor the crispness of Budd Boetticher's direction. Nor the course of the hero's career, as he rises from a smalltime thief to be the personal bodyguard of Arnold Rothstein, uses the two women who are willing to love him and, finally, meets his doom at the hands of a rival crime syndicate.

Irene Thirer of the *New York Post* wrote (January 28, 1960), "Budd Boetticher's direction is swift indeed; sordid to the gory core... [This is] hardly family entertainment. ... [Steele] does a capable job as the distraught, unhappy Alice."

Hazel Flynn of the *Beverly Hills Citizen* (March 23, 1960) found it to be "the most brutal film of its type yet encountered…. I naturally do not recommend it for any except those with strong extra innards." Philip K. Scheuer in the *Los Angeles Times* (January 31, 1960) wrote, "In the last rat race, we realize, even Legs had feet of clay." He gave Steele a good review, saying she "rises gradually to a real poignancy, rare in such a melodrama."

The *Los Angeles Mirror News* (March 24, 1960) wrote, "Budd Boetticher gets a lively, noisy gangster film in the mode of about 30 years ago." And the *Los Angeles Examiner*'s Ruth Waterbury opined, "Danton's performance gives it stature. I think you ought to see it." According to *Variety* (January 25, 1960), "There is more emphasis on the rise than on the fall," but predicted it "should turn a profit for Warner Bros." (It did.) *Variety* also said that Budd's direction "could well have tipped the scales further in favor of the story's grimmer side, but in all it is good both in the light and hard tones."

For Boetticher, *The Rise and Fall of Legs Diamond*s proved that he was capable of making much more than just B Westerns. But shortly after the film's release, he turned his back on Hollywood and headed to Mexico to start his long-planned Carlos Arruza project. By the time he came back in 1968, Jack Warner had retired, the studio system was just about dead, and it was clear that neither Karen Steele nor Ray Danton would become a star.

Danton worked steadily in television and on the stage, later turning to directing TV shows and low-budget European nonsense like *Hannah, Queen of the Vampires*. He died of kidney disease at the age of 60 in 1992—a little over 30 years after the cinematic highlight of his career, directed by Boetticher, was released. Now and then in interviews, Boetticher would say that Gilbert Roland and Ray Danton were the only two actors he didn't like, but he rarely specified why. He told me he thought Danton abused Julie Adams in some way, but supplied no details. Perhaps he just didn't like a man who had won the heart of a woman who he, Boetticher, loved. Or maybe he disliked Danton because he won the part because of Budd's affection for Julie Adams.

Budd called his three years with Karen Steele "the saddest three years of my life. Because I was such an idiot." He later told aspiring directors and interviewers, "Don't ever sleep with your leading lady—unless it's the last night of the production." He claimed his affair with Steele led him to cast her in three of the four films she made with him and he regretted it, but Steele certainly showed verve and spark in *Ride Lonesome* and *Decision at Sundown* and graces *The Rise and Fall of Legs Diamond* with a nicely balanced portrayal of a woman who sold herself out for love and discovered she was not loved in return.

She worked steadily through the 1960s, almost exclusively in television, including parts in *Lawman*, *Bronco*, *Bonanza*, *Get Smart*, *Mannix* and *Star Trek*. After a supporting turn as a divorcee in Richard Brooks' 1969 film *The Happy Ending*, Steele, not quite 40, pretty much called it quits. Budd and film historian Jon Tuska both told me she suffered from mental illness and ended up in an "insane asylum," but she later married a doctor and retired in Arizona, where she died of cancer at age 57 in 1988. It's a shame no one ever interviewed her about her relationship or work with Budd—or Randolph Scott, with whom she made three films.

A Time for Dying (FIPCO, 1969, 67 minutes; it was never really released, though it showed up in film festivals in the 1980s) Written and Directed by Budd Boetticher. Producer: Audie Murphy. Cinematographer: Lucien Ballard. With Richard Lapp (Cass Bunning), Anne Randall (Nellie Winter), Bob Random (Billy Pimple), Beatrice Kay (Mamie), Victor Jory (Judge Roy Bean), Audie Murphy (Jesse James), Ron Masak (Bartender), Walter Reed (Mayor) and Walt LaRue (Shotgun Guard).

Synopsis: Would-be gunman Cass Bunning learns that if there is a time for killing, there is a time for dying.

A Time for Dying is a sad, frustrating film that gives us a glimpse into Budd's mindset following eight years of self-exile in Mexico. Reaching back to the movies he made with Burt Kennedy a decade before, he uses the oft-told story (a young gunfighter looks to make a name for himself) as a springboard to examine the importance of having a mentor in your life. Here, there is no father figure for the well-meaning fast-draw Cass Bunning to rely on. There's a brief encounter with an aging Jesse James, well played in a cameo by producer Audie Murphy, but Bunning learns nothing from Jesse or even from rival Billy Pimple. And for all his fast draw practicing, when the time comes to kill someone, Cass' hands sweat up, he drops his guns and he's a dead man.

A Time for Dying is one of those movies that is more fun to write about than view. Budd said he made it as a rescue mission, to help Audie Murphy out of a financial jam. Budd was lying ill in a hospital bed in Mexico in the summer of 1966, after Carlos Arruza died in a car crash, when Audie Murphy showed up to tell him he wasn't going to die; the actor gave him a check for $5500, $5000 of it for bills Budd had to pay off for *Aruzza*. Budd asked Murphy what the extra $500 was for. "Well, you gotta eat," the Texas war hero said. Budd didn't forget that gift and a few years later, when Murphy said he needed a movie to regain his financial footing, Budd wrote and directed *A Time for Dying*.

When Budd wrote the script is a mystery, though a February 1, 1967, *Variety* story reported that he planned it as a Mexican production with roles for Frankie Avalon, Nancy Sinatra and Peter Fonda. A final shooting script, housed in the Margaret Herrick Library at the Academy of Motion Pictures Arts and Sciences, is not dated. Budd always said he initially wanted Fonda to play the young gunman but I'm not sure that would have come to fruition. Budd agreed to join Murphy in the newly formed First International Planning Company, or FIPCO, to co-produced a series of films. FIPCO set up an office in the Franklin West Towers of Los Angeles, where Budd was renting an apartment and where he met his third and last wife, Mary Chelde.

By Budd's account, Murphy was at least $250,000 in debt. Murphy told the press around this time that he lost about that much in oil investments following the Six Day Arab Israeli War, so that part seems true. Budd also claims that Murphy wanted to make the film simply as a write-off for his taxable income, and that he never intended to release it. Murphy's son Terry, who plays a horse thief who ends up swinging by his neck on a rope in *A Time for Dying*, said that was not so. His father, he said, was working to find money to finish and release the film at the time of his death in May 1971.

"He came to me, he needed money and he was in real trouble," Budd told me of Murphy. "I got my 'A' company group (of crew) together with Lucien Ballard and put a picture together that was never supposed to be released." Murphy, Budd said, didn't want to be in the film but agreed to perform the cameo for some box office insurance. "I thought he'd be a deadly Jesse James," Budd said. "He was a very good actor."

Budd told me the money that Murphy raised came from the mob. "The only distasteful thing about the deal was, I didn't care for [Murphy's] associates and financiers, but I didn't have to spend any time with them so… what the hell," Budd wrote in his autobiography. Murphy, he said, told him, "It's really shady money."

Budd told Sean Axmaker that he asked John Wayne to play Judge Roy Bean in the movie. Wayne, Budd said, was insulted. "You don't think for a fucking minute that I'm gong to play a bit in one of your god-damned pictures, do ya'?" Wayne asked Budd.

Boetticher said Wayne was a shmuck to turn the role down: "I thought, 'Goddamn, you'll win an Academy Award.' He would've been wonderful… [I]t would have been a great thing for his image. If he would have helped me, it would have made the picture."

If we take that story at face value, it's hard to imagine that Budd and Murphy never intended to release *A Time for Dying*. And the fact that Murphy spent several years trying to raise money to make the picture better sug-

Producer Audie Murphy (left, with beard), Boetticher (center) and cinematographer Lucien Ballard (right) discuss a point on the set of *A Time for Dying*, Murphy's last film.

gests that Budd's account is questionable. And why would Budd, who so badly needed a comeback movie, waste time and energy on a not-good film that was never intended to be seen? In Sue Gossett's *The Films and Career of Audie Murphy* (Empire Publishing, 1996), she writes that a Universal executive screened the film with an eye toward releasing it, but reported, "Too little Audie and a plot that seemed to go nowhere." This doesn't sound like a tax write-off project to me.

Other stories about the making of the film don't quite add up either. Actor-artist Walt LaRue said that Budd brought the film in 15 minutes too short for distribution because the script girl didn't keep track of how long the film was running. Actress Anne Randall, a 1967 *Playboy* Playmate, told the same story to Tom Lisanti for *Glamour Girls of Sixties Hollywood* (McFarland, 2008). She said Budd hired the inexperienced daughter of an old friend for the job and she "didn't take notes very well and after filming was completed, it turned out the movie was too short. Per Budd, it was too difficult to get more money to shoot more scenes to extend the running time."

Terry Murphy acknowledges the film came in short:

> There was a screening. The audience wanted to see more of Audie Murphy as Jesse James. That would of course go beyond the structure of the piece. But to get it released, the film had to run longer. An old friend of Audie Murphy's, Ewing "Lucky" Brown, a character actor and low-budget producer, thought he could set up a scene where Frank and Jesse carry out a hold-up, thus extending screening time and giving Audie Murphy more face time.

All of this may be true, but Budd's 158-page shooting script was pretty much shot as written, so I don't know why anyone would blame anyone else but Budd. He was accustomed to making movies that ran 70 or 80 minutes, so maybe he figured that was still acceptable in Hollywood.

Another odd story surrounding the making of the film suggests that once *A Time for Dying* was in the can, everyone realized they needed about five more minutes of footage to expand it, so the crew and some of the cast returned to Apache Junction, Arizona, where filming took place. There they reportedly shot the scene where Jesse James and his gang come across Cass Bunning and his wife Nellie (Randall). But when they got to the set, this story goes, they discovered it had burned down shortly after they finished filming. It is true that Apache Junction did go up in flames in May 1969, shortly after *A Time for Dying* wrapped, but Budd's script incudes that sequence pretty much as it was shot, and Terry Murphy said the fire had nothing to do with the film's problems.

The truth is that neither Budd or Audie were bankable entities in 1969. Budd had been away from Hollywood for nearly a decade and told one journalist that he wasn't even sure he still had the spark and fire to make a good motion picture. He told *Film World* that he hoped *A Time for Dying* would be "the last...short budget picture I'll ever make." He was right, because it was also the last feature film he would make, not including the documentaries *Arruza* and *My Kingdom For...*

And Murphy's career was in trouble. Budd honestly told *Film World* that Murphy had "bastardized his career by making pictures just to make money, and some of them were pretty bad and ruined the career of Audie Murphy." He said Murphy had invested all of his money in horses, but what he didn't say was that Murphy was actually investing all of his money into horse *racing*, and he was losing. A habitual gambler, Murphy's need for money led him to make some poor professional decisions in the early 1960s when he started making not-good films for studios other than Universal, where he was under contract from 1950 to 1965. Few Audie Murphy fans would want to attend a film festival made up of such stinkers as *Battle at Bloody Beach* (1961), *Gunfight at Comanche Creek* (1963), *The Quick Gun* (1964) and *Arizona Raiders* (1965). Murphy had last stepped before the cameras in the summer of 1966, appearing in another poor picture called *40 Guns to Apache Pass*. The titles of these movies say it all: Murphy's career was not just stalling, but regressing. It's too bad, because he had made some small inroads along the way in serious pictures like John Huston's *The Red Badge of Courage* (1951) and *The Unforgiven* (1960) and an underrated adaptation of Graham Greene's novel *The Quiet American* (in 1958).

By the early 1970s, Murphy was telling journalists that he never was a good actor but that he was tough enough to beat his enemy called Hollywood. He died at the age of 45 in a plane crash over Memorial Day weekend in 1971. His son Terry said Audie was on that flight for a business proposal that maybe would have helped raise money toward *A Time for Dying*.

What should we make of the film, shot in about three weeks in Apache Junction in April and May 1969, on a budget that screams "cheap"? It's the tale of a young gunman and a young naïve gal who think they can tame the West, but the West tames them, killing him and sending her into a life of prostitution. There is a whorehouse waiting to claim the innocence of the heroine, and a bartender who drinks an egg-filled beer for breakfast, and a pointed realism to the isolated shacks and tent cities that our protagonists frequent. Victor Jory, as Judge Roy Bean (the part John Wayne supposedly turned down), seems to be having more fun than you have ever seen him do in his entire film career as a human vulture with a sense of humor. There's a terrific bit, clearly influenced by a similar scene in Sam Peckinpah's *Ride the High Country* (1962), wherein the judge forces the youngsters to get married and ends his marriage sermon with, "May God have mercy on our soul!" and then takes back the donated wedding ring he gave to Cass Bunning to make the whole thing legal and proper. Silver City, where our young leads find themselves, is the sort of sordid, dark place you wish Randolph Scott had encountered when he rode into Agrytown ten years earlier in *Buchanan Rides Alone*. Audie Murphy in his cameo is spot-on, suggesting a career as a character actor if he wanted it.

The movie has a lot of problems. The hero is passive and reactive. Budd throws in a pointless and confusing bank robbery sequence that lacks the verve and focus of his best action films. The potential for a strong finale is dampened by a lengthy Mexican standoff and a downbeat ending—which Budd telegraphed to the press before the film was completed. You may not be too sure that you care about the two young leads, but they seem to deserve better than they got here, both on and off camera. Lapp did a few more film roles before disappearing from the scene. Randall did the same, and eventually became a land-use advocate in Southern California. Neither of them became stars, or semi-stars, or almost stars. Budd told me that he had nothing but trouble with the untrained and untested Lapp in the lead role:

> He came into my office and he had a portfolio and it had every picture that Audie had ever done.... I put him in the picture because I figured it would never get released.
>
> And the last day comes when he dies and this guy.... I told him what I wanted, how I wanted him to fall. He said, "I don't want to do it that way." It was 12 o'clock at night. The last day. I said, "What do you mean, you don't want to do it?" He said, "I'm the star. I don't want to fall on my face, I want to fall on my back. You can come in with the camera and come in on my dead face."
>
> I said, "You don't want to die my way?" He said, "No, I'm not gonna do it." I said, "Well, I've been waiting three weeks to tell you this and the whole crew knows it. You don't die the way I want you to, you son of a bitch, I'm gonna kill you."
>
> So he died my way.

Randall said Lapp was "odd" and that he told her that one way to ensure a lot of close-ups was to blow her lines in medium and long shots. He also told her that when she was in the background she should make faces so everyone was looking at her. She didn't play along. "He did that and if you look at his face, he looks like an idiot," she said years later. A *Los Angeles Examiner* article from August 1971 said that Lapp was trying to invest another $50,000 in the film to extend its running time so it could be released. Budd later said that Lapp erroneously believed he owned the rights to the film.

Ron Masak, who played the bartender, said,

"Unfortunately for Lapp, he started thinking of himself as the STAR and started being standoffish and the veteran crew wasn't pleased.... Anne was extremely beautiful and put herself totally in Budd's hands and gave a lovely performance."

The film opens with a close-up of a rattlesnake preparing to strike a bunny. The reptile gets its head shot off. Actor Walter Reed told me that Murphy—who he described as "a little weird"—insisted on shooting the snake himself. "He wanted to shoot the thing. He just blew its head off. But he was a nice, nice person. Anybody that's as big a hero as he was in the war has got to be expected to have a little problem after the war."

Randall recalled Murphy as pleasant: "I thought he gave a great performance. I had a manager at the time who years later went to one of those Western conventions and the door prize question was, 'Who was the last leading lady in an Audie Murphy Western?' It was me and he was the only one who knew, and he won a TV."

In the book *Five Directors* (1970), Boetticher, interviewed early in 1969, spoke of his years away from Hollywood and his plans for *A Time for Dying*:

> I think I've been gone during the period when Hollywood took a chance on a lot of young, inexperienced talent. A very small percentage of them actually had talent. Now I don't think I'll have to fight as hard because they'll think I'm 65 years old when they look at how long I've been directing. I started to direct when I was 25. So I think that if I make a couple of good pictures, there won't be many fights. It should be a comparatively easy road in the future. I may be wrong, and if I do have to fight, I'm sure as hell equipped for it.... I really want to get back to making westerns.

He went on to say that in *A Time for Dying*, "I kill off the leading man at the end of the picture.... He's not Clyde in *Bonnie and Clyde*. He's a great guy. But he just doesn't have it. This is a Western about all the unmarked graves, about all the kids who had everything but just didn't win."

Budd would not make a comeback of any kind. The Western was growing up fast.

Budd didn't grow with it. He had been gone too long.

A Time for Dying popped up in film festivals here and there, and I found an IMDb user who claims he saw it in a drive-in some time in the early 1970s, which may be true because the American Film Institute reports that the film did get some bookings in various Texas cinemas. Ultimately it disappeared for decades before popping up on a cheap home video release in the early 1990s. It's not good. You might even call it bad.

Terry Murphy (to the author):

> I know Dad was disappointed all the way through... He saw the rushes. He hated Lapp's performance... My dad admired Budd tremendously but he thought he had been let down.
>
> I remember the night Dad came back from a casting session with Budd. I said, "Who's the

This French film poster for Budd Boetticher's last Western, 1969's *A Time for Dying*, prominently plays up the role of Audie Murphy as producer, though he only made a cameo. The film's production history was troubled and it was never really released.

lead?" He gave me the name. His shoulders sagged. "Budd thinks he can do something with him." I think he knew at this point that the film was lost... As far as my part went, I was terrible, terrible, terrible. It was a Michael J. Pollard part and I was still trying to be the handsome guitar player back in school.

On the set, Budd would adjust to the situation and the personalities involved. Sometimes he would coax Victor Jory down a notch, sometimes bring him up. He fired a pistol to get an extra to react correctly. When Frank and Jesse come upon the kid [Lapp] practicing his shooting, Budd changed the location from a ridge to a depression.

My hanging scene went well, but everyone was just being kind. I told Budd that I'd seen a picture of a young man who strangled to death as opposed to getting his neck broken. That's what we went for. I have no idea if this came across, but by this time it didn't matter.

Budd, Terry Murphy said, was one of just three directors his dad felt simpatico with (the other two being John Huston and Don Siegel). Interestingly, none of those directors, despite having made two films each with Murphy, really succeeded with the films they made with him.

Ron Masak told me that Budd treated his veteran cast members with respect and

> led the new ones through their paces... We shot night for night so the feeling of times in the Old West was real. Audie was on the set a lot. My impression of him was one of total respect. He drove my wife and me to the location a few times and enjoyed driving fast. His relationship with Budd was one of friendship, trust and understanding.

Budd's energy, Masak said, was "quick, accurate and totally enjoyable. If I remember right, he finished a day early. While filming one day, Carlos Arruza's horse Pieropoo was delivered to Budd, who immediately got on him and put him through his paces."

Few critics saw the film at the time of its making. Philip Strick in *Films and Filming* (August 1969) wrote that Budd let Victor Jory go over the top and "allowed both the writing and the playing of it to run away with him rather further than the film can bear...." Most critics had to wait until the early 1980s, when *A Time for Dying* played at film festivals, to comment on it.

Vincent Canby, reviewing the film for the *New York Times* in the summer of 1982 (when it played at the Joseph Papp Public Theater as part of a Boetticher retrospective), wrote that it was "a classic of sorts" and called Ballard's cinematography "straight on—unfancy but vivid." Canby also noted,

> The film contains two large holes where the performances of Mr. Lapp and Miss Randall should be. Mr. Lapp, a handsome young man, seems to be doing an imitation of Mr. Murphy, but with none of Mr. Murphy's unaffected, natural ease. [True.] Miss Randall behaves as if she were an ingénue in an old Republic Western. It's to Mr. Boetticher's credit that, in spite of these large failings, *A Time for Dying* is a fascinating film.

Roger Ebert, seeing the film around the same time, did not agree. "I cannot recommend *A Time for Dying*... the movie is too slight, too flat and too unintentionally ludicrous. ...[It] combines immaturity and cynicism in such a weird way that there is not another film like it. To see it is to see all the conventions of the Western crumble to pieces."

Phil Hardy's *The Overlook Film Encyclopedia—The Western* calls the movie "the most playful of Boetticher's series of games with the genre," a baffling comment to me. Hardy goes on to call it "a marvelous film, full of wonderful details."

Boyd Magers, in *The Films of Audie Murphy* (with Bob Larkins, McFarland, 2004), wrote, "It was an artistic try, if not a commercial success. Murphy... was excellent in his brief appearance as Jesse James."

Arruza (Avco Embassy, 73 or 90 minutes, released in the United States in May 1972) Writer-Producer-Director: Budd Boetticher. Cinematographers: Lucien Ballard and Carlos Carvajal. With Carlos Arruza, Maria del Carmen Arruza, Carlos Arruza, Jr., Manuel Arruza, Mari Carmen Arruza and a host of other bullfighters and their coteries. Narrated by Anthony Quinn or Jason Robards, depending on which version you see.

Synopsis: Famed Mexican *torero* Carlos Arruza, tired of retirement, returns to the ring as a *rejoneador*—a bullfighter on horseback.

Wouldn't it have been a wonderful thing if the director of The Agony and the Ecstasy *had Michelangelo instead of Charlton Heston?—Budd Boetticher, on* Arruza

I had my own private genius for eight years… you don't get that very often in a career.—Budd Boetticher, on Carlos Arruza.

Budd's Arruza *script seems like a map with no treasure at the end. A journey with no real destination.—Sean Bartok, L.A. After Midnight blog*

The documentary *Arruza* (and it is a documentary, despite following something resembling a script) is the story of a man named Budd Boetticher who was obsessed with telling the story of a man named Carlos Arruza. I wrote in the initial draft of my book *The Last of the Cowboy Heroes*—which covered the postwar westerns of Randolph Scott, Joel McCrea and Audie Murphy—that Boetticher set out to make a film about his idol Carlos Arruza, but Budd called me and chided me: "Understand this: no man is my idol."

But I still can't help but think that Carlos Arruza was Budd's idol. At the peak of his career, Arruza was the equivalent of a movie star with a loving family, adoring fans of both genders and the ability to command money, fame and the best table at any restaurant in Mexico.

Arruza is also a film made by a bullfighter for bullfighting fans. As such, its appeal remains limited, but the footage in the arena is stunning to watch, especially as you realize there was no way Budd or anyone involved in that film could have choreographed the action of the bulls. Watching the film, one should not ask, "Did Budd's bullfighting experience influence his Westerns?" but rather "Did Budd's Westerns influence *Arruza*?" because, as the film unfolds, Carlos Arruza becomes Randolph Scott, with the bulls filling in for the Richard Boones of the world and the crowded arena of death substituting for the empty expanse of Lone Pine.

By Budd's own account, he began filming background bullfighting footage in the spring of 1958. He put together a first draft of a script roughly a year later. He shot the movie's last sequences in February 1967. It took another four years to get a mostly finished print together to premiere in Tijuana, Mexico, and another year before the film received limited distribution (in May 1972).

Some critics have suggested that Budd ended up like Don Quixote, wearily swinging away at windmills, while others liken him to the character of Capt. Ahab in *Moby Dick*, obsessed with finding and killing a mythological white whale. You can find tragedy in Budd's sojourn south to make *Arruza*, but he did emerge semi-triumphant, with a product to be proud of and the wisdom and experience to realize that he didn't have to take crap from anyone ever again. Then again, that may have brought little solace to him, given *Arruza* was his last full-length commercial film project.

"I wanted to make a real bullfight film with a real *torero* fighting the bull," Budd wrote in his autobiography. "And I knew from experience that whoever the *torero* turned out to be, he'd have to be a close personal friend of mine." That narrowed his choices down to two men: Carlos Arruza in Mexico and Luis Miguel "Dominguin" in Spain, who Budd had known since 1954. A chance phone call from Arruza in November 1956 turned the tide. Arruza, who had formally retired as a bullfighter in 1953, invited Budd to Mexico and told him he was returning to the ring as a *rejoneador*. It was the horse angle that grabbed Budd: "I could create something truly different, something entirely new with the pageantry of medieval times, with the colors of Picasso and with the horses—Portuguese Lusitanos—the most excitingly beautiful horses in the world."

Working with cinematographers Carlos Carvajal and Lucien Ballard, Budd began filming on May 25, 1958, initially racking up about 11 hours of film footage. His star was mostly cooperative, taking credit for some of the mistakes caught on camera: "If his fiery horse would rear up on his own, Carlos would make it look like it was his idea," Budd recalled.

In the interim, Budd and his wife Emily divorced, he kept shooting Randolph Scott Westerns for Harry Joe Brown, and he fell in love with Karen Steele. He stumbled out of that relationship and, thanks to Ballard, went out on a date with actress Debra Paget, then nearing the end of a contract with 20th Century-Fox that often saw her playing earnest Indian girls who suffer death or loss or similar tragedy. Budd fell in love with her, married her and decided to cast her as Arruza's wife Maria. After fending off an offer to finance the film by Jack Warner—who would do so only under the condition that Budd cast someone like Tony Curtis as Arruza and fictionalize the tale—Budd and Paget drove across the border into Mexico on May 7, 1961, to officially start making the movie.

The couple was divorced by the end of that year, and in November Budd was behind bars for failing to pay some $2636 for cocktail parties he hosted for the press. Budd told the press his imprisonment was all "a misunderstanding" but it was the first of a series of such setbacks that would impede his progress on the film and distance him from Hollywood, where he might have made a bigger impact with the right films.

Budd next took up with the actress Elsa Cardenas, and decided she would play Maria. Despite shooting some footage of her, that idea fell apart fast. The fall-outs with both Paget and Cardenas were just the beginning of an odyssey of misfortune, and Budd lays them all out in his autobiography: illness, alcoholism, incarceration in a madhouse, poverty and more jail time for failing to pay more hotel bills. But Budd prevailed, sticking to his guns as he worked on what he called "the *Red Shoes* of bullfight pictures…. I wanted to smell the bulls and sweat out the stench of impending destruction and death."

He succeeded there. As with *Bronco Buster*, Budd had several camera pits dug in the arenas where Arruza was appearing, to capture that smell, sweat and stench. The picture includes some amazing shots taken behind the defensive bulls as they face off against Arruza on horseback. Budd told journalist Drake Stutesman that he and Arruza would lay out all the scenes the day before Arruza rode into the ring to fight. "Where would you like me to die for you?" Arruza once sarcastically asked Budd.

While Budd shot the film, Mexican producers tried to screw him out of the rights while American producers said they'd turn it into the best film he had ever made *if* he turned over the final edit to them. Budd went through money fast and ended up halting filming while he scrambled to find more. "I was the only director I know of in the world who went from a Rolls-Royce to a bus," Budd later recalled. "And it was kind of charming." How did he survive?

Carlos Arruza struts about the arena in this shot from *Arruza*, Boetticher's last theatrical release—and one that got very limited distribution.

> I just locked myself up when I thought I would have to go to a psychiatrist or lose my mind or start to scream. I'd get about four or five bottles of tequila and a lot of beer. Then I'd close the door and just get stoned for two or three days. Then I'd wake up and feel awful, because I don't drink, and then I'd start over for another six

Score one for the *rejoneador*, as Carlos Arruza proves victorious against a charging bull in Boetticher's homage to Arruza, called, quite logically, *Arruza*.

months of hard labor and mental anguish. That way, it never got to me. I found it was a great catharsis. I can't recommend it, because if I hadn't had a strong heart, I would have died of a heart attack many times.

He nearly did die, in a Mexican hospital, of a lung infection. Budd refused to give up, even though one day some of his friends and supporters gathered around his bed to recite the Last Rites. "Maybe Death is wrong," Budd later wrote. "Anybody can make a mistake. Hell, maybe Death's got the wrong room number."

And just when success, in the form of a completed film, seemed within reach, misfortune struck again. In May 1966, with just one last scene to shoot, Carlos Arruza died in a car accident. Budd then went to Arruza's widow Maria and asked her to play herself in the film. He gave her a suitable amount of time to grieve for her husband and then shot new footage of her and her now-grown children and tried his best to match it to footage of her and Arruza that was taken years before. Over the years, most of the crew of *Arruza* died too, leaving Budd as more or less the last man standing when the film finally played a limited engagement some six years after Arruza's death.

Budd cobbled together a first cut and set about finding a distributor. While still living in Mexico, he visited the set of John Sturges' film *Hour of the Gun* to discuss a production deal. Sturges was enjoying the tail end of a long career at the top when he made the film—which would turn out to be a box office disappointment—and he agreed to look at four reels of *Arruza*. Impressed with the footage, Sturges agreed to release the film through his Alpha Corporation, financing the completion of the film in the deal.

So far, so good. But then Sturges brought Budd back to Hollywood, where Sturges' production manager Nate Edwards told Budd they were disappointed in the finished film. Budd proclaimed delight at this news, saying, "Whenever really bright folks are disappointed with what I do, I know I've got a hit." Sturges laid it out a little more bluntly to Budd: "*Arruza* is just deadly in the beginning, amateurishly edited and doesn't—in any way—live up to its potential." Sturges told Budd to run back to Mexico and leave the film in his hands and the result "just might win you an Academy Award."

Budd had heard that story long before, with John Ford's editing of *Bullfighter and the Lady*, so he stood his ground. The two men agreed to hold a preview screening for Hollywood insiders to see what they thought of Budd's cut. Budd invited about 300 people who he knew, leading Sturges to cynically suggest the screening was "fixed." Budd said the screening received a standing ovation.

Sturges also stood his ground and re-edited the picture, hiring Jason Robards—who played Doc Holliday in *Hour of the Gun*—to read a rewrite of Budd's narration. Budd didn't like that idea and, maintaining artistic control of the picture, re-edited the picture back to the way he wanted it and hired Anthony Quinn to speak the narration (Quinn did the job for free). Budd told Quinn that Robards' narration didn't work because the actor was going through a divorce and his heart wasn't in the job.

Budd ended his partnership with Sturges and, in May 1971, arranged for the film's world premiere in Tijuana, Mexico. Joseph Levine of Avco Embassy showed interest in the film and agreed to release it the following year. Though Levine had distributed or produced some big hits—like the original Italian version of *Hercules* and more highbrow pictures like *The Graduate* and *The Producers*—he and his marketing team realized early on that they would have a tough time selling *Arruza*. And they did. Avco Embassy publicity materials promoted the fact that it was "a many faceted love story"—one between director and star, one between the camera and star, and one between Carlos Arruza and his wife. The picture, Avco Embassy insisted, "will hit its audiences in the solar plexus."

Not many audiences got the chance to take the hit. The movie came and went fast following a brief release in art houses and a few larger cinemas in some of the big industry cities, including Los Angeles and New York. "It got almost no publicity and drew almost nothing," wrote Winfred Blevins, Entertainment Editor and critic for the *Los Angeles Herald-Examiner.* "Avco-Embassy, the distributor, simply did not handle the film well." In a separate review of the film, Blevins called it "a minor classic"—a quote Budd repeated often in the years to come.

Perhaps Levine did not get behind the film as much as he should have. Budd, in his autobiography, writes of making the mistake of criticizing Levine's production of *Carnal Knowledge* because of its frank depiction of sex. "I knew I had blown a lot of Joe's enthusiasm for *Arruza* with my own personal views about his picture," Budd recalled. When the Los Angeles Film Festival offered to screen *Arruza*, Levine turned down the offer, saying, "Sweetheart, I've always had lousy luck with film festivals. Trust me."

At that point, Budd said, "I knew I was a dead duck. When the top executives call you 'sweetheart' and end with 'trust me,' you're in real trouble."

And he was. The film played those few major markets and then Levine withdrew it. A few years later, Levine left Avco Embassy, which in turn shut down by the mid-1970s. Budd maintained the distribution rights to the film and, hoping to redistribute it, kept the original print locked in a shed in his backyard. He would sometimes pull it out for film retrospectives about his career, and thus some lucky fans got to see his original version.

Unfortunately, I was not one of those folks. With that original print pretty much out of reach, I had to settle for the version that Sturges edited, which is not without its appeal. Fortunately, Kirk Ellis, an Emmy-winning television producer and writer who knew Budd and hosted several film festivals honoring him, had seen Budd's cut at one of those festivals. Ellis watched the Sturges version with me and offered insight into the differences.

To start with, Jason Robards narrates in a dry, dispassionate voice that fails to excite us about the life of Carlos Arruza. Ellis said Anthony Quinn did a much livelier job, imbuing the narration with passion and a feel for the culture, sport and land. To make matters worse, Sturges apparently made much tighter cuts between some key sequences and, in the first third of the film, allowed some sequences to run without providing proper context or explanation for what is going on. An example: Arruza, working his ranch, suddenly jumps into his open-air Jeep to take off across the plains, a modern-day Randolph Scott searching for…what? The sequence just ends. Likewise, one lengthy sequence of three strange men riding through Mexico City streets gives you no hint that they are going to review the bulls. Rather, they look like hit men with some nefarious plan as they pass children playing in the streets.

But, Ellis said, the first third of the film still retains a lot of Budd's spirit, as does the last third. It is the middle section that often comes across as a jumble, where viewers are left scratching their noggins and asking, "What the hell is going on here?" Sound effects are missing, as in a vibrant sequence involving a thunderstorm, minus the thunder. Close-ups of seemingly unimportant people sitting in the stands (they may have been financial backers) take away from the excitement of the arena. Long shots of Arruza watching over his children as they play *torero* at his ranch suggest the use of a "fake Shemp" filling in for our hero, since they were likely shot after his demise. And it is jarring to see the Arruza children growing up so fast from scene to scene, aging from kids to adolescents to teens as they did over the course of some ten years of filmmaking. Staged shots of them sitting at home and applauding as they watch Daddy fighting bulls on the television screen in their living room come off as artificial.

But the last third, even in the Sturges version, is visually stimulating and dramatically satisfying. According to Ellis, Sturges left that part alone and it plays out exactly as Budd wanted it. You feel the anxiety of the horses, bulls and spectators in the moments leading up to the bullfights. You enter the territory of the bulls as they try their best to avoid death and inflict some violence of their own upon the horses. They pant, bleed and die, scared and valiant and heroic, as Arruza remains the last man standing, the gunman who has vanquished all rivals in a string of shoot-outs. You can tell Budd knew the contours of the arena well, capturing the conflict in real time and well aware that anything could go wrong. His camerawork is assured, and his abrupt cuts

Carlos Arruza strikes a pose during the shooting of *Arruza*. He died in 1966, right before filming ended.

and use of music play up the fact that tension and fear are constant companions in the ring. At its best, *Arruza* shows how much Budd Boetticher had matured as a filmmaker. It is an assured piece, even with John Sturges playing a meddling role in the project, and shows that Budd could have segued into more complex, character-driven films had he been given the chance.

The film received scant distribution and most critics offered faint praise, often focusing their reviews on Budd's lengthy efforts to get it made and released. *The Hollywood Reporter* said that while it might make an "attractive second feature…it is not strong enough—in subject matter, at least—to be a first feature in general circulation in the U.S." *Variety* noted, "There is no real story," but said the film, "though short, will make its mark, especially in the Latin world."

The New Republic's Stanley Kauffman, in a September 23, 1972, column, said the film has too many bullring shots for the average audience member to enjoy. "There are other dull elements," he wrote, citing Quinn's narration and the sequences at Arruza's hacienda with his wife and children, "all done with the waxiness and shadowless lighting of a Busby Berkeley musical." (That comment must have enraged Budd.)

Roger Greenspan in the *New York Times* called it a "magnificent" documentary and noted the old-fashioned cinematic style that Budd used:

> *Arruza* is not much given to mythologizing and its interest in the bullring has more to do with the camera's field of view than with anybody's depth of interpretation. *Arruza* avoids almost all false rhetoric, including the false rhetoric of too much plainness. For this, and for the genuine complexities revealed in its spare and lovely style, it may belong among the last great examples of classical filmmaking.

All of these reviews have merit, and I found something to agree with in each one of them. But *Arruza* would remain a disappointment in the career of Budd Boetticher. He had been gone too long from a business that quickly forgets, and he had come back with something no one quite understood: part-documentary, part-feature film, with a topic of limited interest to an American audience becoming accustomed to more adult fare—like *Carnal Knowledge*. His filmmaking days were, for the most part, over. But he had one more small little personal project to complete before he called it quits.

My Kingdom For… (A Lusitano, Ltd., Production; it played in some film festivals and was released on VHS, 85 minutes) Directed, written and produced under the auspices of Lusitano, Ltd. With Budd Boetticher, Mary Chelde Boetticher, Robert Stack, Rosemarie Stack, Alison Campbell, Gloria Allyn and Carlos Arruza, Jr.

Synopsis: Budd Boetticher shows visitors Robert and Rosemarie Stack how he and his wife Mary train Lusitano and Andalusian horses to fight (or avoid) bulls.

A strangely compelling documentary, despite its many flaws, *My Kingdom For…* is a little-seen film that Budd financed and produced in the mid-1980s, combining new video footage from the mid-1980s with 16mm and 35mm film clips that date back to perhaps as early as 1972. If *Arruza* is a film made by Boetticher about Carlos Arruza, then *My Kingdom For…* is a film made by Boetticher about Boetticher, with our director-actor now playing both the Carlos Arruza and Randolph Scott roles. In one thrilling shot, Budd, pushing 70, is in the ring on horseback, nearly spilling out of the saddle to prove that he can still get the job done.

This curious work allows Budd to reference his earlier work without drawing direct attention to it: His wife Mary looks amazingly like Budd's old paramour Karen Steele in both attire and style. In one sequence, Budd spends the night tending to an ailing horse, echoing a similar sequence in his 1959 film *Ride Lonesome*. In *My Kingdom For…*, the loose narrative shows Budd and his wife serving as mentors to two young girls who want to learn how to be great horsewomen, a nod to the role Randolph Scott's character played to reckless and restless youth in most of the Boetticher-Scott Westerns. And the ghost of Carlos Arruza haunts the film as Budd tries to help the late bullfighter's son Carlos, Jr., stage something of a comeback during some horse exhibitions at Budd's Ramona-based home and arena. Finally, film clips from both *Arruza* and *Bullfighter and the Lady* pepper the documentary, playing up Budd's continued respect for the art of both the *torero* and the *rejoneador*.

The picture is narrated by Robert Stack, who also appears as himself in some clumsily scripted sequences in which he and his wife Rosemarie show up at Budd and Mary's spread to watch an exhibition, only to learn that they are expected to be part of the show and help tell the story. Stack's affection for Budd after all those years is still evident as the two engage in some forced comic banter about their own professional failures, with Budd at one point saying of his own films, "I always thought they should have been better."

But *My Kingdom For...* is not about Budd Boetticher, the filmmaker—though it is a Budd Boetticher film—but about Budd Boetticher, horse *aficionado*. He calls the warrior-like Lusitano breed "the most athletic...in the world...the most special horse there is." It's clear he is in love with these horses, and he's still having fun with them long after Hollywood gave up on him, or visa versa.

The background of the film is a little difficult to figure out after all these years. Film producer and screenwriter Kirk Ellis, who spearheaded the filming of the new (mid-1980s) video footage of the exhibition, recalls working on it in the summer of either 1984 or 1985, shortly after he graduated from the University of Southern California's Film and Television program. Budd, he recalled, phoned him and asked him to bring a small camera and production crew to shoot some footage of Budd and Mary showcasing their horses during a Sunday afternoon exhibition in Ramona, California, where they lived. Budd told Ellis he was working on a documentary about the training of Portuguese Lusitano horses. Ellis and his crew shot not only footage of the horse show (which is often stunning) but of poorly scripted sequences of Budd and Mary, and Budd and protégé Alison Campbell, interacting as if in a true-to-life documentary. That shoot, Ellis said, took about three days.

"To be on that shoot, if only for a weekend, was to experience the full force not only of Budd's outside personality, but also his undiminished talent," Ellis said in the autumn of 2017, after watching the film for the first time in decades. He continued,

> Budd chose every camera set-up, even down to the bridging sequences and walk-throughs he later dubbed. No director then living was better at filming horses, and certain shots in the stable sequences recall some of the best compositions in the Ranown films. Budd was absolutely precise and resolute in his choices. He had an instinctive feel for what angle would best display the action, and he knew from *Arruza* just where cameras should be placed around the ring to pick up individual moments.

What Budd did not tell Ellis is that he (Budd) had compiled archival footage of his work with the horses dating back to the early to mid-1970s, footage shot on 16mm and/or 35mm—perhaps by cinematographer Lucien Ballard, who is credited on the film as cinematic camera consultant. Budd wrote, directed and produced the film without taking credit, Ellis said, later editing in the older footage to create a patchwork documentary spanning at least a decade that sometimes jars the viewer as characters grow older or younger scene by scene. It doesn't help that neither protégé Alison Campbell or Gloria Allyn—seen in footage dating back to the 1970s, before Ellis and company came on board—are good actresses, so their efforts to project excitement, disappointment or pride pretty much fail. But once they get in the saddle, they prove themselves to be excellent horsewomen.

The film was intended for a direct-to-video release, though it was also seen in some film festivals honoring Budd over the years. The copyright date on the film is 1988, but most online sources, including film festival catalogues, give the production date as 1985. Correspondence dating to 1983, housed in the Margaret Herrick Library at the Academy of Motion Pictures Arts and Sciences, reveals that a Robert Sandstrom agreed to put up $9260 for Budd to shoot the film—which did not yet have a title—in three days. Sandstrom told Budd that he was concerned about the lack of coverage on such a short shooting schedule and with such a tight budget. Around the same time, Budd was writing to independent producer Stanley Margolies, looking for financing for both his script for *A Horse for Mr. Barnum* and *My Kingdom For...*. In one letter, Budd says he is "absolutely certain that one day, *A Horse...* will go into production. I hope, with all my heart, it is with you." He goes on to say he wants James Coburn as Tango, one of the lead characters in *Barnum*, Joel McCrea's son Peter as Mustang, another lead, and R.G. Armstrong as Barnum. He had also penciled in Elizabeth Stack, daughter of Robert and Rosemarie Stack, for the part of Theresa. (Had she done the film as scripted, she would have had to perform a naughty nude swimming scene with another woman.) Budd told Margolies that Peter McCrea was "not too excited about becoming an actor," but that wasn't dimming his enthusiasm for the project.

Budd would never get *A Horse for Mr. Barnum* made, not even after it looked like Italian film producer Dino De Laurentiis would back it. That leaves *My Kingdom For...* as his final film, his valediction, an homage to both his life's work and his personal joy at being who he was: Budd Boetticher. As Stack says in the film's narration, Budd's "craziness is so natural that 'excitement' and 'danger' are simply two words in the dictionary."

And as Budd's career, including *My Kingdom For...* makes clear, that's a pretty spot-on description, and a fitting epithet.

Television

Television was not a medium that Budd Boetticher felt suited for. Not only would he dismiss much of his television work, but most journalists—including me—overlooked it as well when interviewing him. Budd felt that television didn't afford him enough time or money to make a good show. And he realized early on—perhaps while directing three *Maverick* episodes for Warner Bros.—that eventually the stars, and not the directors, would control TV. "I think television is not a director's medium," he told interviewer Ronald L. Davis in the late 1980s. "Today if a star is the star of his show 40 weeks a year and the director does every third picture, you don't think for one minute the director is going to come in and be able to tell the guy what he wants."

In an interview from the 1990s, Budd said, "You go in and make a *Maverick* picture in eight or ten days and then the next poor guy comes in and does it in six. That wasn't for me." And if the next guy could in fact do the show in six days, then Budd would have been expected to do the same on any ensuing shows. He had cut enough corners at Columbia, Monogram and Eagle-Lion and probably did not want to do the same for a network television program.

For the most part, Budd's television work is accessible, but I won't claim that this is a full list. For example, many sources say he directed at least one episode of *77 Sunset Strip*, and Budd claimed he directed the pilot episode, but that's not true. Warner Bros., which produced the series, gave that job to studio contract director Richard L. Bare. I could find no evidence that Budd directed a *77 Sunset Strip*. On the other hand, Budd is credited with directing the episode "Escape" for *Public Defender*, but Erle C. Kenton directed that one (and the majority of that series).

In his autobiography, Budd barely discusses his television work, and the filmography in that book simply notes, "Between 1955 and 1960, Boetticher made a number of television programs: the 'pilot' show for *Maverick*, with Jack Kelly, four episodes of *The Dick Powell Show*; *The Count of Monte Cristo*; 'Captain Cat'" (the latter an episode of the series *Hong Kong*).

That is an incomplete list that does not include the six *Public Defender* shows or a 1961 *Rifleman* episode, "Stopover." And Budd directed five, not four, shows for Dick Powell. The actual title of the *Hong Kong* episode is "Colonel Cat," not "Captain Cat." Budd directed three episodes of *Maverick* and Jack Kelly does not appear in any of them.

Here is a mostly complete list of TV shows directed by Budd Boetticher.

The Magnavox Theater: The Three Musketeers. Director: Budd Boetticher. Producer: Hal Roach, Jr. Screenplay: Roy Hamilton, based on the novel by Alexandre Dumas. With Robert Clarke (D'Artagnan), John Hubbard (Athos), Mel Archer (Portos), Keith Richards (Aramis), Paul Cavanagh (Richelieu), Don Beddoe (King Louis), Marjorie Lord (Queen Anne), Lyn Thomas (Constance), Kristine Miller (Lady DeWinter), Charles Lang (Buckingham) and Peter Mamakos (Rochefort). 51 or 52 minutes. The show first ran on various regional television stations in late November 1950 and continued running through the end of 1950. It was re-edited into a short feature and released by Howco International (aka Howco Productions) in 1953.

Synopsis: Musketeer cadet D'Artagnan joins the famed "Three Musketeers" to save the reputation of Queen Anne by foiling the nefarious plotting of Prime Minister Richelieu. Swordplay ensues.

This adaptation of Alexandre Dumas' classic tale served as Budd's introduction to the world of television. In his memoir, Boetticher recalled, "Nothing, absolutely nothing was happening with my directorial career" when Hal Roach, Jr., called him in 1950 to request a favor.

"And what a favor!" Budd wrote. "Hal had just signed a contract with Ford [Theater] Magnavox and was going to produce the very first one-hour motion picture specifically designed for television." The show was a sort of *Reader's Digest* abbreviated version of *The Three Musketeers*, slated for a four-day shoot on a budget of just under $24,000. Budd agreed to do it for $500—a financial decision he later regretted.

Archival documents from the Hal Roach studio housed in the Cinema Arts Library at the University of Southern California reveal that filming began at eight a.m. on October 24, 1950. Budd recalled that the production was scheduled for three days and he went over schedule by a half day, but the Roach files indicate it was planned for four days from the start. The studio paid writer Roy Hamilton $750 for his script. Star Robert Clarke received $500 and the rest of the cast got about $50 a day. Overtime wages accounted for another $100, wig rentals cost $440, the set design was a whopping $200, and meals cost a total of $60 over the four-day schedule. (Sandwiches again!)

A page of "casting possibilities" found in the Roach archives indicates Budd wanted Robert Stack, Scott Brady or Gig Young for D'Artagnan, but I'm guessing they where way out of his price range. (I sure can't see Brady in the role). Leif Erickson, Alan Hale, Jr., and Raymond Burr were all considered for the role of Porthos, played by Mel Archer, and among the actresses considered for the queen were Charles Lang's wife Helen Parrish (remember her from *The Wolf Hunters*?), Ellen Drew, Eva Gabor and Joy Page—who Budd had just directed in *Bullfighter and the Lady*. Vincent Price was the number one choice for the conniving Cardinal Richelieu (a role he played in MGM's 1948 version of *Three Musketeers*), but his salary was out of Roach's range so Paul Cavanagh got the part. Budd cast old pals John Hubbard and Charles Lang in prominent roles. The wardrobe budget included two outfits for D'Artagnan, King Louis and Richelieu, three for the queen and basically one for everyone else—aside from the bit players who had to enact several parts.

The news that Roach, Jr., was going into television production and making these shows as if they were motion pictures attracted a lot of attention from many name directors in Hollywood. Not that John Huston, Alfred Hitchcock or George Stevens were seeking work in the still-new medium. The Roach studio files are full of recommendation letters for Jean Yarbrough, Ralph Murphy, Robert Aldrich, Norman Foster, Tim Whelan, Bruce Humberstone and Reginald LeBorg. Michael Curtiz wrote Roach personally and asked him to consider hiring Curtiz's lesser-known brother David as a director. Studio archives indicate that Roach granted an interview to David, who had worked mostly as an editor or second unit director, but I have found no evidence that Roach ever hired him for any job.

There is nothing in the Roach files to indicate that someone pitched Budd as a director—just a one-page résumé of Budd's that notes that he just finished shooting *Bullfighter and the Lady*, described as "a million dollar picture" (not true), and a sentence stating he had worked at the Hal Roach Studios in the past "as an assistant casting director and second assistant director."

The turnaround on the show was fast. Roach, Jr., had it ready for broadcast by Thanksgiving Day, 1950, and set up the first select preview screening of it at the Parish

Theatre on Hollywood Boulevard on November 22. "I believe it is a major development in the process of establishing Hollywood as the capital of television production," Roach wrote at the time, and in retrospect he was right.

On October 30, 1950, Roach, Jr., asked his accounting department to cut a $500 check for Boetticher, so Budd got paid right away. In his autobiography, Budd says that when he went to see Edward Dmytryk's 1959 military drama *The Young Lions,* he was shocked to discover that the second feature, titled *The Sword of D'Artagnan,* was a thinly disguised re-edit of his Magnavox program, padded out to 54 minutes. "I was so damn angry," Budd wrote, that he called Roach, Jr., the next morning and asked the producer to give him a check for $34,500 "for directing your fucking picture… [M]y present salary is $35,000. I've been advanced 500 and now I'd like the rest of my money."

To which Roach, Jr., replied, "My boy, a deal's a deal."

And, based on Hal Roach, Jr., studio archives documents, it seems Roach was right. Boetticher signed on for $500, and there was no provision for paying him extra should the television show be released theatrically.

Budd got the timing of the Howco screening wrong. Howco, a short-lived enterprise that originated out of New Orleans and basically distributed low-budget pictures that nobody else wanted to touch (*Mesa of Lost Women* comes to mind), placed the picture in select theaters some time in 1953 under both the title *Blades of the Musketeers* and, as Budd noted, *The Sword of D'Artagnan*. But *The Young Lions* was not released until 1959, and it makes little sense that Roach, Jr., would wait nearly a decade to try to make any more money off of a television program that would have seem dated by that time.

Budd wrote in his memoir that the experience making the show was "degrading." He also notes that he had not yet filmed *Bullfighter and the Lady,* but his timing is off there. He shot that picture for Republic in the spring and summer of 1950, months before he agreed to helm the Roach show. That picture would be released to critical acclaim and good box office the following spring, so perhaps looking back, Budd realized that the *Musketeers* show was a career misstep that might make him look as if he were desperate. Maybe he was.

In any event, the *Musketeers* show is not an embarrassment, and given the short shooting schedule and condensing of the Dumas source material, it's not a bad second-tier adaptation of the classic.

The plot follows the first part of the Dumas book, with Robert Clarke's D'Artagnan joining the King's Musketeers Athos, Porthos and Aramis in retrieving some stolen diamonds that, if not replaced on a necklace in the nick of time, will humiliate Queen Anne and lead her husband, King Louis, to disown her and start a war at the urging of his double-dealing prime minister.

Although Clarke is no Errol Flynn—or Cornel Wilde or Victor Mature, for that matter— he exudes enthusiasm and flashes a becoming smile as he recites old-fashioned dialogue and crosses swords with the bad guys. The rest of the cast members certainly give it their all, and Hubbard succeeds in making Athos an introspective character given to subtlety. It's a nice character turn and makes you wish Hubbard hadn't so often been cast as oily salesman-type villains, as he was in several Boetticher productions.

But the tight running time—not even an hour, given the need for commercials—limits both plot and character development, with Keith Richards' voiceover narration as Aramis helping to bridge very large narrative gaps. A bit player, enacting the role of a fisherman, contributes plenty by providing lots of "this sure sounds crazy!" plot points to a confused D'Artagnan late in the proceedings. As for the sets, Clarke recalled that Roach, Jr., had access to set pieces left over from the 1948 Ingrid Bergman version of *Joan of Arc,* and that gives this television film some needed class.

The dialogue is mostly unmemorable. "To a professional musketeer, danger is life!" D'Artagnan proclaims at one point, and there are a lot of variations on the old "Get out of here—we'll hold them off!" variety. The next thing you know, the 50-some minutes is over and you are enjoying the end credits, in which close-ups of the various actors are screened with their names superimposed over their images.

The biggest problems are the limited sets and what seems to be a reliance on just one camera. There's not much Budd or any director could do with swordfights in which the camera cannot move, so basically we watch as our heroes fence with anonymous actors playing anonymous bad men in a tight hallway or a small tavern. Some of the actors do move out of camera range, but the camera doesn't move with them. As a nod toward maintaining civility and cutting down on violence, just about everyone who is stabbed is wounded, not killed, so death is kept to a minimum.

Once the show was in the can, Roach Jr., went to work advertising it. He wrote letters to friends, professional colleagues and TV station owners around the country in an attempt to generate interest. He even wrote newspaper magnate "Randy Hearst" (William Randolph Hearst), asking if he could suggest someone in his newspaper empire's advertising department for Roach, Jr., to contact. Hearst replied within days, suggesting one R.L Litchfield and saying he himself would keep an eye out for the program "and will be glad to tell you what I think of it." There is no record of Roach replying to that offer.

By Thanksgiving, *The Three Musketeers* was airing on CBS-affiliate television stations in select cities, including the Chicago area. On Christmas Day, it played in the Los Angeles area. It was just one of about a half-dozen Magnavox anthology series that CBS put its weight behind and the only one Boetticher directed.

Robert Clarke, in his very engaging autobiography *To "B" or Not to "B"—A Film Actor's Odyssey* (written with Tom Weaver), recalls hearing that Scott Brady would play D'Artagnan and sending Roach, Jr., a telegram suggesting he play the role instead. Once he was hired, Clarke asked Roach if his telegram made a difference and Roach said yes. "In truth, I've always suspected that Scott Brady simply refused to work for the kind of money that the rest of us did," Clarke wrote. Clarke recalled with pride that famed makeup artist Jack Pierce worked on the production and fashioned a spirit-gum mustache for Clarke that never fell off or gave him trouble, though it made him maintain a very stiff upper lip throughout the shoot. He said he took fencing lessons on the side, which he paid for and could scarcely afford. "I thought I came off fairly well, all things considered," Clarke wrote. "I am not putting myself in the class of an Errol Flynn, but for this small production I was able to come up to what was expected."

Of the other cast members, Clarke recalled Hubbard as "a very smooth, professional actor and also a pleasant guy. He was a light leading man type who had been under contract to Roach, Sr., years before and had starred for Roach in a movie with Carole Landis called *Turnabout*." Clarke went on to say that one day Hubbard pointed out a sizable dressing room on the Roach lot and said, "That was built for me..." Clarke: "And there he was, back on that very lot, doing this little TV thing for just $55 a day." It's a bit sad to realize that Hubbard was on the verge of film stardom just a decade before, giving engaging comic performances in the Roach productions *Road Show* and *Turnabout*.

Clarke said Mel Archer had a voice like a canary and had to be looped, hence the deep, low voice coming from his mouth "sounding like it was coming out of a barrel and it was so terrible that it became distracting." (True.) Clarke felt that actor Paul Cavanagh was unhappy to be acting in such a low-budget production, "which to him was belittling, probably. He didn't let it be known through his acting, he did not stint in any way in his efforts. He was letter perfect in his lines, a consummate actor and just by being in it he lent some dignity to the proceedings."

Budd, Clarke wrote,

> was the type of director you liked to be around.... [H]e was gung ho and enthusiastic, very much for the project, and ... tried to get a variety of shots, to try different camera moves, to use a dolly when he could.... Budd wanted to make it

look the very best he could; he didn't treat it as something to be sloughed off or run through as fast as possible. He was a fun-type guy who loved to make pictures and gave the actor the first nod insofar as priority.

Clarke also recalled the show being released to cinemas but harbored no hard feelings toward Roach: "There were no residuals when it went to the theaters and no residuals when it played who-knows-how-many-time on television. But I was excited about getting to do it, and if I'd had the money, I'd have paid Hal Roach, Jr., $55 a day to let me do it."

The only possible beneficiary from the Howco cinematic release of the show—besides Roach, Jr.—may have been screenwriter Roy Hamilton, who had worked something into his contract regarding extra payment should the TV show go into cinemas, as Roach Jr., glumly noted in a letter to studio executive Herb Gelbspan. Roach, Jr., wrote that they would "unfortunately" have to make a compromise "adjustment" to Hamilton's salary, though the letter does not cite a figure.

Decades later, Budd told Wheeler Winston Dixon that after Roach, Jr., said, "A deal's a deal," he never saw the producer again or spoke with him. Not true. Budd went back to work for Roach, Jr., on the *Public Defender* television series in 1954–1955, although it is possible that's because Roach, wishing to make amends, wanted to give Budd some steady-paying work during a time of transition between the Universal series and the Randolph Scott Westerns.

The *Public Defender* series (Hal Roach, Jr., production, 1954–1955). Though the 1963 Supreme Court case Gideon v. Wainright proved to be the landmark ruling that guaranteed that an indigent defendant would receive free legal counsel in the courtroom, the County of Los Angeles is credited with opening the first public defender's office way back around 1913 or 1914. Some 40 years later, Hal Roach, Jr., teamed with producer Carroll Case to put together the short-lived but often fascinating television series *Public Defender,* starring character actor Reed Hadley as public defender Bart Matthews. The series based its stories on real-life cases from around the country and sometimes public defenders other than Matthews anchored the proceedings. Tobacco giant Philip Morris was the show's main sponsor, which may explain why Hadley and a lot of other characters continually light up during the shows. For all the commercialization, however, *Public Defender* did an admirable job of spotlighting the work of the in-the-shadows champions of the downtrodden and poor.

The episodes tackled then-topical issues that, in many cases, remain relevant today, including juvenile delinquency, high-school hazing, bullying, "cutting" (a person intentionally uses a sharp object to slice up their body) and the challenges facing parents (sometimes single moms) who are losing control of their teen charges. To the show's credit, sometimes the well-meaning but guilty protagonists went to jail, and sometimes the bad guys stole off into the night.

While a lot of no-name young actors popped up in small roles throughout the series, *Public Defender* also utilized a lot of familiar character actors including Charles Bronson, Dick Foran, Harry Carey, Jr., Adele Jergens, Hugh Beaumont, John Qualen, Percy Helton and Ben Weldon. Natalie Wood appeared in one episode, and both of *Superman*'s Lois Lanes, Phyllis Coates and Noel Neill, played in (unfortunately) separate episodes. The titles were catchy too, including "Baby for Sale," "Return of the Dead" and "Out of the Past." Hadley was hardly the leading-man model, and his near-cadaverous look may make you wonder if he wasn't over-indulging in the smoking, but he embodied a no-nonsense approach that worked well for the program.

Boetticher directed at least six episodes of the series, which ran from March 1954 to June 1955. He later said his fee for directing TV shows in that time period was $1500. Still licking his wounds from the fiasco of *The Americano*, he no doubt saw the work as an opportunity to re-establish himself in the business, make some money and see if this TV industry had potential.

Public Defender: "The Prize Fighter Story"

(April 8, 1954) Director: Budd Boetticher. Producers: Hal Roach, Jr., and Carroll Case. Teleplay: John Tucker Battle. With Reed Hadley (Bart Matthews), Richard Jaeckel (Dave Davis), Tom Brown (Soapy), Ben Welden (Donny), Henry Kulky (Murphy), Mary Beth Hughes (Eve), Lou Lubin (Willie) and John Qualen (Ames).

Synopsis: When an honest boxer refuses to take a dive, the syndicate frames him for peddling dope. Public defender Bart Matthews takes a hand.

"The Prize Fighter Story" maintains interest because of the high-powered performance of Richard Jaeckel and its gallery of stereotypical gangster types. Typical of the series' penchant for not shying away from taboo topics, "The Prize Fighter Story" sees its protagonist framed not for murder, but for peddling drugs, and it even lets the blonde temptress seductively enter the innocent good guy's apartment for some sexual byplay.

Naturally the public defender gets involved and clears everything up for the boy, but in a novel touch, some of the bad guys hightail it to Mexico and aren't punished. Boetticher stages a peppy boxing match sequence despite the cheap sets, and all the players—including Mary Beth Hughes—perform with a gusto that suggests they were putting on a production of *Richard III*.

Public Defender: "The Stepchild" (May 27, 1954) Director: Budd Boetticher. Producers: Hal Roach, Jr., and Carroll Case. Teleplay: Marianne Mosner. With Reed Hadley (Bart Matthews), Barbara Whiting (Torry), Argentina Brunetti (Mrs. Derek), Michael Hale (Chuck), Paul Bryar (Policeman), Fred Essler (Steiner), Lizz Slifer (Mrs. Griffin) and Richard Deacon (Truant Officer).

Synopsis: Hysterical teen Torry claims her mother attacked her with a knife. Public defender Bart Matthews discovers that the emotionally disturbed girl inflicted the wounds herself.

Way ahead of its time in its depiction of "cutting," "The Stepchild" is a disturbing edition of the series. Hadley's Bart Matthews warns us in his opening narration that this is the grim story of "a child—and a child-beater" and the teleplay kicks into high gear immediately with the terrified Torry (Barbara Whiting) desperately pounding on the apartment doors of her neighbors in an attempt to escape her mother who, Torry claims, locked her in the closet and tried to kill her. In an unfortunately disappointing denouement, Matthews discovers that Torry has come under the influence of the evil Circle Gang! This group of overage juvenile delinquents—the precursor to Eric Von Zipper's inept Rat Packers from the 1960s *Beach Party* films—spout such jive dialogue as, "Hey baby, you're real hep!" and put aside fighting to indulge in some juke-box dancing. But the teleplay still packs a punch with some harrowing automobile accident scenes and a finale that sees our young troublemaker doing time for her scheming ways.

Public Defender: "Think No Evil" (August 16, 1954) Director: Budd Boetticher. Producers: Hal Roach, Jr., and Carroll Case. Teleplay: William P. Rousseau. With Reed Hadley (Bart Matthews), James Lydon (Wade Foster), Hugh Beaumont (Ed McGrath), Helen Ford (Mrs. Blair), Will Wright (Horace Bascomb), Marjorie Owens (Margo) and Marshall Bradford (Judge Knox)

Synopsis: Accused of armed robbery, Wade Foster maintains he was in Las Vegas when the crime took place in Los Angeles. Public defenders Ben Matthews and Ed McGrath must prove his innocence.

"Think No Evil" boasts a novel idea wrapped up in a teleplay of humorous intention. It is the liveliest and funniest of the six *Public Defender* shows that Budd directed, and everyone in it seems to be having a grand time despite its serious subject matter: the potential conviction of a seemingly innocent man. The William P. Rousseau script and Budd's direction keep things hopping, as in a very amusing interrogation scene involving a ditzy socialite who matter-of-factly explains that she can't be blamed for misidentifying a culprit because she left her glasses in the car.

Hilarious, too, is a sequence in which public

defender Ed McGrath (Hugh Beaumont) tries to question the owner of a small Las Vegas motel who insists on vacuuming the floor during the interrogation. ("Move your feet!" she barks at him.) When McGrath tells her that she may be called into court to testify, she says her price is $25 per day plus expenses—since that is what she gets paid for serving as a witness in all those divorce cases that come out of Las Vegas!

James Lydon's portrayal of the fresh-faced realtor who insists he is innocent is solid. The script has a nice last-minute plot turn or two that lend realism to the series.

Budd also directed Beaumont in the pilot for *Alias Mike Hercules*, a show that never got off the ground. Later in the *Public Defender* series, Dick Foran enacted the role of Ed McGrath.

Public Defender: "The Last Appeal" (August 30, 1954) Director: Budd Boetticher: Producers: Hal Roach, Jr., and Carroll Case. Teleplay: Donald S. Sanford. With Reed Hadley (Bart Matthews), Richard Jaeckel (Jimmy Morse), Robert Armstrong (Father Duffy), James Seay (Sam Copeland), Emile Meyer (Haynes), Benny Rubin (Hoff), Merry Anders (Agnes Fay) and Ron Kennedy (Fred Mackey).

Synopsis: With the minutes ticking away toward the time of his execution, young hellion Jimmy Morse wonders if the public defender and Father Duffy will save him from a date with the electric chair.

"The Last Appeal" features strong performances from its ensemble cast, but struggles to deliver realism against all odds in a teleplay that relies way too much on coincidence and last-minute bluffing on the part of our supposedly heroic public defenders. This time around, our normal protagonist, Bart Matthews, recedes into the background to let visiting public defender Sam Copeland handle the heavy (and dirty) work. At one point, desperate to prove that Death Row inmate Jimmy is innocent, Copeland strong-arms a suspect into just-in-the-nick-of-time confession by threatening, "You'll tell it to the warden if I have to wring every word out of you!"

Cigarettes pop up everywhere in this episode—in the jail cell, the pool hall, the supper club and a taxi cab. Philip Morris must have loved this one. Benny Rubin is pretty amusing as a cab driver who does not understand what all the fuss is about (Jimmy being framed). The teleplay's emphasis on rainy city streets, nocturnal crimes, barroom deals and poolroom muscle suggest a 1930s Warner Bros. movie, and Budd kept it moving along at a snappy clip.

Public Defender: "A Call in the Night" (July 15, 1954) Director: Budd Boetticher. Producers: Hal Roach, Jr., and Carroll Case. Teleplay: David Dortort. With Reed Hadley (Bart Matthews), Barbara Whiting (Ellie Black), Claudia Barrett (Sue), James Flavin (Jim Black), Ruth Lee (Alice Black), Robert Patten (Don), Sally Fraser (Peg), Tom Irish (Chuck) and Gloria Donovan (Cora).

Synopsis: Anxious to work her way into the high-class world of the high school gang The Night Riders, Ellie Black resorts to burglary and assault with a deadly weapon.

"A Call in the Night" features some disturbing scenes that still pack power today, including a humiliating hazing incident in which innocent Ellie is publicly coerced to her knees and forced to pledge allegiance to the gang—even if it means giving herself up sexually to high school heartthrob Don. But despite a winning performance by Barbara Whiting, this episode is reduced to being just a hoot to watch. Budd must have had salacious fun with a girls' locker-room sequence in which Ellie, anxious to strip down to get into the pool, is visited by a couple of her new "girlfriends," whose eyes roam up and down her half-clad body as they entice her to forsake the swim for some gang fun. As Ellie grows more enthused about the prospect of joining the girl gang, the older Sue (Claudia Barrett) lets her eyes drop down to Ellie's bra-covered bosom and says, "Your excitement's showing!"

But the girl gang members' continual put-downs of Ellie ("The original square from Square Land") grow tiresome after a while, and Ellie's last-minute conversion to a near-suicidal speed freak is unconvincing. It doesn't help that most of the actresses playing high school snobs were in their early to mid-20s while actor Robert Patten, playing 18-year-old Don, was pushing 30. Offsetting these faults is a nice turn by character actor James Flavin as Ellie's beer-guzzling working-class dad, who clearly cares about his daughter and has a much better idea of what she is up to than his shallow wife. Upon hearing that Ellie plans to join the Night Riders, an after-school club, he expresses his concern: "Sounds like a gang of cutthroats!" He's not far off base.

This episode ends with a panning shot of the accused teens and their concerned parents all awaiting judgment as Hadley somberly intones, "Rich or poor, kids are kids wherever you find them—until they get trapped by the wrong side of ideas." And once again, some of the perpetrators do get some jail time for their misdeeds, though it seems like a light slap of justice to me.

Low-budget horror movie fan alert: Actress Claudia Barrett had just appeared in the cult stinker *Robot Monster* while Sally Fraser would appear in some late 1950s shockers including *It Conquered the World, Giant from the Unknown, War of the Colossal Beast* and *The Spider*.

Public Defender: "When Credit Is Due" (October 14, 1954). Director: Budd Boetticher. Producers: Hal Roach, Jr., and Carroll Case. The episode I viewed did not include a credit for teleplay, but some online sources say it was written by Mort R. Lewis. With Reed Hadley (Bart Matthews), Don Megowan (Eddie McGowen), Margo Karin (Greta McGowen), Percy Helton (Leo Jason), Walter Reed (Doctor) and Forrest Taylor (Judge).

Synopsis: Greta McGowen falls behind in her bills as she strives to support her injured husband and two children. The public defender's office steps in to help before she drowns in debt.

In his opening narration, Bart Matthews explains that three times as many people come to the public defender's office seeking help with civil matters rather than criminal cases. That sounds like, "Ladies and gentlemen, this story is more common than you think but a lot less interesting than stories about gangsters and grifters."

As a result, "When Credit Is Due" is the least interesting of Budd's *Public Defender*s, dealing as it does with the average housewife sinking under a pile of bills and hiding the financial shame from her husband, who cannot work because of a car accident. But in its own way it features one of the vilest villains of the series in Percy Helton's avaricious businessman, who, upon hearing that Greta can't pay her bills, garnishes her wages and fires her. "I'm not running a kindergarten here," he sharply tells Bart Matthews. "Hard cash on the barrel!"

The extent to which Matthews and a judge go to help Greta borders on conflict of interest: making some phone calls to get her a job, bringing her husband a Christmas present, stepping in to stop Eddie from shooting evil Helton and so on. Maudlin and melodramatic, "When Credit Is Due" is a negligible entry in the Budd Boetticher television canon.

The Count of Monte Cristo: "The Affair of the Three Napoleons." Director: Bud [sic] Boetticher. Producer: Sidney Marshall. Story and Teleplay: Marshall. Executive Producer: Hal Roach, Jr. With George Dolenz (Edmond Dantes, aka the Count of Monte Cristo), Fortunio Bonanova (Mario), Nick Cravat (Jacopo), Faith Domergue (Renee Morrell), Paul Cavanagh (Morrell) and John Sutton (De Villefort).

Synopsis: Mystery woman Renee Morrell asks Edmond Dantes, the infamous Count of Monte Cristo, to find out who murdered her father. Clutched in his dead hands were three strange French coins.

One can question the wisdom of putting together a television series based on a famous French literary classic—Alexandre Dumas' *The Count of Monte Cristo*, later memorialized in countless film and television adaptations. But that's what producers Sidney Miller, Leon Fromkess, Dennis Vance and Hal Roach, Jr., decided to do in the mid–1950s. The novel deals with a nobleman who vows vengeance on the men whose false accusations sent him to prison. The series picks up that idea and sees the count (George Dolenz, father of Mickey Dolenz of The Monkees) still out for vengeance while getting sidetracked helping others who have been wronged.

Budd Boetticher—or *Bud* Boetticher, as he is inexplicably credited on this one—really doesn't belong in the world of swashbuckling noblemen or dueling pirates. He's as out of place with material like this as he was with Monogram's *Killer Shark*. In an interview, he passed the episode off as a favor to Roach, Jr.

Some sources say this episode served as the pilot for the 39-episode series, but other sources note that it was not aired until near the end of the program's brief 1955–1956 run. Since the first 12 episodes were shot on the Hal Roach lot and surrounding region, I bet Boetticher did direct this as either the pilot or an early episode, since the last 27 episodes were filmed on location in England, and somehow I can't see him traveling that far for such a small pay-off.

"The Affair of the Three Napoleons" is just plain stupid. It may make sense that our hero Dantes wants to find out who killed his best friend Morrell (Paul Cavanagh), but the ensuing skullduggery is both hard to follow and hard to swallow, especially when Morrell's mysterious daughter shows up in the enemy camp. Morrell's murder ties in with undercover efforts to unmask the three leaders of a plot to overthrow the king of France in 1854. Dantes is aided by two sidekicks who appeared throughout the series, Mario (Fortunio Bonanova) and Jacopo (the always-mute Nick Cravat), but the pair do little to help him and mostly seem to get in his way. As with Boetticher's 1950 version of *The Three Musketeers*, here we encounter a bit player enacting the role of a snitch who conveniently discloses all the major plot points for both Dantes and the audience to consume. And would you really believe that the evil mastermind plotters would leave a piece of paper with "the details of our plan and the names of our ringleaders" in the top drawer of an easy-to-access nightstand?

Special guest star Faith Domergue looks pained throughout; she isn't in it more than a few moments and one can't imagine her remembering the job a year later. Weather note: it looks cloudy in all the outdoor scenes, making me think Budd got stuck with a forecast of "overcast, chance of rain." So does the audience.

Alias Mike Hercules (Air date some time between July and September 1956). Director: Budd Boetticher. Producer: Hal Roach, Jr. Teleplay: Herbert Margolis. With Hugh Beaumont (Mike Hercules), Reginald Denny (Prof. Thayer), Anne Kimbell (Vivian Harding), Marie Windsor (Lydia Brady), Rex Roberts (Walter Harding), Dan Haggerty (Leo Brady), Greg Martell (Max Capallo), Ellen Corby (Birdie) and Victor Sen Yung (Charlie)

Synopsis: Ex-convict turned detective Mike Hercules, who lives on a houseboat, works with his pal Prof. Thayer and cab driver Charlie to help a rich woman rescue her father from kidnappers.

Alias Mike Hercules isn't quite the Holy Grail of Budd Boetticher's TV works, but it's still tough to see. The only copy I could find is housed at the University of California–Los Angeles' Film and Television Archives, and wouldn't you know it: Every time I went out there on a research trip for this book, the archives were either closed or that particular episode was not available for viewing. It was shot in 1954 at the Hal Roach Studios, and when the pilot failed to sell, ABC ran it as a stand-alone in a short-lived 1956 summer series of one-shot pilot episodes that never went anywhere. (I love that idea.) General Electric sponsored that series. Beaumont, who appeared on several of the *Public Defender* series, played the title character in yet another bid to attain television stardom. He eventually did so, playing Ward Cleaver in the popular *Leave it to Beaver* series of the late 1950s and early 1960s. An ordained minister, he worked as an actor until a stroke in 1972 curtailed his career.

Though I could not see *Alias Mike Hercules*, my Los Angeles–like friend Pete Kaminski, a film editor and movie buff and historian, viewed it at the archives in December 2016. He happily provided me with a write-up of the episode:

> Beaumont, as Mike Hercules, looks the part. He looks like he's been in fights, he looks plenty tough, and he even looks a little bit like Chris Isaak. But his acting is best described as being somewhere between terrible and stiff. He makes a wooden Indian look like Danny Kaye.
>
> The rest of the cast is made up of accomplished craftspeople but they all disappoint here, which is puzzling, given the credits some of them racked up in movies and other television shows. But the story is well-paced and often exciting, if sometimes complicated and full of coincidences (it turns out Mike Hercules and the kidnapped man spent time in the same jail cell on Alcatraz!). There are some nice touches, as with Ellen Corby's character of Birdie, an old grifter whose apartment is full of cages of chirping birds. One effective moment has Birdie, having suddenly sung like a bird to reveal some much-needed information, die with a peaceful smile on her face among her beloved birds.
>
> The technical credits, including the work of cinematographer Jack Mackenzie and film editor Gene Fowler, Jr., are solid. The camerawork looks good, including during the extensive and probably difficult-to-shoot location sequences, replete with civilians staring into the camera. (At one point, even Marie Windsor does this before quickly looking away, as if she wasn't aware the camera was filming her.) The staging, stunting and lighting are all up to snuff and the location footage in San Francisco lends credibility to the story.
>
> The set-up for a weekly program is actually great. Mike's complex past (though he was a jailbird, he was innocent) has high potential and having his home and office be a houseboat leads to miles of story possibilities and rich visuals. But Beaumont was miscast and the actors needed some much-missing direction by Boetticher. The presence of a much more charismatic lead—think Dick Powell or even Howard Duff—might have helped the pilot take off into a full season. And why would Charlie the cab driver, who has seemingly nothing else to do, drive Mike from place to place around town, other than for the contact high he may get from his proximity to Mike's exciting adventures? It doesn't help that the particulars of at least one story point—a second kidnapping leads to a third kidnapping, which in turn leads to the professor and Charlie barging in to save the day—are somewhat unclear.

***Maverick* (Warner Bros.–ABC Television, 1957–1962).** Budd Boetticher directed the pilot and two subsequent episodes of the popular Western-comedy series about a con man and gambler (James Garner) who roams the West on a vague mission and ends up helping (and sometimes hurting) the people he encounters. According to Budd, he agreed to direct the pilot and then, because he liked Garner, decided to stick around to do two more episodes, which turned out to be the first three shows aired in the autumn of 1957.

You can find a lot of information about the creation and programming of *Maverick* both online and in your local library—including Garner's 2011 memoir *The Garner Files* (with Jon Winokur). But going too in-depth about the rise and eventual fall of this series makes little sense when looking at Boetticher's career. He was out of the picture by Episode 4 and never returned to the show, which underwent cast changes and endured legal controversies over the years. Producer Roy Huggins—who had directed Randolph Scott in an interesting 1952 Columbia Western called *Hangman's Knot*—pitched the idea for *Maverick* to Warner Bros. as the antithesis of the studio's *Cheyenne* series, in which hero Clint Walker always did the right thing. Huggins wanted a show where the hero was always doing the wrong thing, be it a sensual seduction of a woman he shouldn't be chasing or a double-cross of a new partner. And if gunplay erupted, maybe the hero would duck out the nearest window rather than pull his six-gun.

Warner Bros. went for it. ABC bought it. Warners insisted on full control, which in turn meant producer Huggins had full control. Well, almost. He turned in a pilot script called "Point Blank" but the studio heads told him they did not want him to be credited with creating the series, or he might ask for royalties down the line. (At least the studio was honest with him.) At that time, it was common for Warner Bros. to insist that all new series be based on properties the studio already owned. Huggins found a book called *War of the Copper Kings* by C.B. Glasscock that the studio owned. Huggins adapted it for a *Maverick* script, "War of the Silver Kings," for the pilot episode. The studio talked with Budd about perhaps directing a picture there. (The Warner Bros. Archives at the University of Southern California indicate that both sides were discussing a project called *Garden of Evil*. Given that's the title of a 1954 20th Century–Fox Western starring Gary Cooper and Richard Widmark, I imagine they would have changed the title had it been produced.) Budd said he could do no wrong with Jack Warner. "I always liked the tough guys and they liked me," Budd said of Warner. Warner, he said, told him about the upcoming show *Maverick* and asked him to direct the first episode.

By Boetticher's account, one day Warner asked him to come to a screening room and watch a reel of film between Marlon Brando and contract player James Garner from the film *Sayonara*, then shooting in Japan. In the footage, shot by director Josh Logan, Brando asks all sorts of inane questions, like "Where do I look?" and causing about nine minutes of grief before they get to his brief scene with Garner. When the reel was over and the lights came up in the screening room, Budd turned to Warner and said, "There's Maverick."

Warner said, "I wouldn't work with that son of a bitch again as long as I live."

"Who are you talking about?" Budd asked.

"Brando," Warner said.

"I'm not talking about Brando," Budd said, referring to the still-unknown contract player named Garner who was earning $250 a week. "What's his name?"

"James Garner."

And so, Budd claims, "that's how [Garner] got the job." It's unclear in this retelling if Warner wanted Budd to weigh in on the scene or wanted his opinion about Brando or Garner.

In his memoir, Garner simply says that upon returning from shooting *Sayonara* in Japan early in 1957, the studio asked him to test for the role. "They picked me, probably because they saw the *Sayonara* dailies and figured, 'Hey, we've already got this guy under contract, we might as well save some money.' That's how they 'discovered' me to play Bret Maverick," he wrote.

Huggins told a different tale, claiming he saw Garner play a con man in an obscure science fiction show that the studio produced, "The Man from 1999." Though Huggins had previously seen Garner's work and found

Actress Carla Merey and actor James Garner added pep and humor to "War of the Silver Kings," the pilot episode for the popular television series *Maverick*, directed by Budd Boetticher (Photofest).

him "stiff," he loved the comedic energy Garner brought to it and recommended him for the part of Bret Maverick. Warner, he said, "was all for it."

Budd was assigned to shoot the pilot for the new one-hour show, which would take six to eight days to film, and soon necessitated the hiring of a second actor—Jack Kelly—to play Bret's brother Bart so they could alternate shows and give each actor a rest.

Budd and Garner agree that together they played around with the scripts for two of the first three shows, changing the dialogue to fit their needs and incorporating physical and verbal shtick wherever possible to lighten the tone. Budd, accustomed to working this way with Burt Kennedy, Harry Joe Brown and Randolph Scott, probably assumed it was equally kosher to do so in the deadline-driven world of television. It wasn't. They got away with it on "War of the Silver Kings," stuck closer to the original script with Huggins' "Point Blank" (which became the second show of the series) and then returned to their carefree antics for Budd's third show, "According to Hoyle."

Huggins, in a 1999 Archive of American Television interview, said Budd crossed the line by playing fast and loose with the scripts. Midway through the shoot of "According to Hoyle," Huggins watched some dallies and noticed with dismay that Budd was giving all the heroic lines designated for actor Leo Gordon—playing Bret's amiable sidekick Mike McCord in the early episodes—to Garner. Budd also gave all of Garner's anti-heroic lines to Gordon. Huggins said he called Budd up that night to chide him, and Budd simply said, "I'm the director, this is what I do." Since it was too late to reshoot all those sequences, Huggins let it go. But, he said, "I never used [Boetticher] again."

In truth, the two shows Budd and Garner goofed around on are much more entertaining than Huggins' somber and slow-moving "Point Blank." Huggins eventually caught on. As Garner wrote in his autobiography: "By the fourth episode Roy was writing for it and [the episodes] got a lot more amusing."

Maverick: "War of the Silver Kings" (September 22, 1957) Director: Budd Boetticher. Producer: Roy Huggins. Teleplay: James O'Hanlon, based on C.B. Glasscock's *War of the Copper Kings*. With James Garner (Bret Maverick), Edmund Lowe (Phineas King), John Litel (Joshua Thayer), Leo Gordon (Big Mike McCombs), Carla Merey (Edie Stoller), Fred Sherman (John Stoller), John Hubbard (Bixby), Robert Griffin (Kennedy) and Bob Steele (Jackson).

Synopsis: Drifting gambler and con man Bret Maverick inadvertently gallops into a conflict over control of the mining town of Echo Springs.

"War of the Silver Kings" is arguably Budd's best television production. Instilled with a confidence gained from the recent string of films he had made with Randolph Scott, he tackles the project with a child-like verve of discovery and imagination. The show is filled with humor and some then-daring touches that showcase a very different kind of Western hero. Maverick introduces himself as a "grass inspector…the type that always looks greener in the other fella's yard." In one sequence, determined to learn who set him up for an ambush, he marches into a barber shop and accosts the thug sitting under the barber's razor with a six-gun—which fits right into the hapless bad guy's mouth.

"You're in my room!" Maverick declares when he finds drunken ex-judge Thayer (John Litel) in his bed.

"So are you!" Thayer responds with perfect comic timing.

The show includes a hilarious would-be seduction scene where the semi-homely Edie Stoller (played by now-forgotten actress Carla Merey) attempts to convince Maverick to marry her. It also features a lot of wonderful comic byplay between Garner and Leo Gordon, who, for once, is allowed to play it funny as an agreeable Irish barkeep.

In the end, Maverick uses common sense, bravado and humor to overcome all obstacles, then riding off toward the next town, with new pal Mike McComb (Gordon) in tow. This new hero was always on the run—and, you sensed, he liked it that way.

James Garner (left) and Leo Gordon paired well in the pilot episode for the *Maverick* television series, entitled "War of the Silver Kings." It was one of three *Maverick* episodes that Budd Boetticher directed (Photofest).

Maverick: "Point Blank" (September 29, 1957) Director: Budd Boetticher. Writer-Producer: Roy Huggins. With James Garner (Bret Maverick), Karen Steele (Molly Gleason), Mike Connors (Ralph Jordan), Richard Garland (Sheriff Wes Corwin), Benny Baker (Mike Brill), Robert Foulk (The Moose), John Harmon (Nelson) and Peter Brown (Chris Semple).

Synopsis: Bank teller Ralph Jordan schemes with fiancée Molly Gleason to rob the bank and frame Bret Maverick—who will be conveniently shot dead and thus be unable to defend himself.

A dull, dark and dreary affair, "Point Blank" offers almost no comic interchanges and features a plot right out of a mid–1940s Republic Western. Budd managed to draw a soft, sensitive portrayal out of Karen Steele, but there is almost nothing else going on here to recommend a viewing of the show. Maverick defends himself in a gunfight and ends up in jail. Bar owner Mike bails him out and asks him to oversee his gambling establishment and keep it honest. A pair of bad guys who seem inconsequential to the plot show up and get caught cheating, and then break jail and beat up Maverick, who is saved by the sheriff, who then fights with Maverick, who then hightails it back to town to discover that his new girlfriend is up to no good, and…

Budd and Garner tried to interject one interesting bit of physical humor by having Maverick and the sheriff disappear behind some bushes to carry on a fistfight, but now that business just seems confusing. If you saw it in an old Buster Crabbe PRC Western, you'd probably groan.

Though Leo Gordon's Mike McCombs rode out of town with Bret Maverick at the end of Episode 1, setting up a sequel, McCombs does not return until Episode 3. But it's odd that Bret Maverick encounters another bar owner named Mike (played by Benny Baker) who helps him out in Episode 2.

Maverick: "According to Hoyle" (October 6, 1957) Director: Budd Boetticher. Producer: Roy Huggins. Teleplay: Russell Hughes. With James Garner (Bret Maverick), Diane Brewster (Samantha Crawford), Leo Gordon (Mike McCombs), Ted De Corsia (Joe Riggs), Jay Novello (Henry Tree), Tol Avery (George Cross), Esther Dale (Ma Braus), Walter Reed (Bledsoe) and Tyler McVey (Hayes).

Synopsis: Anxious to learn why gambler Samantha Crawford is trying to ruin him, Bret

Maverick joins forces with her to oust yet another gambling rival, the crooked Joe Riggs.

The title for this episode comes from *Hoyle's Book of Games* (1876) and sets this teleplay up for comic possibilities as Bret Maverick and other experienced gamblers find themselves flustered by a Southern belle whose knowledge of poker games follows strict Hoyle guidelines; none of her gambling opponents has apparently read the book in years, if ever. About halfway through the show, that idea is set aside as Maverick and Crawford team to do away with stereotypical town boss Joe Riggs, leading to a not-very-exciting saloon brawl primarily made up of footage from director Michael Curtiz's 1939 *Dodge City*.

Everyone involved in this production—except the unfortunately somber Ted De Corsia, who had played the same sort of role countless times—imbues their characterization with subtle comic touches, adding to the fun. Jay Novello in particular is a delight as a middleman who discreetly deals himself into every new set-up, regardless of who is behind it. Budd brings a tension and excitement to the poker games, cutting to close-ups of the other players and spectators as Bret Maverick does five-card-stud battle with his tablemates. The last shot of the show offers a beautiful comic pay-off.

The character of Samantha Crawford popped up again on the show, as did Leo Gordon's Mike McComb. And for poker players, it's a good reminder to occasionally look at the rulebook regarding card games.

One thing Warner Bros. did with their television shows—for better or worse—was to give them a veneer of class by throwing in stock footage from previous A-Westerns. Shots from 1952's *Carson City* show up as background in "War of the Silver Kings" and here we get extensive footage from 1939's *Dodge City*, which looks very out of place when compared to poorly shot close-ups of *Maverick* actors observing as though they were caught up in the destruction. Garner later joked that viewers knew any time they saw more than two actors in a Warner Bros. television show, it was stock footage.

Hong Kong: "Colonel Cat" (A 20th Century–Fox Television production. Air date: November 11, 1960) Director: Budd Boetticher. Producer: Herbert Hirschman. Created and Written by Robert Buckner. With Rod Taylor (Glenn Evans), Lloyd Bochner (Neil Campbell), Jack Kruschen (Tully), Teru Shimada (Colonel "Cat" Okamara), Herbert Marshall (Sir John Dolman), Sarah Marshall (Kit Dolman) and John Lasell (Roger Dolman).

Synopsis: Japanese war criminal Col. Okamara returns to Hong Kong 15 years after the end of World War II for some nefarious reason. Journalist Glenn Evans and his bartender pal Tully work to find out why.

Hong Kong was an unusual series for its time in that its locale was the British Crown Colony of Hong Kong, which added a touch of the exotic to the usual stories of gamblers, smugglers, mystery women and dope dealers. That in turn gave series protagonist Glenn Evans (Rod Taylor) the opportunity to play an international crime reporter, always conveniently stumbling upon a criminal act or crafty heist of some sort. Fortuitously, Evans made fast friends with British police chief Neil Campbell and barkeep Tully, both of whom provided a wealth of inside information that helped Evans land one front-page story after another.

Driving a flashy sports car and often donning a white tuxedo, star Rod Taylor—on the verge of stardom thanks to the success of 1960's *The Time Machine*—came off as an admirable and natural television version of James Bond as he engaged in sleuthing and slugging to get his stories. Much of the show was shot on the Fox back lot, but Taylor did journey to Hong Kong for some generic background footage. One of the goofy pleasures of watching Budd's sole directorial effort for the series is spotting the double takes of the locals as they suddenly notice star Taylor walking through their slum streets. In "Colonel Cat," one little Hong Kong boy suddenly spies the camera up on a platform and flashes an impetuous and delighted grin as Taylor almost bumps into him on the street.

Those amusements aside, "Colonel Cat"

makes good use of an offbeat script. Budd's direction—including some fast-paced cross-cutting—builds tension as our heroes work together to find more clues to Okamara's whereabouts and mission. Typical of the series, this episode is full of fortune-telling Asian mystics and pistol-wielding mystery men, and there's plenty of violence, including a karate match, to keep things moving along at a swift pace. Shot in a straightforward *noir* style by Budd, the final brawls include some effective close-ups and exertive physical exchanges, most of which seems to have been done by the principal actors and not their stunt doubles. There's one great shot of a character suddenly catching sight of Okamara's face in the glow of a lit cigarette; it's downright spooky.

Taylor later called the one-hour ABC show a success that ran for a couple of years, but it ran just one season, from September 1960 through September 1961. Taylor enjoyed a limited sense of stardom through the 1960s before finding himself lounging about in supporting roles in the 1970s, including a nice turn as an aging cowpoke riding along with John Wayne in 1973's *The Train Robbers*, directed by Burt Kennedy.

Rod Taylor, on "Colonel Cat":

> Budd Boetticher was a dear friend of mine.... [M]y relationship was a lot concerned with the fact that he admired that as a young and stupid punk I did all my own stunts and I was kind of pretty good at it. And of course Budd was fighting bulls and all this stuff himself and so this brought us together. He kind of respected and admired me. He said, "I've got a great stunt...it's for the next fight. You'll do anything?" "Sure!"
>
> So he dug a trench, the son of a bitch, filled it with water and I fought two Chinese ... thugs for an hour up to my neck in water. I got out, I couldn't breathe, I was frozen, and he said, "That was great, that was great, Rod, that's the kind of stuff we need." And it's a TV show for Christ's sake. Anyway, that was Budd.

That story may be true since the trench serves little other purpose in the plot other than as a place to stage a watery fight. But Taylor's memory is a bit off: He only fights one thug in the water.

An ill-looking Herbert Marshall plays almost all of his scenes sitting down. His daughter Sarah, who mostly worked in theater and television, plays his character's daughter, but she isn't given much to do and one wonders if the old boy didn't insist upon a "two for one" deal to help her break into the business.

The Rifleman: "Stopover" (April 25, 1961) Director: Budd Boetticher. Producers: Arthur Gardner, Arnold Laven and Jules V. Levy. Teleplay: Arthur Browne, Jr. With Chuck Connors (Lucas McCain), Johnny Crawford (Mark McCain), Adam West (Christopher Rolf), Gordon Jones (Vince Medford), Bethel Leslie (Tess Miller) and Joe Higgins (Scotty).

Synopsis: A trio of morally compromised stagecoach passengers take refuge at the McCain ranch during a fierce winter snowstorm.

"Stopover" is an adequate episode of the then-popular ABC Western series that ran from the autumn of 1958 into the spring of 1963. It allows Chuck Connors, as Lucas McCain, to serve as a moral anchor who has to keep three unexpected guests in line. In an unusual turn, one of the overnighters is a schoolteacher turned gunfighter (Adam West) who, like Lucas, lost his wife in a senseless tragedy. The crux of the conflict shifts between his character and the alcoholic booze peddler Vince Medford (Gordon Jones, also in Boetticher's *The Rise and Fall of Legs Diamond*) and between Medford and his female companion Tess Miller (nicely played by stage actress Bethel Leslie). Greed, suspicion and the hope of earning a fast buck nearly leads to a shootout in the McCain barn.

Boetticher used some offbeat camera angles to give the episode a sense of claustrophobic scope. (One shot, taken from the roof of McCain's home, captures the snow-covered stage pulling in.) West gives a simple, straightforward performance as the emotionally tortured gunman, and Jones is more believable than usual as a desperate loser who chases one last slim chance at success.

The teleplay features a very amusing and naughty sequence in which adolescent Mark is forced to share his bedroom with the mature Tess. Lucas ensures Mark that he will hang a blanket on a clothesline in the room to separate them. "Just a blanket?" the boy asks with a horrified look. Later, the camera, set up on this side of Mark's bed as he faces the audience, captures Tess' bare feet and legs as her clothes drop to the floor (behind the blanket, of course). Mark, catching just a glimpse of the disrobing, buries his head under the covers out of shame. Good, too, is the slight touch of realism as Mark discovers that a snowstorm means he may not have to go to school the next day.

Sam Peckinpah wrote the pilot script for *The Rifleman* for Dick Powell's *Zane Grey Theatre*. That show aired in March 1958. ABC picked it up as a series and it had a healthy five-year run. Peckinpah contributed several scripts in the early years, but this is the only *Rifleman* episode I know of that Budd Boetticher directed. He didn't mention it much in later years.

Johnny Crawford to the author:

> Budd was a good guy, a really good guy. We went over schedule on that one—I think we shot it in four or five days and we usually shot an episode in three days—and [the producers] never used him again. We both owned horses in Burbank and we would ride around together in Griffith Park. While we were shooting that episode, he was married to a beautiful woman, an actress named Debra Paget. She was very sweet. I was impressed—they were a great couple. That was a good episode. I was very fond of him. I didn't spend a lot of time with him on the set. He was busy setting up scenes while we were working and I was busy myself as I sometimes used rehearsal time to "build up my education," spending three hours with a welfare worker getting my education. I didn't have a lot of time to associate with the other actors [Adam West and Gordon Jones]. Budd later invited me to see that film he was working on about the bullfighter, *Arruza*. He's got a great reputation for his work and deservedly so.

***Dick Powell's Zane Grey Theatre* (CBS, 1960–1961).** Dick Powell was one smart man. He was a top star in Warner Bros. musicals of the 1930s. When that wave ran out, he struggled for a few years before reinventing himself by playing hard-boiled detective Philip Marlowe in RKO's 1944 screen adaptation of Raymond Chandler's *Murder, My Sweet*. That success led to five or six years of film noirs and action films, including the underrated 1948 Western *Station West*, in which Powell is so convincing as a cowboy that I'm curious why he did not make more Westerns.

Then in the mid-1950s, Powell joined forces with actors David Niven and Charles Boyer to create Four Star Television, a prescient move that secured Powell's position in the industry for nearly a decade. "Four Star was the brainchild of Don Sharpe, a prolific radio package and talent agent," Christine Becker wrote in her illuminating book *It's the Pictures That Got Small: Hollywood Film Stars on 1950s Television*. Sharpe had already put together an anthology radio series called *Four Star Playhouse* in 1949. He then approached clients Powell and Joel McCrea about following suit with a television version of that show. McCrea reportedly shot one episode before dropping out, but Powell stayed on and convinced Niven and Boyer to join the show, organizing Four Star Productions in the process. Actress Ida Lupino later signed on to co-host the series, but she was not a producer or profit participant in the enterprise.

"The program's anthology series ran the gamut of genres, from thrillers to romances to comedies," Becker wrote. But as television companies produced more and more Western series, Powell launched *Dick Powell's Zane Grey Theatre* for CBS in 1956. Four Star also produced such popular Western series as *Trackdown* and *Wanted: Dead or Alive*. The *Zane Grey Theatre* spawned several spin-offs, including *The Rifleman* and *The Westerner*.

Western film and television historian Boyd Magers wrote on his *Western Clippings* website that Powell was a fan of Zane Grey's Western stories. "Although he obtained the rights to all the Grey novels and stories, the problem was trying to adapt Grey's works into a 30-minute TV format," Magers wrote. "Instead, the writers devised characters and incidents from Grey's stories and wrote tightly scripted new material that captured the essence of Grey's western writings."

As both a producer and a long-time Hollywood player, Powell could pick up the telephone and ask name stars to appear on the show. Joan Crawford, Edward G. Robinson, Walter Pidgeon, Robert Ryan, Van Johnson and Ronald Reagan all played parts in the series, some of them making return appearances. Powell also appeared in several of them, including two that Boetticher directed.

Budd told film historian Ronald L. Davis that Powell phoned him some time in the spring of 1960 and said, "There's no one in the world other than you that I would like to have direct." Budd said he replied, "Mr. Powell, how much do I have to pay you?" He signed on to direct five shows in the fifth and last season of the program. Budd said he liked both Powell and producer Aaron Spelling.

As of this writing (the autumn of 2017), the first three seasons of *Zane Grey Theatre* have been released on DVD, but Seasons 4 and 5 have not. Still, I tracked down four of the five Boetticher episodes. As with the rest of his television work, his *Zane Grey Theatre* output remains a mixed bag.

Zane Grey Theatre: "Desert Flight" (October 13, 1960) Director: Budd Boetticher. Producer: Aaron Spelling. Teleplay: James and Joseph Byrns. With Dick Powell (Mike Brenner), James Coburn (Charlie Doyle), Ben Cooper (Sandy) and John Pickard (The Sheriff).

Synopsis: Bank robber Mike Brenner, who prides himself on never shooting anyone, hires two young hellions for a big job. As a result, someone gets killed.

"Desert Flight" is the first and best of the four Budd Boetticher *Zane Grey Theatre* shows that I viewed. Powell reached back to his hard-edged noir persona to shade in a sharp portrait of an aging bank robber who tries to set a moral tone for two young whippersnappers. What I find fascinating about the show is how comfortably it fits into the realm of the Budd Boetticher-Burt Kennedy-Randolph Scott Westerns. "Too bad somebody don't give them a helping hand before it's too late," one character says of the two young guns, a line that bears close resemblance to the type of dialogue Burt Kennedy wrote for the Scott Westerns. The casting of Coburn from *Ride Lonesome* strengthens that connection. Ben Cooper, an underrated and natural performer, turns in a strong performance as the naïve farm boy turned outlaw. The finale is melancholy and surprising, and the producers aimed for realism with the sweaty brows and chapped lips on the characters.

Zane Grey Theatre: "Ransom" (November 17, 1960). Director: Budd Boetticher. Producer: Aaron Spelling. Teleplay: Harry Julian Fink. With Lloyd Bridges (Dundee), Claude Akins (Simmy), Anita Corsaut (Amy) and Ed Nelson (Tantasi). Host: Keenan Wynn.

Synopsis: Comanchero Simmy saves the life of a white captive of the Comanches for reason that are not initially clear.

"Ransom" comes close to slipping into the horror genre with a disturbingly tense three-character dinner sequence deftly played by Bridges, Akins and Corsaut (who would soon gain television fame as Andy Griffith's girlfriend in his long-running series). The show kicks off with a brutal Comanche ambush and then survives a goofy bit of byplay between Akins' smiling trader and Ed Nelson's Hollywoodized turn as a Comanche chief. Then the story rides straight into the frightening depths of a gothic horror novel. Corsaut really proves herself as a disturbed pioneer woman who has been living in an emotional torture chamber and wants Bridges to join her there.

Zane Grey Theatre: "Ambush" (January 5, 1961) Director: Budd Boetticher. Producer: Aaron Spelling. Teleplay: Richard Fielder. With Dick Powell (Col. Blackburn), Jack Elam (Dirk Ryan), Arch Johnson (Dutch), Dean Stanton (Private Brock), Conlan Carter (McKenzie), Charles Fredericks (Confederate Captain) and Don Dubbins (Lt. Homeyer).

Synopsis: Union Colonel Blackburn leads a half-dirty-dozen band of deserters, miscreants and killers on a suicide mission to deliver a treaty to the Comanche during the Civil War.

"Ambush" needs more than the 24 minutes allotted to it to fully flesh out its complicated notions. The story jams too much information into its brief running time, giving the actors little chance of infusing their characters with anything more than broad brushstrokes of rage, cynicism and cowardice. Budd was hampered by both the script and phony-looking exterior sets obviously shot on a sound stage. Powell delivers a one-note turn. Little is done to create and maintain conflict between the characters. And why would Comanche warriors come charging out of a dark forest on foot with no weapons in their hands to take on soldiers on horseback who sport rifles and pistols? "Ambush" is a big step down from the heights set by "Desert Flight."

Zane Grey Theatre: "The Long Shadow" (January 19, 1961) Director: Budd Boetticher. Producer: Aaron Spelling. Teleplay: Richard Fielder. With Ronald Reagan (Major Will Sinclair), Nancy Davis (Amy), Scott Marlowe (Jimmy Budd), Roberta Shore (Laurie) and Walter Sande (Sgt. Luke Muldoy)

Synopsis: Cavalry Major Will Sinclair has the tough job of explaining to widow Amy Lawson how her son died under his command.

Another *Zane Grey Theatre* misfire for writer Richard Fielder and Budd, "The Long Shadow" does not even start out with much of a good idea. It's heavy on coincidence too: Amy's late husband was in the army with Major Sinclair, and then her son joins up with Sinclair and gets killed, and she and Sinclair have some vague emotional connection and there's an old friend of the dead son who is trailing Sinclair, and a comic-relief sergeant who knows all the characters, and…

Reagan's authoritative military martinet doesn't move one to empathize with his actions. But Nancy Davis was spot on as the grieving widow and you can tell she was really attracted to her real-life husband Reagan as they played out their romantic scenes together. Marlowe and Shore, as the youngsters, over-emote in a Method-style acting manner that is at odds with Reagan and Davis' energy. A clumsy fight sequence, obviously staged with doubles and an all-too-fake knife blade (it bends like cardboard when it hits the wall), mars the climax.

The fifth *Zane Grey Theatre* episode that Budd Boetticher directed, "The Last Trumpet," stars Robert Cummings as a cavalry officer trying to make peace with Geronimo. I could not find a copy.

Boyd Magers said that *Dick Powell's Zane Grey Theatre* had little competition from the rival networks in its first few years of production, but by the beginning of Season 5, NBC threw *Bat Masterson* against it while ABC scheduled *The Real McCoys*, both popular shows that bit into *Zane Grey Theater*'s ratings. Dick Powell's death from cancer in 1963 "dealt the heaviest blow to the company's fortunes," Becker wrote. Charles Boyer later said, "When Dick Powell died, it was no longer the same."

In the spring of 1959, Budd teamed with Burt Kennedy to film a TV pilot called *Wildcatters* for John Wayne's Batjac company. A one-page memo housed in the University of Southern California's film archives says that Claude Akins, Karen Steele, L.Q. Jones and Sean McClory appeared in the 30-minute pilot episode, which Budd created and directed and Burt wrote and produced. Sam Thurm, an executive vice-president for advertising for Lever Brothers, who sponsored a number of television shows at the time, screened the pilot in March and apparently did not like it, according to the memo. To the best of my knowledge, the pilot never aired. I can't imagine there's a copy of the show floating around out there in the Black Hole of lost television programs, but who knows?

Bibliography

Books

Adams, Julie. *The Lucky Southern Star: Reflections from the Black Lagoon.* Hollywood: Hollywood Adventures, 2011.

Arness, James, with James E. Wise, Jr. *James Arness: An Autobiography.* Jefferson, NC: McFarland, 2001.

Atkinson, Barry. *Six-Gun Law: The Westerns of Randolph Scott, Audie Murphy, Joel McCrea and George Montgomery.* Baltimore: Midnight Marquee Press, 2015.

Balio, Tino. *United Artists: The Company That Changed the Film Industry.* Madison: University of Wisconsin Press, 1987.

Becker, Christine. *It's the Pictures That Got Small: Hollywood Film Stars on 1950s Television.* Middletown, CT: Wesleyan University Press, 2008.

Best, James, with Jim Clark. *Best in Hollywood: The Good, the Bad and the Beautiful.* Albany, GA: Bear Manor, 2009.

Boetticher, Budd. *When in Disgrace.* Santa Barbara, CA: Neville Publishing, 1989. A must-have for any Boetticher fan, though he talks more about bullfighting and his private life than his film career.

Clarke, Robert, and Tom Weaver. *Robert Clarke: To "B" or Not to "B," a Film Actor's Odyssey.* Baltimore: Midnight Marquee Press, 1996.

Dick, Bernard F. *Columbia Pictures: Portrait of a Studio.* Lexington: University Press of Kentucky, 1992.

Dixon, Wheeler Winston. *Collected Interviews: Voices from 20th Century Cinema.* Carbondale: Southern Illinois University Press, 2001.

Epstein, Dwayne. *Lee Marvin: Point Blank.* Tucson: Schaffner Press, 2013.

Eyman, Scott. *John Wayne: The Life and Legend.* New York: Simon & Schuster, 2014.

Fagen, Herb. *Duke, We're Glad We Knew You.* New York: Citadel Press, 2006; New York: Kensington, 2009 (reprint).

Fernett, Gene. *American Film Studios: An Historical Encyclopedia.* Jefferson, NC: McFarland, 2001

Fitzgerald, Michael. *Universal Pictures.* New York: Arlington House, 1979.

Fitzgerald, Michael G., and Boyd Magers. *Ladies of the Western: Interviews with Fifty-One More Actresses from the Silent Era to the Television Westerns of the 1950s and 1960s.* Jefferson, NC: McFarland, 2002.

Fitzgerald, Michael G., and Boyd Magers. *Westerns Women: Interviews with 50 Leading Ladies of Movie and Television Westerns from the 1930s to the 1960s.* Jefferson, NC: McFarland, 1999.

Flynn, Charles, and Todd M. McCarthy. *Kings of the Bs: Working Within the Hollywood System, an Anthology of Film History and Criticism.* New York: E.P. Dutton, 1975.

Ford, Peter. *Glenn Ford: A Life.* Madison: University of Wisconsin Press, 2011.

Garfield, Brian. *Western Films: A Complete Guide.* New York: Rawson Associates, 1982.

Garner, James, with Jon Winokur. *The Garner Files: A Memoir.* New York: Simon & Schuster, 2012.

Gossett, Sue. *The Films and Career of Audie Murphy.* Madison, NC: Empire Publishing, 1996.

Goudsovzian, Aram. *Sidney Poitier: Man, Actor, Icon.* Chapel Hill: University of North Carolina Press, 2004.

Graham, Don. *No Name on the Bullet, a Biography of Audie Murphy.* New York: Viking, 1989.

Hardy, Phil. *The Overlook Film Encyclopedia: The Western*, 2d ed. Woodstock, NY: Overlook Press, 1994.

Hinkle, Robert, with Mike Farris. *Call Me Lucky: A Texan in Hollywood.* Norman: University of Oklahoma Press, 2005.

Hirschhorn, Clive. *The Columbia Story.* London: Hamlyn, 1999.

Hirschhorn, Clive. *The Universal Story.* London: Octopus Books, 1983

Horwitz, James. *They Went Thataway.* New York City: E.P. Dutton, 1976. A great love affair of a book between author and B Westerns.

Joyner, C. Courtney. *The Westerners: Interviews with Actors, Directors, Writers and Producers.* Jefferson, NC: McFarland, 2009.

Kaminsky, Stuart M. *Don Siegel: Director.* New York: Curtis Books, 1974.

Kemper, Tom. *Hidden Talent: The Emergency of Hollywood Agents.* Berkeley: University of California Press, 2010.

Kennedy, Burt. *Hollywood Trail Boss.* New York: Boulevard Books, 1997. This reads more like an engaging string of anecdotes, but here and there Burt reveals some nuggets about his relationship with Budd Boetticher and Randolph Scott, plus there's a great photo of Angie Dickinson stepping out of a tub.

Kitses, Jim. *Horizons West.* Bloomington: Indiana University Press, 1969. Another must-have book for any serious Western film fan.

L'Amour, Louis. *Education of a Wandering Man.* New York: Bantam Books, 1990.

Lyons, Arthur. *Death on the Cheap: The Lost B Movies of Film Noir!* Boston: Da Capo Press, 2000.

Magers, Boyd, Bob Nareau, and Bobby Copeland. *Best of the Badmen: Polecats, Varmints, and Desperadoes of Western Films.* Madison, NC: Empire Publishing, 2005.

Magers, Boyd, with Bob Larkins. *The Films of Audie Murphy.* Jefferson, NC: McFarland, 2004.

Matlin, Leonard. *Behind the Camera.* New York: Signet Books, 1971. This collection of interviews includes one with cinematographer Lucien Ballard.

McCarthy, Todd, and Charles Flynn. *King of the Bs.* New York: E.P. Dutton, 1975. A great, all-over-the-place collection of interviews, essays and information about the B movie business.

McClelland, Doug. *Forties Film Talk: Oral Histories of Hollywood.* Jefferson, NC: McFarland, 1992.

McGilligan, Patrick. *Backstory 1: Interviews with Screenwriters of Hollywood's Golden Age.* Berkeley: University of California Press, 1986.

Miller, Don. *Hollywood Corral.* New York: Big Apple Film Series, Popular Library, 1976. One of my favorite books on B Westerns.

Mitchell, Charles P., and Paua Parla. *Scream Sirens Scream!* Jefferson, NC: McFarland, 1999.

Nott, Robert. *The Films of Randolph Scott.* Jefferson, NC: McFarland, 2004.

Nott, Robert. *Last of the Cowboy Heroes: The Westerns of Randolph Scott, Joel McCrea and Audie Murphy.* Jefferson, NC: McFarland, 2000.

O'Hara, Maureen, with John Nicoletti. *'Tis Herself: An Autobiography.* New York: Simon & Schuster Paperbacks, 2005. Just a paragraph on *The Magnificent Matador,* which says a lot about what O'Hara thought of the film.

Parish, James Robert. *The Great Movie Series.* Chicago: A.S. Barnes, 1971

Parish, James Robert, and Ronald L. Bowers. *The Golden Era: The MGM Stock Company.* New York: Bonanza Books, 1972.

Poitier, Sidney. *This Life.* New York: Ballantine Books, 1981.

Quinn, Anthony, with Daniel Paisner. *One Man Tango.* New York: HarperCollins, 1996.

Rhodes, Gary, and Robert Singer. *The Films of Budd Boetticher.* Edinburgh: Edinburgh University Press, 2017. The first serious look at Boetticher's films, this collection of essays, while heavy on scholarly analysis and plot description, is a must-have for Budd Boetticher fans, and includes some insightful write ups about some of Budd's less appreciated films, including *The Killer Is Loose* and *Decision at Sundown.* Highly recommended, though it does not cover all of Budd's films, focusing on the Randolph Scott Westerns, the bullfighting trilogy and less than a handful of his crime dramas and film noirs.

Rubin, Martin, and Eric Sherman. *The Directors Event: Interviews with Five American Film-Makers.* New York: Atheneum, 1970.

Schickel, Richard. *Clint Eastwood: A Biography.* New York: Vintage, 1996.

Silver, Alain, and Elizabeth Ward. *Film Noir: An Encyclopedic Reference to the American Style.* Woodstock, NY: Overlook Press, 1979.

Silver, Alain, with James Ursini and Robert Porfirio. *Film Noir Reader 3: Interviews with Filmmakers of the Classic Period.* New York: Limelight Editions, 2004.

Stack, Robert, with Mark Evans. *Straight Shooting.* New York: Macmillan, 1980. This is a surprisingly lively and well-written memoir from a second-tier star who seemed to have had a hell of a fun life.

Tuska, Jon. *The Filming of the West.* Garden City, NY: Doubleday, 1976.

Ward, Richard Lewis. *A History of the Hal Roach Studios.* Carbondale: Southern Illinois University Press, 2005.

Weaver, Tom, David Schecter, and Steve Kronenberg. *The Creature Chronicles: Exploring the Black Lagoon.* Jefferson, NC: McFarland, 2014.

Magazine and Newspaper Articles

A note: I did my best to cite newspaper, magazine and online articles that I drew material from throughout the text of this book, and see no need to credit them again here. But following is a list of some pieces that stand out and should be utilized by any Budd Boetticher historian. In addition, Budd Boetticher: A Man Can Do That, *Bruce Ricker's 2005 documentary, deserves mention as a prime source for any Budd Boetticher historian.*

Arnold, Jeremy. "How I Got to Call the Shots" features a lively interview with Burt Kennedy. First published in March 2000 on JWayne.com, an unofficial fan site of the late movie star.

Axmaker, Sean. "Budd Boetticher: Lost Interview with a True Hollywood Maverick," published in issues 126 and 127 of *Filmfax* magazine in 2011. Anything Axmaker writes is worth reading, as far as I am concerned.

Axmaker, Sean. "Burt Kennedy: Writing Broadway in Arizona," in the Nov. 6, 2008, edition of the *Parallax View.*

Axmaker, Sean. "Ride Lonesome: The Career of Budd Boetticher," published in *Senses of Cinema* in February 2005.

Boetticher, Budd. *The Hollywood Reporter* articles. Between 1954 and 1956 Budd Boetticher wrote several first-person pieces for *The Hollywood Reporter,* which I find interesting given that was a period of flux for him. Three that are worth seeking out are "Toreros, Toreros!" (Nov. 12, 1954), "Time Out for Bullfighting" (Nov. 14, 1955) and "The Perennial Western" (Nov. 19, 1956).

Coonradt, Peter. "Boetticher Returns," in the December 1968 issue of *Cinema.*

Dixon, Wheeler Winston. "Budd Boetticher: The Last Interview," published in the spring 2002 edition of *Film Criticism.*

Film World. Author unknown—A profile of Budd Boetticher, circa spring of 1969. I found a copy of this article in the Margaret Herrick Library at the Academy of Motion Picture Arts and Sciences, but it does not cite an author. It was published about the time Budd was completing shooting on *A Time for Dying.* It's terrific in capturing Budd's mindset following some eight years in Mexico.

Francis, Patrick. "Wise Guys," published on April 26, 2002, in *LA Weekly.* Francis may have been the last writer to interview Budd before his death in November 2001.

Gill, Ted. "Synthetic Bullfighting," a short profile of Budd Boetticher and actor John Hubbard that ran in the May 4, 1941, issue of *The Sun-Baltimore.* It may be the first newspaper article written about Budd, who was still toiling away at the Hal Roach Studios, where Hubbard was a rising star, when this piece ran.

Kehr, Dave. "Welcome Back Boetticher," *Chicago Reader,* March 1982. An affectionate homage to Budd, hopeful in its belief that maybe, just maybe, he could still stage a comeback.

Othman, Frederick C. "Ex Office Boy Loses Pants but He Directs a Movie," for the United Press (UP), published June 10, 1944. Of interest in that it may be the first newspaper story on Budd Boetticher's career as a director, conducted while he was shooting *One Mysterious Night* for Columbia Studios.

Schwartz, David. "A Pinewood Dialogue with Budd Boetticher," a transcript of an interview that Museum of the Moving Image curator Schwartz conducted with Budd in October of 2000.

Sherwood, Lynn. "An Interview with Budd Boetticher," for the *Bullfight World* column of the *San Diego La Presna.* The publication date is June 16, 2006, some years after Budd's death.

Index

Numbers in **_bold italics_** indicate pages with illustrations

Abbott (Bud) and Costello (Lou) 15, 25, 68
Adams, Julie (aka Julia) 17, 77, 89, 90, 91, **_91_**, 92, **_92_**, 97, 98, 99, 146, 149, 152
The African Queen (1951 film) 68
Akins, Claude **_145_**, 183, 184
The Alamo (1960 film) 92
Alias Mike Hercules (1955 television pilot) 175–176
Allen, Lewis 115–116
Allyn, Gloria 165
Alperson, Edward L. 102, 103, 106, 107
Angel and the Badman (1947 film) 54, 115
Archer, John 127
Archer, Mel 168, 170
Archer, Pam 63
Arena (1953 film) 67
Arness, James 79, 115
Arnold, Jack 17
Arnow, Max 26
Arthur, Jean 10, 11, 34
Arruza (1972 film) 19, 20, 21, 53, 153, 158–164, **_160_**, **_161_**, **_163_**
Arruza, Carlos 6, 19, 105, 152, 153, 159, 160, **_160_**, 161, **_161_**, 162, 163, **_163_**, 164
Arruza, Carlos, Jr. 164–165
Arruza, Maria 161
Assigned to Danger (1948 film) 14, 37–40, **_38_**
Avalon, Frankie 153
Avco Embassy 162

Bakaleinikoff, Mischa 25, 123
Ball, Suzan 85, 86, 87, 94–95
Ballard, Lucien 106, 108, 129, 130, 151–152, 154, **_154_**, 158, 159, 165
Bannon, Jim 26, **_26_**, 27
Barry, Don "Red" 12, 36, 116
Beaumont, Hugh 173, 175, 176
Behind Locked Doors (1948 film) 14, 39, 40–42, **_41_**
Benedict, Billy 30, 32, 33
Berke, William 11, 12
Best, James 61, 62, 63, 82, 83, 135, **_136_**, 138

Bischoff, Robert 9
Black Patch (1957 film) 129
Black Midnight (1949 film) 42–46, **_43_**, **_44_**
Blanke, Henry 139
Blood Alley (1955 film) 114
Blood and Sand (1941 film) 7, 8, 9
Boetticher, Budd 14, **_16_**, **_18_**, **_20_**, **_91_**, **_147_**, **_154_**; biography 1–3, 5–22; birth and early childhood 5; career decline 19–22; at Columbia Pictures studio 9, 10, 11, 12; death 22; at Eagle Lion Studios 14, 37–38; at Hal Roach Studios 7, 8, 13, 14; marriage to Debra Paget 19; marriage to Emily Cook 12, 13; in Mexico 6–7, 19, 159–161; military service 12–13; at Monogram Studios 14–15, 42–43; relationship and work with Burt Kennedy 2, 17, 18, 19, 110–113, 114, 124–125, 138, 143, 145–146; relationship and work with Harry Joe Brown 17, 18, 19, 114, 124, 137; relationship and work with Randolph Scott 18, 19, 113, 114, 115, 139, 141; television work 167–184; at Universal Studios 15, 16, 17, 64, 67, 76, 96, 98, 99, 100
Boetticher, Georgia 5, 7, 13, 17
Boetticher, Mary (Chelde) 2, 21, 22, 153, 164, 165
Boetticher, Oscar 5, 13, 17
Boggs, Johnny D. 61
Boone, Richard 119, 120, 121, 123, **_123_**
Boyer, Charles 182, 184
Boyle, Donald (creator of Boston Blackie) 23
Brady, Scott 64, 65, 66, 68, 69, 90, 168, 170
Brand, Neville 90–91
Brando, Marlon 177
Braun, Judith **_79_**
The Brave Bulls (1951 film) 58
Bremer, Lucille 40, 41, **_41_**, 42
Brice, Monte 35, 37
Briones, Luis 55

Broidy, Steve 42
Bromfield, John 63
Bronco Buster (1952 film) 16, 64–70, **_65_**, **_66_**, **_70_**, 75, 76, 90, 160
Brooks, Rand **_44_**, 45, 46, 61, 63, 114, 146
Brown, Harry Joe 9, 10, 17, 18, 19, 110, 111, 114, 118, 120, 124, 134, 136, 137, 139, 140, 145, 148; work and relationship with Budd Boetticher 17, 18, 19, 114, 124, 137
Brown, Harry Joe, Jr. 124, 134, 146
Buchanan Rides Alone (1958 film) 2, 48, 49, 67, 128, 129–134, **_130_**, **_132_**, **_133_**, **_139_**
Budd Boetticher: A Man Can Do That (documentary) 21
Bullfighter and the Lady (1951 film) 2, 15, 17, 21, 52–59, **_53_**, **_55_**, **_56_**, 64, 67, 161, 165, 168, 169
Busch, Niven 92, 93

Cagney, James 62, *102*
Califa (unrealized Budd Boetticher project) 21
Calvert, John **_31_**, 32, 33
Camacho, Manuel Avila 6
Camacho, Maximilo Avila 6
Campbell, Allison 165
Campbell, William 115
The Canadians (1961 film) 148
Capra, Frank 9, 10, 12, 13
Captain Scarface (1953 film) 103
The Captives (1955 short story) 121
Cardenas, Elsa 160
Carlson, Richard 12, 37, 40–42, **_41_**, 81–82
Carr, Barney 8
Carroll, John 127, 128
Carter, Janis 12, 24, 26, **_26_**
Case, Carroll 106, 171
Castle, William 11, 14, 17, 24, 30, 101
Cavanagh, Paul 168, 170
Chandler, Jeff 16, 64, 72, **_72_**, 73, 74, **_74_**, 94, 95
Chinatown (1973 film) 21
Chinook the Wonder Dog 46, 47, **_47_**, 49

189

Index **190**

The Cimarron Kid (1952 film) **18**, 48, 59–64, **60**, **61**
City Beneath The Sea (1953 film) 13, 17, 48, 84–88, **85**, **87**
Clark, Dane 13
Clarke, Robert 168–169, 170, 171
Clayton, Jan 47, 48, **48**
Coburn, James 21, 137, 183
Coffeyville raid 60, 61
Cohen, Albert J. 76
Cohn, Harry 10, 11, 36, 45, 124, 125, 132, 134, 137
Collins, Cora Sue 31, **32**, 33, 34
Columbia Pictures 10–12
Comanche Station (1960 film) 1, 2, 19, 64, 112, 114, 121, 130, 134, 137, 138, 142–148, **144**, **145**, **147**
The Comancheros (1961 film) 148
Connors, Chuck 181
Cook, Emily 12, 13, 45, 125, 126
Cooper, Ben 183
Corey, Wendell 107, **108**, 109
Corsaut, Anita 183
Cotten, Joseph 107, **108**, 109
The Count of Monte Cristo (television series) 174, 175
Cover Girl (1944 film) 11
Crawford, Johnny 181, 182
Curwood, James Oliver 46, 47

Dalton gang (brothers) 60, 61
Dante, Michael 140, **140**, 141, 142
Danton, Ray 57, 149, 150, **150**, 151, 152
Darnell, Linda 9
Davis, Nancy 184
Decision at Sundown (1957 film) 2, 48, 49, 125–129, **126**, 131, 134
Decision at Sundown (short story) 125
de Cordova, Frederick 15
de Corsia, Ted 180
Denning, Richard **105**, 106, 107
The Desperadoes (1943 film) 9, 90
The Devil with Hitler (1942 film) 7
Diamond, Legs 149
Dick Powell's Zane Grey Theatre 182–184
Dickerson, Dudley 35
D'Laurage, Ruth 6–7
Dmytryk, Edward 24
Dolenz, George 175
Domergue, Faith 125
Donaldson, Ted **35**
Donovan, James 91
Doolin, Bill 60, 61
Drake, Charles 73
Draper, Jack 57
The Duel at Silver Creek (1952 film) 62
Dugay, Yvette 62
Duggan, Andrew 128

Eagle Lion Studios 14, 37, 38, 40
East of Sumatra (1953 film) 75, 93–96
Eastwood, Clint 21
Egan, Richard 114
Ellis, Kirk 52, 162, 163, 165

Escape in the Fog (1944 film) 12, 27, 28, **28**, 29, **29**, 30

Feather Nest (unrealized Budd Boetticher project) 21
Feldman, Charles 39
Fellows, Robert 122
Fenady, Andrew J. 118
Field, Betty 13
Film Classics (studio) 38
A Fistful of Dollars (1964 film) 131, 134
Fix, Paul 58
Flavin, James 174
The Fleet That Came to Stay (U.S. Navy film) 13
Fleming, Rhonda 107, **108**, 109
Fluharty, Vernon L. 125
Foch, Nina 10, 23, 27, 28, **28**, 29
Fonda, Peter 153
Ford, Glenn 9, 10, 16, 17, 88, 89, 8**9**, 90, 91, **92**, 93, 100, 101, 102, 115
Ford, John 13, 15, 17, 21, 54, 57, 58, 59, 75, 76, 92, 116
Ford, Peter 89, 90, 101, 102
Foster, Harve 8
Four Star Television 182
Fowley, Douglas 40, **50**, **51**, 52
Foy, Bryon 14, 37
Francis the Talking Mule 15, 67, 92
Freeman, Kathleen 41
French, Valerie 127
Fuller, Sam 14

Galando, Nacho **51**
Garden of Evil (unrealized Budd Boetticher project) 177
Garner, James 176, 177, **177**, 178, **179**, 180
Garza, Lorenzo 6, 7
Gates, Nancy 104, 143, 144, 145, 146, **147**
Girl in the Case (1944 film) 11
Goetz, William 15, 98
Gomez, Thomas **102**, **103**
Gonzalez, Gonzalez, Pedro 97, 98, 99
Good Luck, Mr. Yates (1943 film) 11
Gordon, Leo 129, 178, **179**, **179**, 180
Grady, William 71
Grahame, Gloria 94
Grant, James Edward 15, 54
Grant, Kirby 45, 46, 47, **47**, 48, 49
Grey, Virginia **53**, 54, 56, 58, 59
Grossman, Jack 63
A Guy, a Gal and a Pal (1944 film) 16, 34–37, **35**

Hadley, Reed 171
Hale, Barbara 82, 83
Hamilton, Roy 168, 171
Hangman's Knot (1952 film) 176
Harolde, Rolf **38**, 41
Hawks, Howard 11
Hayward, Lillie 64
Hayworth, Rita 7, 9, 10, 11
Heflin, Van 16, 90, 96, 97, 99
Helton, Percy 174
Hinkle, Robert 69, 70

Hitchcock, Alfred 13
Holden, Jennifer 67
Holden, Joyce 64, 66, 67, 68
Holt, Nat 139
Homeier, Skip 122, 145
Hong Kong (television series) 180–181
Horizons West (1952 film) 76–80, **77**, **78**, **79**
A Horse for Mr. Barnum (unrealized Budd Boetticher project) 21, 166
Hour of the Gun (1967 film) 161, 162
How Green Was My Valley (1942 film) 45
Howco 169, 171
Hubbard, John 8, **53**, 54, 56, 58, 59, 63, 122, 168, 169, 170
Hudson, John 63
Hudson, Rock 15, 16, 36, 64, 79, **79**, 80, **81**, 81, 82, 83
Huggins, Roy 176, 177, 178
Hunnicutt, Arthur 1, 122
Hunter, Ross 15, 34, 35, **35**, 36
Huston, John 55, 62

I Shot Jesse James (1949 film) 14
Ibanez, Vicente Blasco 8

Jack Slade (1953 film) 42
Jaeckel, Richard 172
Johnson, Bubber 71
Johnson, Tor 40, 41
Jones, Gordon **43**, 45, 181
Jones, L.Q. 1301–131, 133, **133**
Jory, Victor 89, 156, 158
Joy, Tom 6–7
Jurado, Katy 59

Karlson, Phil 11, 14, 15
Kelly, Gene 11, 12
Kelly, Jack 167, 178
Kennedy, Arthur 100, 101
Kennedy, Burt 1, 16, 17, 19, 64, 79, 80, 109, 110, 111, 112, 113, 114, 115, 116, 118, 120, 121, 122, 123, 124, 125, 129, 130, 131, 134, 135, 136, 137, 138, 141–142, 143, 144, 145, 146, 147, 148, 178, 181, 183, 184; work and relationship with Budd Boetticher 1, 17, 18, 19, 110–113, 114, 124–125, 138, 143, 145–146
Kenny, Joseph 63
The Keys to the Kingdom (1944 film) 45
The Killer Is Loose (1955 film) 17, 107–110, **108**, 114
Killer Shark (1950 film) 15, 43, 46, 49, 50–52, **50**, **51**, 54, 84
Kosleck, Martin 39
Krim, Arthur 37, 38
Kruger, Otto 28

Lamont, Charles 15, 17
L'Amour, Louis 74–75, 94, 95
Landers, Lew 12
Landis, Carole 8, 170
Landon, Joseph 150, 151, 152
Lane, Richard 24

Lang, Charles (writer-actor) 46, 47, 48, 49, 103, 125, 129, 130, 131, 168
Lapp, Richard 156, 157, 158
LaRue, Lash 37
LaRue, Walt 155
Leonard, Elmore 118, 121, 122
Leone, Sergio 131, 134
Levine, Joseph 162
Ling, Eugene 14
Lovejoy, Frank 101
Luez, Laurette 51, 52
Lund, John 64, 65, 66, 68, 69, 90
Lupino, Ida 182
The Lusty Men (1952 film) 67
Lydon, James 173

MacDonald, Jeanette 39
Macready, George, 23, 25, 26, 27, **27**
Madison, Guy 116, 117
The Magnificent Matador (1955 film) 17, 100–107, **101**, **102**, **103**, **104**, **105**
Malone(y), Dorothy 25
Mamoulian, Rouben 8, 9
The Man from the Alamo (1953 film) 15, 16, 80, 88–93, **89**, **91**, **92**
Mann, Anthony 3, 14, 19, 25, 37, 76, 110
Margolis, Stanley 166
Marshall, Herbert 181
Marshall, Sarah 181
Marvin, Lee 82, 112, 116
Marx, Groucho 98
Masak, Ron 156, 157, 158
Matador (Barnaby Conrad novel) 103
Matador (unrealized John Huston film) 55
Mature, Victor 8, 85, 107
Maverick (television series) 176–180, **177**, **179**
Maxwell, Marilyn 94, 95
Mayo, Virginia **140**, 141
Mazurki, Mike 25
McCoy, Horace 64, 67, 69
McCrea, Joel 2, 11, 34, 114, 166, 182
McCrea, Peter 166
McDaniel, Sam 35
McDowell, Roddy 42, 43, **43**, 44, **44**, 45, **50**, 50–52,
McLaglen, Andrew 15, 52, 54, 55, 117, 118
McLain, Barbara 9
McLeod, Mary 35
Merley, Carla **177**, 178
Merrick, Lynn **35**, 36
Mimieux, Yvette 21
The Missing Juror (1944 film) 12, 25–27, **26**, **27**
Mitchell, Steve 115
Mitchum, Robert 20, 114, 115
Monogram Pictures 14, 15, 42–43, 45, 46, 47, 49, 51, 52
Monroe, Marilyn 39, 40
Montagne, Eddie 8
Montalban, Ricardo 55
Montgomery, George 129, 147
Montiel, Sarita 100, 101
Moore, Dickie 41, 51

The More the Merrier (1943 film) 2, 9, 11
Morris, Chester 12, **16**, 23, 24, **24**, 25
Morse, Holly 8
Morse, Mel (American Humane Association representative) 57
Muhl, Edward 15, 98
Murphy, Audie 2, **18**, 20, 59, **60**, **61**, 62, 63, 69, 134, 147, 153, 154, **154**, 155, 156, 157, 158
Murphy, Terry 154, 155, 156, 157, 158
My Friend Flicka (1943 film) 45
My Kingdom for... (1985 film) 53, 164–166

Nagel, Conrad 36
Nash, Noreen **38**, 39, 40
Nazarro, Ray 54
Neal, Tom 11
Nicol, Alex 73, **74**, 75
Niven, David 182
Norris, Edward 17, 48, **48**
Norton, Jack 35
Novello, Jay 180

O'Brian, Hugh 62, 63, 71, **81**, 82
Of Mice and Men (1939 film) 7
O'Flynn, Damian 43, **43**, 44
O'Hara, Maureen **101**, **102**, **103**, **104**, 104, **105**, 105, 106, 107, 146
One Mysterious Night (1944 film) 12, 23–25, **24**
Osceola (Seminole chief) 81, 84
O'Sullivan, Maureen 122, 123, **123**
Owens, Jesse 6

Page, Joy 54, **55**, 57, 59, 168
Paget, Debra 19, 160, 182
Palma, Joe 36
Palmer, Gregg (aka Palmer Lee) 63, 74, 75
Parrish, Helen 48, 49, 168
Parsons, Lindsley 15, 42, 43, 45, 46
Pastoral (1939 play) 49
Peckinpah, Sam 3, 75, 76, 114, 128, 137, 144, 156, 182
Pevney, Joseph 15, 17, 116
Poitier, Sidney 71, 72, 73, 74
Powell, Dick 114, 182, 183, 184
Power, Tyrone 7, 8, 9
Powers, Mala 85, 86, **87**
PRC (Producers Releasing Corporation) 37, 38
Preston, Robert 114
Price, Vincent 168
Public Defender (television series) 17, 167, 171–174

Quinn, Anthony 9, 82, 83, 84, 85, **85**, 87, 94, 95, 100, **101**, 102, **102**, **103**, 104, **104**, 105, **105**, 106, 107, 162

Randall, Anne 155, 156, 157, 158
Rank, J. Arthur 37, 38
Raye, Martha 12
Raymond, Gene 37, 38, **38**, 39
Reagan, Ronald 183, 184
The Rebel (1960s television show) 118

The Red Badge of Courage (1951 film) 62
Red Ball Express (1952 film) 70–76, **72**, **74**, 93, 126
Red Ball Express (World War II military operation) 70, 71, 72, 73
Reed, David 31, 33
Reed, Walter 59, 88, 91, 115, 116, 157
Return to Paradise (1953 film) 96
Reynolds, William 62, 63, 64
Richmond, Ted 25, 67
Ricker, Bruce 21–22
Ride Lonesome (1959 film) 2, 19, 63, 112, 114, 130, 134–138, **136**, 142
Ride the High Country (1962 film) 114, 128, 144, 148, 156
Riefenstahl, Leni 150
Rieseberg, Harry E. 86
The Rifleman (television series) 181–182
The Rise and Fall of Legs Diamond (1960 film) 30, 126, 148–153, **150**
Roach, Hal, Jr. 6, 13, 14, 103, 168, 169, 170, 171, 174
Roach, Hal, Sr. 6, 7, 8, 9, 13
Road Show (1941 film) 8, 170
Robards, Jason 162
Roberts, Pernell 137
Robinson, Ann 45–46, 63
Rodeo (1952 film) 67
Roland, Gilbert 53, 54, 57, 58
Romero, Cesar 100, 101
Root, Elizabeth 48, **48**
Rosenberg, Aaron 15, 91
Rossen, Robert 58
Russell, Gail **111**, 115, 116, 117, 118
Rust, Richard 143, 144, 146–147
Ryan, Robert 16, 76, 77, **77**, 78, **78**, 80, 84, 85, 86, 87

Sands of Iwo Jima (1949 film) 54
Sawyer, Geneva 9
Sayonara (1957 film) 177
Scott, Randolph 1, 2, 9, 10, 11, 16, 17, 18, 19, 25, 26, 34, 36, 44, 64, 110, 111, **111**, 112, 113, **113**, 114, 115, 116, 117, 118, **118**, 119, 120, **120**, 121, **121**, 122, **123**, 124, 125, **126**, 127, 128, 129, 130, **130**, 131, **132**, **133**, 134, 135, **136**, 138, 139, 140, **140**, 141, 142, 143, 144, **144**, **145**, 146, 147, 148, 156, 159, 163, 164; work and relationship with Budd Boetticher 18, 19, 113, 114, 115, 139, 141
Seminole (1953 film) 80–84, **81**, 116
Seven Men from Now (1956 film) 2, 3, 11, 17, 52, 58, 59, 80, 109, 110–119, **111**, **113**, 134, 135, 143
7 Men from Now (1956 paperback book) **118**, 119
Sharpe, Dave 63
Shayne, Konstantin, **28**, **29**
Sheridan, Ann 36
Siegel, Don 20, 43, 62
Siegel, Lee 40
Silva, Henry 1, 122, 135
Sinatra, Nancy 152
Sinclair, Eric 30, **31**, **32**, 33
Six Black Horses (1962 film) 147

Index

Sky King (television series) 49
A Song to Remember (1945 film) 10
Space, Arthur 88
Sperling, Milton 149, 152
Spitz, Leo 15
Stack, Elizabeth 166
Stack, Robert 21, *53*, 55, *55*, 56, *56*, 57, 58, 59, 97, 165, 166, 168
Stack, Rosemarie 165, 166
Steele, Karen 125, 126, 127, 128, 129, 135, 141, 142, 149, 151, 153, 160, 179, 184
Stevens, Craig 130, *130*, 132, 133–134
Stevens, George 9, 11, 12, 13
Stevens, Louis 76
Stewart, James 3, 17, 97, 110
Stillman, Robert 99, 100, 101
Stone, George E. 23, *24*
Sturges, John 11, 137, 161, 162, 163, 164
Submarine Raider (1942 film) 11
Sweethearts of Sigma Chi (1946 film) 36
Swerling, Jo 8

The Talk of the Town (1942 film) 10
The Tall T (1957 film) 1, 2, 63, 112, 118, 119–125, *120*, *121*, *123*
Taylor, Rod 180, 181
Tequila Sunrise (1988 film) 21
Thomas, Lyn 45–46, 52
3-D (film process) 96–97, 99

The Three Musketeers (1950 television production) 167–171
Tibbs, Casey 68, 69
A Time for Dying (1969 film) 20, 30, 64, 153–158, *154*, *157*
Tomorrow's Almost Over (1946 Budd Boetticher screenplay) 13
Towne, Robert 21
Triesault, Ivan *28*, *29*
Trilling, Steve 141–142
Triumph of the Will (1935 film) 150
Turnabout (1940 film) 8, 170
The Two Jakes (1990 film) 21
Two Mules for Sister Sara (1970 film) 20, 21, 99
Tyler, Beverly *60*, 63

U-Boat Prisoner (1944 film) 12

Van Cleef, Lee 135, 138
Vidor, Charles 9, 10, 11

Wake of the Red Witch (1949 film) 115
Ward, Jonas 129, 131
Warner, Jack 96, 114, 137, 149, 152, 160, 177
Wayne, John 11, 15, 17, 54, 55, 56, 57, 58, 59, 80, 92, 109, 114, 115, 116, 117, 118, 119, 122, 124, 130, 148, 154, 181
Welles, Orson 107, 109
West, Adam 181

Westbound (1959 film) 2, 19, 64, 84, 128, 134, 138–142, *140*
When in Disgrace (Budd Boetticher autobiography) 5, 7, 19, 21, 54, 125–126, 129
Where Are the Elephants? (Budd Boetticher unpublished autobiography) 21
Whiting, Barbara 173
Wildcatters (unsold 1959 TV pilot) 184
Williams, Guinn "Big Boy" 9
Wills, Chill 67, 68, *70*, 89, 92, *92*
Wings of the Hawk (1953 film) 70, 96–100
The Wolf Hunters (1949 film) 43, 45, 46–49, *47*, *48*
The Wolf Hunters (novel) 46, 47
Wright, William 28, *28*, *29*
Wynant, H.M. 128

Yates, Herbert 15, 54, 57, 58, 59, 92
Yolanda and the Thief (1946 film) 40–42
Yordan, Philip 150
You Bet Your Life (television series) 98
Young, Gig 168
Young, Robert R. (producer) 37, 38
Youth on Trial (1945 film) 30–34, *31*, *32*
Yukon Gold (1954 film) 49

www.ingramcontent.com/pod-product-compliance
Lightning Source LLC
Chambersburg PA
CBHW081558300426
44116CB00015B/2929